Im Blickpunkt: Niederlande
The Netherlands in Focus

Beispielhafte Ideen und Konzepte für Stadt und Landschaft
Exemplary ideas and concepts for town and landscape

Edition Topos

Callwey Verlag
München

Birkhäuser
Basel · Boston · Berlin

Inhalt
Table of contents

Station Square Enschede
Design: okra landscape architects
Photo: Frank Colder

Topos

Robert Schäfer

„Modellfall Niederlande" nannten wir die Ausgabe 31 von "Topos – European Landscape Magazine". Ein Land war Gegenstand näherer Betrachtung, dessen Architektur, Stadt- und Landschaftsplanung bereits viele Seiten in Fachzeitschriften füllte und Stoff für eine unüberschaubare Reihe von Publikationen bot. "Topos" widmete sich diesem planerischen Musterländle seit 1993 regelmäßig, stellte Projekte und Planungen vor, die weit über die Niederlande hinaus diskutiert wurden. Einige dieser Beiträge haben wir nun in dem vorliegenden Buch zusammengefasst. Sie belegen exemplarisch einige besondere Grundzüge des Planens und Bauens in Holland.

Was ist nun das Besondere an diesem kleinen Land, das in einem stetigen Überlebenskampf mit dem Element Wasser zu leben scheint? Der Architekturkritiker Bart Lootsma ging in seinem vielbeachteten, im Jahr 2000 erschienenen Buch „SuperDutch" dieser Frage für den Architekturbereich nach. Dass der unbescheidene Titel von seinem englischen Verleger kam, ist ein Zeichen für das Phänomen, dass die besondere Rolle, die die niederländischen Architekten in den 90er Jahren einnahmen, primär in der Betrachtung von außen lag. Lootsma schilderte die Zweite Moderne der holländischen Architektur, analysierte die vergangene Dekade und stellte sie in den geschichtlichen Kontext. In einem Rückblick, nur ein Jahr später erschienen, äußert sich Lootsma sehr skeptisch. Für ihn ist der Boom vorüber, die Exponenten der SuperDutch-Generation bauen und lehren weltweit, während im Lande die Qualität zu sinken drohe. Ganz der Attitüde Rem Koolhaas' folgend, sieht die Avantgarde die Welt als Aufgabenfeld, nicht länger die niederländischen Polder und Hafenanlagen. Für Lootsma sind die Niederlande das Versuchslabor der Internationalisierung, die sich in diesem Land besonders rasch vollzogen hat, allerdings unter Bedingungen, die kennzeichnend für die Niederlande sind: Gesprächskultur, Konsens, hohe Dichte, Künstlichkeit, Regulierung und Pragmatismus.

Umso interessanter ist es also, sich in einem Rückblick, wie in diesem Buch, nochmals einigen Facetten dieser Blütezeit zu nähern. Dabei sind Stadt und Landschaft verwoben. Die Landschaftsarchitektur der Niederlande profitierte vom Planungs- und Bauboom der 90er Jahre wie sonst wohl kein anderes europäisches Land.

Erst 1946 wurde ein Studiengang für Landschaftsarchitektur an der Landwirtschaftlichen Hochschule in Wageningen gegründet. Bis dahin herrschten in Garten und Landschaft Einflüsse aus Deutschland, Frankreich und England vor. Die ersten Polder aus dem 17. Jahrhundert haben zwar die Landschaft grundlegend neu gestaltet, jedoch ohne Mitwirkung von Landschaftsarchitekten.

Erst nach dem Zweiten Weltkrieg erforderten die neuen Polder im IJsselmeer, die Neustrukturierung der Agrarlandschaft und die neuen Wohngebiete diese Planungsdisziplin. Passend, und später idealer Nährboden für Diskussionen über die Moderne und Zweite Moderne oder Überwindung derselben, dass

auch die scheinbar natürlichen Landschaften menschengemacht waren und somit als ideales Spielfeld für die Profession herhalten konnten, die von Beginn an durch die intensive Zusammenarbeit mit Architekten und Stadtplanern mit funktionalistischen Ideen vertraut war.
Die Annahme, das gesamte Land als gebaute oder verstädterte Landschaft betrachten zu können, wo der Gegensatz zwischen Stadt und Land weitgehend aufgehoben ist, führte zu einem pragmatischen Umgang mit der Landschaft. Dies vor allem Ende der 80er Jahre, als sich der Staat allmählich aus der Verantwortung für den sozialen Wohnungsbau schlich und somit auch die Kontrolle über die Qualität neuer Siedlungsgebiete aus der Hand gab. Berühmt wurden die Vinex-Gebiete, benannt nach der "Vierde nota extra", der vierten Änderung des Raumordnungsgesetzes. Bis zum Jahr 2005 sollen im Umkreis der Städte nach diesem Wohnbauprogramm 500 000 Wohnungen entstehen. Diesem gigantischen Verstädterungsprozess wollten etliche Planer andere Konzepte entgegenstellen, Adriaan Geuze beispielsweise, der erkannte, dass der ländliche Raum ohnehin nicht von Bebauung freigehalten werden kann, es also besser sei, ihn geplant zu kolonisieren. Niederländische Landschaftsarchitekten sind der Überzeugung, dass die Stärke der Landschaft in ihrer Wandlungsfähigkeit liegt. Zugleich denken manche, darunter wieder Adriaan Geuze von West 8, dass sich der Mensch, ganz nach Darwin, der Landschaft anpasst, sie so nutzt, wie er sie vorfindet. Es wäre also gar nicht notwendig, die Landschaft nach überholten Bildern umzugestalten oder zu dekorieren.
Geht es um den öffentlichen Raum in den Städten, stoßen die Planer auf eine hohe Regelungsdichte. In Rotterdam reden bis zu 17 städtische Behörden mit, die auch noch unterschiedlichen Dienststellen und Ressorts zugeordnet sind. Dazu kommt das spezielle niederländische Konsensbestreben, das sich im sogenannten „Poldermodell" niederschlägt. Bei diesem Modell werden unterschiedliche Interessen und sogar gegenläufige Planungsauffassungen so lange besprochen und verhandelt, bis ein Konsens gefunden wird.
Architektur und Stadtplanung sind in den Niederlanden ein öffentliches Thema seit den 70er Jahren, als die Bürger mehr Mitsprache einforderten, gegen Bauvorhaben demonstrierten und leer stehende Häuser in Sanierungsgebieten besetzten. Dominierten in der Folge die sozialen und ökologischen Belange bei Planungsentscheidungen, wurde schließlich mit einer Reihe von politischen Entscheidungen der Grundstein gelegt für die kulturelle Komponente des Bauens. 1989 wurde das international renommierte Architekturinstitut in Rotterdam gegründet und 1992 kam der Stimulierungsfonds für Architektur und Städtebau hinzu, sowie etliche individuelle Fördermöglichkeiten für Architekten. Privatisierung und Bauboom einerseits, ein Konzepte, Ideen und jede Menge Publikationen förderndes Klima andererseits schufen so einen Modellfall, den es zu studieren lohnt.

Robert Schäfer

"The Netherlands in focus" was what we called volume 31 of "Topos: European Landscape Magazine". The object of inspection was a country whose architecture and urban and landscape planning had already covered many pages in specialist journals and provided subject matter for countless publications. "Topos" has devoted articles to this little planning model of a country regularly since 1993, presenting projects and planning schemes that were discussed far beyond The Netherlands. We have now collected some of these articles in the present book. They provide examples of the special fundamentals of planning and building in Holland.

What is it that is so special about this small country that seems constantly struggling for survival against the element of water? This question was examined with reference to architecture by the architecture critic Bart Lootsma in his highly regarded book, SuperDutch, published in 2000. The presumptuous title given by his English publisher illustrates the phenomenon that the special role played by Dutch architects of the 90s existed primarily in the perception of outsiders. Lootsma described the second modern age of Dutch architecture, analysed the past decade, and placed it in a historical context. Looking back only a year later, Lootsma published a sceptical review. According to him, the boom is over and the exponents of the 'SuperDutch' generation are building and teaching all over the world while quality is threatening to take a nosedive in the country itself. Taking on Rem Koolhaas's posturing, the avant-garde no longer considers the Dutch polders and harbour areas but the whole world its field of operation. Lootsma sees The Netherlands as a testing laboratory for internationalisation. Although it occurred particularly rapidly in this country, it did so under typically Dutch conditions: a culture of discourse, consensus, high density, artificialness, regulation, and pragmatism.

Hence it is all the more interesting to have another look at certain aspects of this flowering in a review such as ours. The city and the landscape are interwoven. Landscape architecture probably profited more from the planning and building boom of the 90s in The Netherlands than in any other European country. Not until 1946 had a university programme in landscape architecture been set up at the Agricultural University of Wageningen. Until then, gardens and landscapes had been dominated by influences from Germany, France and England. The first polders of the 17th century had fundamentally re-shaped the landscape but without input from landscape architects. Only after World War II did the new polders in the IJsselmeer, the restructuring of the agrarian landscape, and the new housing districts call for this new planning discipline. It was appropriate that even the apparently natural landscapes were man-made. This later formed an ideal basis for the discourse on modernity and the second modern age or overcoming the latter. It hence served as the ideal playground for the profession, which was familiar with functionalist ideas from the start through the close collaboration with architects and urban planners.

The assumption that the whole country could be regarded as built or urbanised landscape, where the contrast between city and country had largely been obliterated, led to a pragmatic approach to the landscape. This was the case particularly at the end of the 80s when the state gradually snuck out of being responsible for subsidised housing and thus gave up control over the quality of new housing developments. The Vinex districts, named after 'Vierde nota extra,' the fourth amendment to area planning law, became famous. This housing construction programme calls for 500,000 residential units to be built near the cities by 2005. A number of planners hope to counter this gigantic urbanisation process with other concepts. Adriaan Geuze, for example, realises that rural space could not be kept free anyway so it had better be colonised in a planned way. Dutch landscape architects are convinced that the power of the landscape lies in its ability to change. Some of them, including Adriaan Geuze of West 8, also think along Darwin's lines that man adapts to the landscape, making use of it in whatever state he finds it. Hence it would be completely unnecessary to redesign or decorate the landscape according to outdated images.

When it comes to public space in cities planners are confronted with a plethora of regulations. In Rotterdam up to 17 municipal administrative bodies, which, moreover, come under several different departments and jurisdictions, all have a say. On top of it all there is the particularly Dutch desire for consensus that is reflected in the so-called 'polder model.' In this model various interests and even contradictory planning approaches are discussed and negotiated as long as it takes to find a consensus.

Architecture and urban planning have been a public issue in The Netherlands since the 70s, when the citizens demanded more of a say, demonstrated against building projects and occupied empty houses in urban renewal districts. While this initially caused social and ecological issues to dominate in planning decisions, a series of political decisions eventually laid the foundations for the cultural component in architecture. In 1989 the internationally renowned architecture institute NAI was founded in Rotterdam.

From 1992 on, funding to stimulate architectural and urban architectural development as well as many different grants and subsidies for architects were available. Privatisation and the building boom on the one hand and a climate encouraging concepts, ideas and any number of publications on the other created an exemplary situation that is worth studying closely.

Grünsysteme in der niederländischen Stadtplanung

Park systems in Dutch town planning

Gerrie Andela
Cor Wagenaar

Debatten über zeitgemäße Freiräume in der Stadt begleiteten Planungen in den 20er und 30er Jahren. Sie sind auch heute noch aktuell.

Debates on the purpose of urban open space accompanied planning in the twenties and thirties and are still of validity today.

Wie auch in anderen Ländern war die Diskussion über die Notwendigkeit von Freiflächensystemen hauptsächlich auf die großen Städte beschränkt, da durch die Industrialisierung, die in der zweiten Hälfte des 19. Jahrhunderts eingesetzt hatte, die Notwendigkeit von Grünflächen in der Stadt fühlbar wurde. Obwohl einige Parks geschaffen worden waren – so der Vondelpark und der Oosterpark in Amsterdam und der Maaspark in Rotterdam – genügten sie doch nicht den Anforderungen einer wachsenden Stadtbevölkerung, da das Leitmotiv für ihre Gestaltung die Stadtverschönerung gewesen war, und nicht der Wunsch, ausreichenden Erholungsraum zu schaffen.

Darüber hinaus lagen sie weit entfernt von den dicht besiedelten Stadtvierteln und ihr landschaftlicher Stil entsprach nicht mehr den neuen Erholungsansprüchen. Wachsendes politisches Bewußtsein, Veränderungen in Technik und Wirtschaft, neue Entwicklungen in der Medizin bewirkten, daß die Notwendigkeit körperlicher Erholung durch Wandern oder Sport und Spiel im Freien immer stärker akzeptiert wurde. Damit rückte auch das Stadtumland ins Blickfeld der Öffentlichkeit, da es dort noch ausreichend Grünflächen für solche Erholungswünsche gab.

Gleichzeitig entspann sich eine lebhafte Debatte über Gestaltung und Inhalt städtischer Parks, und dies ist einfach auf den Einfluß der deutschen Volksparkbewegung zurückzuführen. Diese Entwicklungen trugen dazu bei, daß die städtischen Parks zum Hauptthema im niederländischen Städtebau um die Jahrhundertwende wurden.

Zwei Strategien kennzeichneten den pragmatischen Modernismus in der holländischen Stadtplanung zwischen 1920 und 1940. In Rotterdam betonten Marinus Jan Granpré Molière und Willem Gerrit Witteveen Parks als harmonisierende Elemente der Stadt. Maßgeblich inspiriert wurde Witteveen durch die zeitgenössische Parkbewegung in den Vereinigten Staaten. Die in Amsterdam angewandte Strategie für den Stadterweiterungsplan von 1935 stellte jedoch einen anderen Ansatz dar: eine enge Verbindung zwischen Parks und Wohnquartieren.

In Amsterdam wurden um das Jahr 1908 erstmals Stimmen laut, die einen leichteren Zugang zur stadtnahen Landschaft forderten. Der Biologe Jac P. Thysse legte dar, daß man Spazier- und Wanderwege um die Stadt herum anlegen sollte,

Modern town planning in the Netherlands has developed from two distinct motives: the desire to curb urban sprawl and prevent it from destroying the Dutch landscape, and the necessity to improve the living conditions of the lower classes in the cities. As elsewhere, the discussion of the necessity of park systems has been mostly limited to the larger cities, since it was here that the urbanization that started in the latter half of the nineteenth century made the introduction of green spaces especially clear. Even though some parks were realized, such as the Vondelpark and the Oosterpark in Amsterdam and the Maaspark in Rotterdam, these did not satisfy the needs of the growing population since the primary objective of their creation was the urge to embellish the city, and not to provide sufficient open space for recreation. These parks were often located at a great distance from the populous neighbourhoods, and the landscape style that dominated their layout was incompatible with more recent views on recreation. Growing political consciousness, technological and economical changes and new developments in medical science boosted the case for physical recreation in the form of hiking in natural surroundings, outdoor sports and games. This shift brought the peripheries of the cities, where there was still some natural greenery, to the attention of the protagonists of space for recreation. At the same time, the form and programme of urban parks was heavily debated, as could be traced back to the impact of the German 'Volkspark' movement. These developments helped make the urban park become a major aspect of Dutch town planning around the turn of the century.

In the twenties and thirties, two different strategies came about in the Netherlands, both of

In den 20er und 30er Jahren wurde eine Grünplanung für die Bedürfnisse der Stadtbevölkerung zum beherrschenden Thema in der niederländischen Stadtplanung. Die Brücke bei Bosbaan wurde als traditionelles Landschaftselement in die Planung für Amsterdams neuen Park, den Boschplan (1937), integriert.

In the twenties and thirties, green planning that fulfilled the needs of the urban population became a leading topic of Dutch town planning. The bridge at Bosbaan was integrated into the 1937 Bosch Park plan as a traditional landscape element.

Erholung im Amsterdamer Bos der 50er Jahre. Der Sommertag in der Badeanstalt war ebenso Bestandteil des Freizeitvergnügens wie der Ausflug mit dem Auto, Symbol des neuen Wohlstands.

Recreation at Amsterdamse Bos in the fifties. A summer day spent at the pool was as popular a way of spending free time as an outing with the car, a symbol of the new state of affluence.

und daß diese im Idealfalle mit den vorhandenen Parks und einem großen Landschaftspark im Westen der Stadt verbunden sein müßten.

Eine Kommission der Amsterdamer Baubehörde, in die unter anderem Hendrikus Petrus Berlage und Thysse berufen worden waren, fand diesen Vorschlag zwar nicht besonders realistisch, aber sie unterstützte weitere Überlegungen über mehr Freiräume für die Erholung im Grünen. Sie begründete das damit, daß in dieser Hinsicht Amsterdam hinter anderen Städten im Ausland herhinkte. Dasselbe traf ihrer Meinung nach auf die Stadtplanung zu. So verwendete sich die Kommission auch dafür, daß Berlages Plan für die südliche Erweiterung von Amsterdam, der bereits vom Stadtparlament beschlossen worden war, umgehend verwirklicht würde. In diesem Plan waren der Zuiderpark, große Flächen für Sport, Erholung und Ausstellungen vorgesehen. Darüber hinaus hatte man freien Zugang zu den Flüssen Amstel und Schinkel geplant, die Naturgenuß in Fülle ermöglichten. Es waren zwar im nördlichen Teil der Stadt einige Parks geschaffen worden, aber im Süden war kaum ein Fortschritt zu verzeichnen. Der wurde erst 1921 durch die Eingliederung weiter Ländereien ins Stadtgebiet möglich, wodurch sich die Fläche des Stadtgebiets annähernd vervierfachte.

Grünflächensysteme in Amsterdam. Stadtplanung mußte nun auf regionaler Ebene betrieben werden. Die Vorschläge der Planungsbehörde für Groß-Amsterdam waren jedoch ziemlich oberflächlich und auf die besonderen Interessen der Baugesellschaften zugeschnitten. Da diesen daran lag, wie bisher vierstöckige Mietshäuser zu errichten, hätte dies nur eine Fortführung der Siedlungsstrukturen bedeutet, die Berlages Erweiterungsplan für Süd-Amsterdam prägten. Dieser Plan rief heftige Kritik hervor. Zwei Alternativvorschläge wurden daraufhin entwickelt: die Gegenplanung der städtischen Wohnungsbehörde und ein Plan von Witteveen, der die Kritikpunkte des Holländischen Instituts für öffentliches Wohnungswesen und Städtebau berücksichtigte. Beide zeigten Merkmale amerikanischer Grünflächensysteme: lange Grünzüge, Wohnquartiere mit Erholungseinrichtungen, in der Nähe des Nieuwe Meers ein großer Park.

Die ursprüngliche Planung wurde 1926 abgeändert. Sie übernahm einige Ansätze der Alternativpläne, wie die Lage und Anordnung der neuen Parks. Des weiteren legte sie ein radiales Muster der Stadterweiterung zugrunde, ohne jedoch die urbane Entwicklung der gesamten Region zu berücksichtigen. Eine Reihe engagierter Stadtplaner wurde eingestellt, eine eigene Abteilung für Stadtplanung geschaffen und der Leitung von Corne-

them typical for the pragmatic modernism that dominated Dutch town planning at this time. In Rotterdam, for example, Marinus Jan Granpré Molière and Willem Gerrit Witteveen used parks to underline the city as a harmonious unity, Witteveen's main source of inspiration being the contemporary park movement in the United States, whereby the link between parks and living quarters was much closer in Amsterdam; a tendency that was to culminate in the General Extension Plan in 1935. It is remarkable that both tendencies originated in an extension plan for the western part of Amsterdam originally designed by Witteveen in 1924.

Park systems in Amsterdam. In Amsterdam, the first voices could be heard about 1908, arguing for easier accessibility of the surrounding countryside. The field biologist Jac P. Thysse pointed out the possibilities of making a number of footpaths around the city, which were ideally to be connected to existing parks and a large landscape park in the west. A study committee initiated by the Amsterdam Dwelling Council – to which, among others, people like H.P. Berlage and Thysse were appointed – did not consider this proposal to be very realistic, but it did support the search for more space for outdoor recreation. The committee argued that Amsterdam was lagging behind in this aspect of planning, compared to cities abroad and that the same was true for the development of town planning in general. It therefore urged the immediate realization of Berlage's plan for the southern extension of Amsterdam, which had already been approved by the municipal council. Part of this plan was a park (Zuiderpark), large open spaces for outdoor sports and exhibi-

tions, and easy access to the Amstel and the Schinkel since these rivers offered abundant natural scenery. Even though some parks were now introduced in the northern half of the city, the southern half showed hardly any sign of progress in this respect. Changes were possible only after the annexation of vast territories in

lis van Eesteren unterstellt. Für Van Eesteren, der sich der niederländischen Avantgardegruppe um De Stijl angeschlossen hatte, wurde der Erweiterungsplan zur Lebensaufgabe, und hierdurch wurde er auch langjähriger Vorsitzender des Internationalen Kongresses für Moderne Architektur (CIAM). Der Allgemeine Stadterweiterungsplan stand in der Tradition des pragmatischen Modernismus in den Niederlanden, und ästhetische Prinzipien spielten hier eine wichtige Rolle. Dank der Arbeit Van Eesterens und

Links: Cornelis van Eesterens Allgemeiner Erweiterungsplan für Amsterdam von 1934 beruht auf der Verteilung von Grünflächen nach der Methode von Martin Wagner. Rechts: Der Boschpark, der 1937 als Teil der Amsterdamer Stadterweiterung konzipiert wurde, betonte die funktionalen, erholungsbezogenen Aspekte des Stadtgrüns.

Left: Cornelis van Eesteren's General Extension Plan for Amsterdam of 1934 is based on a calculation of urban green space distribution that was developed by Martin Wagner. Right: Bosch Park, which was conceived as part of the 1937 urban extension scheme, emphasizes the functional aspect of urban green space.

Van Lohuizens wurde die Behandlung urbaner Planungsaufgaben wissenschaftlicher. Umfangreiche Statistiken wurden erstellt, um das Bevölkerungswachstum, den Verkehr, die industrielle Entwicklung und die Hafenerweiterung zu prognostizieren. Die Verteilung von Grün- und Erholungsflächen basierte auf der »Wagner-Methode«, die der spätere Stadtbaurat von Berlin, Martin Wagner, 1915 in seiner Dissertation über städtische Freiflächenpolitik entwickelt hatte. Die Bevölkerungsdichte der Wohnquartiere und die Entfernung zu den Grünflächen lagen Richtwerten für die Größe und Lage der Freiflächen zugrunde, wobei die pro Person verfügbare Fläche der Hauptparameter war.

In Van Eesterens Entwurf für den westlichen Abschnitt des Plans (1929) trat die von ihm vertretene rationale Methode in den Vordergrund. Die »Verkehrselemente« bestimmten die Grundstruktur: eine Eisenbahnlinie, die um die gesamte Stadt herumführte, übergeordnete und regionale Straßen, die Erweiterung des Hafens nach Westen. Darüber hinaus wurden auch die vorgeschlagene Dichte der neuen Wohnquartiere und die Verfügbarkeit von Erholungsflächen berücksichtigt. Es entstand ein beinahe orthogonaler, durch Hauptverkehrsadern gegliederter Plan. Ausgedehnte Grünzonen durchdrangen die Siedlungsgebiete und verbanden sie gleichzeitig mit der Landschaft. Typisch für Van Eesterens Grünflächensysteme war die Betonung der geometrischen Formen der bebauten Zonen gegenüber den freien Formen der Parks, ein Prinzip, das er auch in seinem preisgekrönten Entwurf für »Unter den Linden« in Berlin anwandte. Folglich blieb Natur, obwohl sie in den die Wohngebiete umgebenden Parks neu geschaffen wurde, immer »natürlich«. Dieses Spiel mit Gegensätzen war neu. Die Altstadt von Amsterdam wurde durch einen langen Grünzug, den Rembrandtpark, von den neuen Siedlungsflächen abgesetzt.

Im Gegensatz zu Witteveen schien sich Van Eesteren wenig Gedanken um die Form der neuen Stadt zu machen – er konzentrierte sich auf methodische Fragen.[1] Seiner Meinung nach gab es keinen Grund für die Annahme, moderne Strukturen wie Straßen und Schienenwege seien für die Stadtgestaltung weniger geeignet als Deiche, Mühlen und Kanäle.

Die Analogie ist in der Tat frappierend. Die neuen Stadtviertel sollten den Geist der niederländischen Landschaft widerspiegeln: großzügig, rational und klar. Welche Bedeutung der Erholung im Freien zukam, zeigt ein Zitat aus dem Erläuterungstext zum Plan: »Das Bedürfnis nach Natur, Sonne und Wasser, der Wunsch, seine eigene Stärke in Sport und Spiel mit der

1921, which almost quadrupled the size of the municipality.

It now became possible to adopt a regional approach based on the latest developments in Dutch town planning. As a result, the tradtional city was no longer seen as a comprehensive entity; rather, new settlement structures that incorporated the rural landscape were devised with the traditional urban centres acting as their core. The leading Dutch town planning journals of the time now dealt with issues such as large cities, park systems and the new regional planning approach. However, the proposal made by the Committee for Greater Amsterdam, which was assigned with the task of coming up with a comprehensive extension plan for the city of Amsterdam, did not live up to expectations. This plan was rather superficial and amounted to little more than a commercial project to gratify the interests of building companies. Since the latter were only interested in erecting four-storied tenement buildings as they had always done, this implied a continuation of the patterns originally introduced by Berlage in his much-famed extension plan for the southern part of the city.

The plan provoked serious criticism and resulted in two alternative proposals which proved to be decisive: the Counter Plan by the Director of the Municipal Department of Housing, and a plan by Witteveen, which incorporated the criticism of the Dutch Institute for Public Housing and Town Planning. Despite their differences, both enhanced the American park system concept, with long stretches of green interspersing the urban tissue. Living quarters were placed near recreational facilities, and a large park was planned near Nieuwe Meer.

The official proposal that had triggered the alternative plans was modified in 1926. It contained some of the suggestions made in the alternative plans, not the least important of which concerned the location of the new parks. It also took as its basis a radial pattern of urban extension without taking into account the urban development of the region, however. The Committee handed over its tasks to a professional Department of Urban Planning headed by Cornelis van Eesteren as chief designer. For Van Eesteren, who had been a member of the Dutch avant-garde group centered around *De Stijl,* the General Extension Plan was the apogee of his professional life. It was also the vehicle that made him chairman of the Congrès Internationaux d'Architecture Moderne (CIAM) for many years. The General Extension Plan, however, was strongly rooted in the tradition of Dutch pragmatic modernism, and, contrary to post-war modernism, featured town planning aesthetics to a considerable extent.

Due to the work of Van Eesteren and Van Lohuizen, the approach taken towards urban problems tended to become more scientific, and extensive statistical calculations were carried out in an attempt to apprehend the increase in population, traffic, the development of industry and harbour expansion. The distribution of green spaces and recreation areas was based on the "Wagner method", a systematic method developed by Martin Wagner in his thesis "Städtische Freiflächenpolitik" (Urban Open Space Policy), Berlin, 1915. The density of the living quarters and the distance people had to cover when walking to the parks provided guiding lines for their size and location, the number of square meters per person being the main parameter.

In Van Eesteren's design for the western section of the plan (1929), his rational method came to the fore. The structure was determined by "traffic elements" comprising a circular railroad circumscribing the entire city, national and provincial plans for the construction of new roads and the extension of the harbour to the west. Furthermore, the proposed density of the new living quarters and the availability of areas suitable for recreational purposes were also taken into account. An almost orthogonal plan resulted, structured by the main traffic arteries. Deep wedges of green land penetrated the built-up areas, connecting them to the landscape. A characteristic of Van Eesteren's park systems was that they highlighted the geometry in the built areas (a method which reflected his prize-winning plan for Unter den Linden in Berlin) by contrasting it with the treatment of the parks. As a consequence, nature, although recreated in the parks, remained a backdrop, a setting for the living

Der Kralingse Bos, 1933 von Willem Gerrit Witteveen entworfen, wurde Rotterdams erster Volkspark. Vorbilder für seine Konzeption waren Fritz Schumachers Arbeiten in Hamburg. Ein See ist Anziehungspunkt in der landschaftlich gestalteten Anlage.

Kralingse Bos, designed by Willem Gerrit Witteveen in 1933, became Rotterdam's first *Volkspark* and was conceptually based on Fritz Schumacher's work in Hamburg. A lake forms the main attraction of the landscaped grounds.

anderen zu messen, mit anderen Worten: der Wunsch sich von den Alltagssorgen und -pflichten zu befreien, ist von größter Bedeutung im täglichen Leben geworden. Grün + Wasser + Sonne = Gesundheit, wurde zur Zauberformel unserer Zeit und das Ergebnis – eine kraftvolle, sonnengebräunte Jugend – hat die Gültigkeit dieser Formel bestätigt.«[2]

Der Allgemeine Erweiterungsplan sah umfangreiche Einrichtungen zur körperlichen und geistigen Ertüchtigung und zur Entspannung vor. Eine wissenschaftliche Annäherung an das Thema Erholung fand ihren Niederschlag in einer Hierarchie der Grünflächen: Parks für kleine Wohnquartiere, Stadtteilparks und Parks für das gesamte Stadtgebiet, deren Ausstattungsgrad mit ihrer Bedeutung wuchs. Sport- und Spieleinrichtungen, Grünzüge, Parks, öffentliche Gartenanlagen und Kleingärten waren aufeinander abgestimmt. Als Elemente der Stadtplanung dienten sie zur Strukturierung des Siedlungsnetzes. Ein sogenannter »Boschpark« (Waldpark) beim Nieuwe Meer, einem Ort, der bereits von Thysse zu Beginn des Jahrhunderts empfohlen worden war, unterstreicht die Bedeutung, die der Allgemeine Stadterweiterungsplan bereits für die gesamte Region hatte. Der Waldpark sollte den Mangel an natürlicher, ländlicher Schönheit in diesem Teil der Region ausgleichen. Eine umfangreiche Diskussion entzündete sich an der Möblierung dieses Parks, wobei sich die Kernfrage stellte, welches Image für einen modernen, großflächigen Park angemessen sei. Sollte er eher Familienspaziergängen dienen, ein Wald mit romantisch gewundenen Wegen oder ein geometrisches, der niederländischen Landschaft nachempfundenes Muster sein? Eines war sicher: niemand wollte einen Park des 19. Jahrhunderts imitieren. Von vorneherein war klar, daß der neue Park Möglichkeiten zur aktiven Erholung bieten sollte. Um dieses Problem zu lösen, wurden beispielhafte ausländische Anlagen besucht. Der Hamburger Stadtpark von Fritz Schumacher und einige Landschaftsparks in England hatten schließlich den größten Einfluß auf die Gestaltung: der deutsche Park wegen seines sozialen Programms, die englischen wegen ihrer Art, mit Landschaft umzugehen. Was man als Idee in neuer Aufmachung bezeichnen könnte, wurde ein Erfolg und nach dem Zweiten Weltkrieg in ländlich gelegenen Erholungsgebieten vielfach übernommen. Amsterdams Planungsverständnis prägte die moderne Tradition.

Grünflächensysteme in Rotterdam. Vermutlich machte kein anderer Stadtplaner so häufigen Gebrauch von Grünflächensystemen wie Witteveen in seinen Planungen für Rotterdam. In seinem Erweiterungsplan von

quarters. The old city was separated from the planned extensions by a long park named the Rembrandtpark.

Contrary to Witteveen, Van Eesteren does not seem to have bothered very much with the form of the modern city, but rather concentrated on the method employed[1]. He stressed that in his opinion, there was no reason to assume that basically modern elements (such as the traffic elements that played such a vital role in his project for the western section of the General Extension Plan) were less suitable for creating a satisfactory urban design than dikes, mills and canals.

The analogy is indeed striking. The new parts of the city were to radiate the spirit of the Dutch landscape: magnificent, rational and clear. How important outdoor recreation was thought to be can be illustrated by the explanatory notes accompanying the plan. Here, Van Eesteren wrote: "The need for nature, sun and water, the wish to measure one's strength in sporting or playing games; in other words, the desire to be liberated from the pressure of everyday worries and duties has become an element of the utmost importance in everyday life. Vegetation + water + sun = health has become the magic formula of our time, and the result – a powerful, sunburnt race of young people – has proved the validity of this formula."[2]

In the General Extension Plan, facilities for physical and mental recreation were provided for very generously. The scientific approach taken to recreation resulted in parks for small groups of houses, for entire neighbourhoods and for larger urban areas. Parkways, parks, public gardens and allotment gardens were introduced in a coherent way. As an element of town planning, this system gave structure to the whole plan.

A so-called "boschpark" (wooded park) near the Nieuwe Meer, a location already recommended by Thysse at the beginning of the century, underlines the impact that the General Extension Plan had already had on the entire region, and was to compensate for the lack of natural and rural beauty in this part of the region. A widespun discussion developed on its furnishing, centering around the question of which form would be most appropriate for a modern, large-scale park. Should it become a park suitable for family walks, or take on the form of woods with either romantically curved promenades or a geometrical pattern inspired by the Dutch landscape? Nobody wanted the result to imitate a nineteenth-century park. That it was to include areas for active recreation was clear right from the start. To solve this difficult problem, examples in other countries were visited. The "Stadtpark" designed by Fritz Schumacher in Hamburg and some landscape parks in England proved inspirational; the German park for its social programme, and the English ones for the way they treated landscape. The formula proved to be a success and after the Second World War was copied many times. Planning in Amsterdam played a pivotal role in shaping the modern tradition in the Netherlands.

Park systems in Rotterdam. Probably no other town planner made such extensive use of the park system concept as did Witteveen in his plans for Rotterdam. He exploited the possibilities entailed by this instrument to the fullest extent in his extension plan for the part of Rotterdam situated south of the River Meuse (1926), and in his proposal for Hoboken (1927). Witteveen's plan for Rotterdam's extension south of the river was

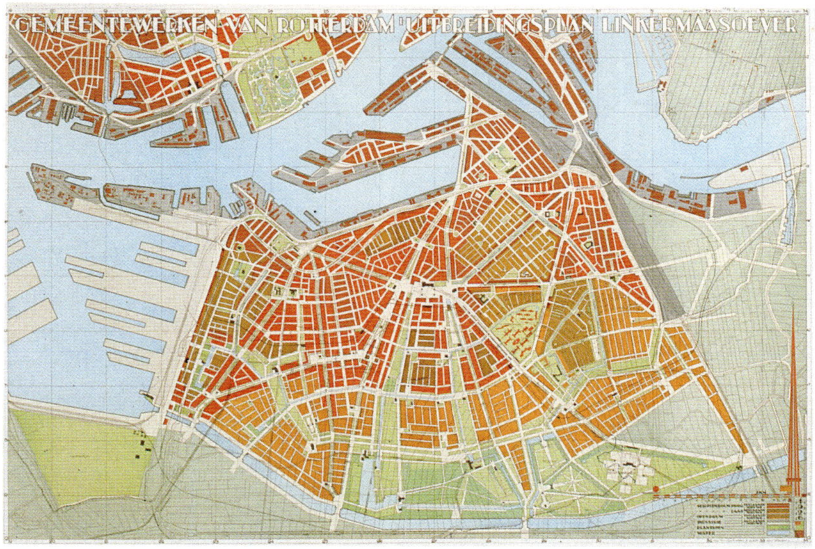

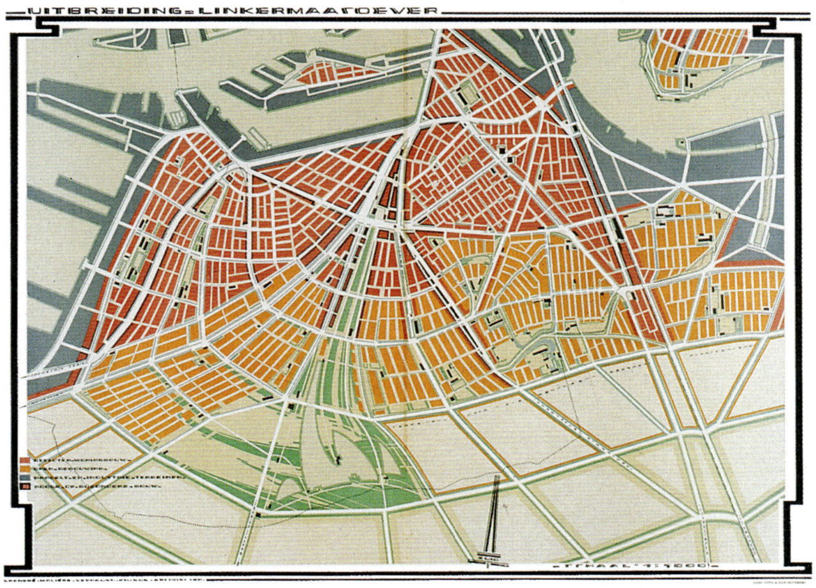

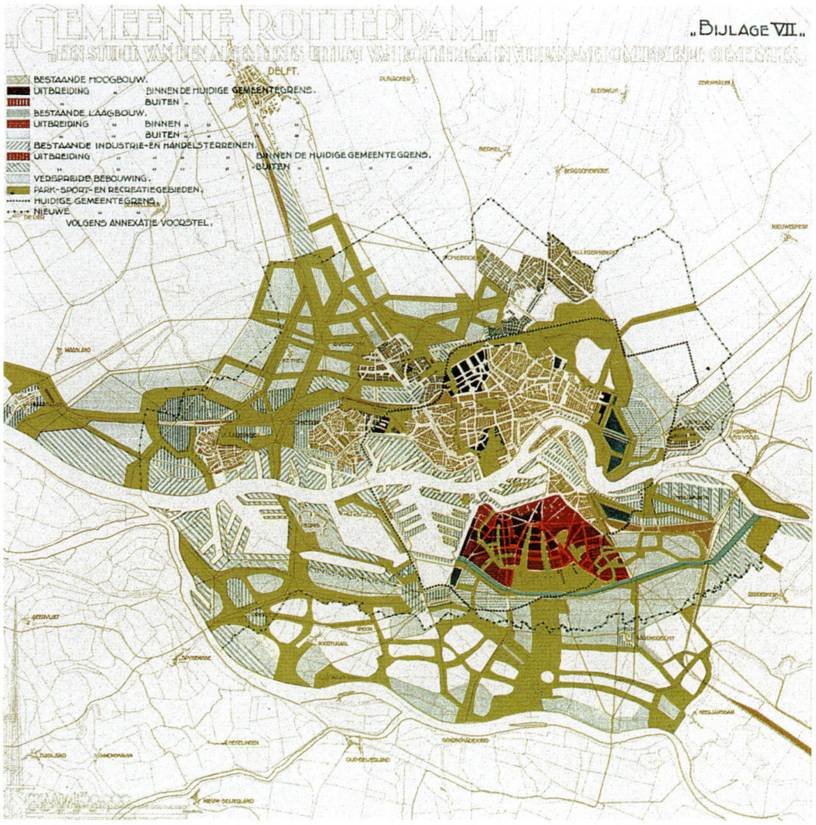

Planungen für das neue Rotterdam der 20er Jahre. Oben: W. G. Witteveens Erweiterungsplan für den Süden Rotterdams von 1926 beruht auf einem früheren Vorschlag von Granpré Molière, Verhagen und Kok aus dem Jahr 1921 (Mitte). Beide Pläne bedienen sich des Parksystems nach amerikanischem Vorbild zur Gliederung der Stadt. Parkways verbinden als Verkehrs- und Grünadern Stadt und Landschaft. Witteveens Plan sieht im Süden zusätzlich einen Kanal als Stadtgrenze vor. Unten: Der allgemeine Erweiterungsplan für Rotterdam, ebenfalls von Witteveen 1928, ist auch durch Parkways strukturiert. (Bearbeitung der aufs Grünsystem und den Erweiterungsplan Süd reduzierten Karte von Joosje van Geest und Gioconda Jager-Mina Quinonez)

Top: W.G. Witteveen's 1926 extension plan for the south of Rotterdam is based on an earlier proposal made by Granpré Molière, Verhagen and Kok from the year 1921 (middle). Both plans made use of the park system developed in America as a means of urban articulation, whereby parkways made up of traffic links and green corridors connect the city to the countryside. Witteveen's plan also included a canal to form the city's southern boundary. Bottom: The General Extension Plan of 1929 for Rotterdam, likewise drawn up by Witteveen, is also divided up by parkways. (Map showing the green system and the extension plan for the south of the city by Joosje van Geest and Gioconda Jager-Mina Quinonez)

1926 für den südlich der Maas gelegenen Teil der Stadt und in seinen Vorschlägen für Hoboken 1927 schöpfte er alle Möglichkeiten aus. Witteveens Plan für die Erweiterung Rotterdams südlich des Flusses basierte auf einem früheren Vorschlag von Marinus Jan Granpré Molière, Piet Verhagen und Anton Kok. Diese Planung spiegelte bereits die aktuellen Ansätze in der Stadtplanung wider. Th. K. van Lohuizen gelang es, die Stadtverwaltung dahin zu bringen, einen von der Planungsbehörde entwickelten Vorschlag zugunsten dieser Planung zurückzuziehen. Der Plan nahm vermehrtes industrielles Wachstum und die Ausdehnung des Hafens entlang des Flusses vorweg, das sich in radial vom Zentrum ausdehnenden Bändern vollzog. Zwischen diesen Bändern erstreckten sich fächerförmig Wohnquartiere in die Landschaft, dicht neben dem Zentrum des Planungsgebiets und gegenüber dem historischen Zentrum am Nordufer zur Landschaft hin geöffnet, die verschiedenen Wohnquartiere durch Grünzüge getrennt. Was Witteveens Plan von dem Plan Granpré Molières, Verhagens und Koks unterscheidet, ist der sparsamere Landverbrauch und die durch einen Kanal markierte, klare Definition der Stadtgrenze. Seiner Ansicht nach sollten der Stadt stark ausgeprägte optische Grenzen gegeben werden, die sie von der Landschaft trennten, während sie gleichzeitig durch das Parksystem mit ihr verbunden war. Parks und Grünzüge bestimmten auch Witteveens Entwurf. Im Unterschied zum Allgemeinen Erweiterungsplan für Amsterdam wurde hier mit den Mitteln der Perspektive gearbeitet: In Witteveens Plan wird das Auge ebenso wie im Plan von Granpré Molière, Verhagen und Kok durch eine Abfolge von Anziehungspunkten, die den Blick entweder auf die Stadt oder auf die offene Landschaft lenken, angeregt, wobei Gebäudefronten an jeder Parkseite und Alleen eindeutig als selbständige Einheiten definiert sind. Anstatt einheitliche Gebäudefronten zu schaffen, entwickelte Van Eesteren ein kompliziertes Zusammenspiel zwischen den Parks und den sie begrenzenden Gebäuden, wobei sich die Betonung des Parks und seinen Blickbeziehungen auf den Parkrand verlagerte. Mit den gleichen Mitteln arbeitete er in Hoboken, einer ländlichen Idylle inmitten der sich rasch ausdehnenden Stadt. Witteveen wandelte diese Freifläche in einer seiner überzeugendsten Grüngestaltungen um. Er beschrieb den Plan ziemlich poetisch: »Hier finden wir Tiefe, die so zwingend ist, daß man sich nicht von der Illusion freimachen kann, sich in einer Metropole zu befinden. Dies schätzen wir hoch ein, denn es scheint uns eine wesentliche Bedingung der modernen Stadt zu sein, daß sie ihre Größe und Ausdehnung einfach

based on an earlier proposal by Marinus Jan Granpré Molière, Piet Verhagen and Anton Kok. This original concept, which inspired Th. K. van Lohuizen to urge the municipality to withdraw an official plan made by the Planning Board, reflected the latest ideas on town planning. The plan presupposed a further growth of industries and harbour facilities alongside the river, and grouped these along radial bands spreading outwards from the center. Between these two bands, a fan-shaped series of living quarters, divided by parkways, streched into the landscape, densely built up at the center (opposite the historical center on the north bank), and opening up towards the landscape. What distinguishes Witteveen's proposal from the plan by Granpré Molière, Verhagen and Kok is the greater economy of land use and the rather hard definition of the city's border, which coincides with a canal. In his view, the city had to be given well-defined visual edges, separating it from the countryside to which it was linked by the park system. Parks and parkways also determined the structure of Witteveen's project. This approach differed from the treatment of the park system in the General Extension Plan for Amsterdam in its use of perspective. In Witteveen's plans, as in those by Granpré Molière, Verhagen and Kok, the eye is guided to the city or to the open landscape, the buildings on the sides of the parks and parkways clearly defining them as autonomous entities. In this way, Van Eesteren created an intricate interplay of the parks and the buildings bordering them, shifting the emphasis to their borders.

The same techniques determined the character of his plan for Hoboken, a rural island in the rapidly expanding city. Witteveen reshaped this

Skizzen für das neue, aufgelockerte Stadtbild Rotterdams nach dem Zweiten Weltkrieg. Witteveens Wiederaufbauplanung sah ein großzügig gestaltetes Zentrum mit grünen Boulevards als urbanen Magnet in der Regionalstadt vor.

Sketches for the new low-density design of Rotterdam in the aftermath of World War II. In order to provide the regional city with an urban magnet, Witteveen's reconstruction plans included a generously laid-out city centre with green boulevards.

open land into one of his most convincing parkways. In one of his rare moments of verbal lucidity, he described his plan rather lyrically: "Here we find a degree of depth so commanding that one has the impression of being in a city. This we value greatly, because we feel that a primary condition of the modern city is the easy and inconspicuous way in which it manifests its size and expanse in a well-defined space. We feel the greatness of a city only when open spaces point towards it, when its size becomes visible in quiet and worthy surroundings. What strikes us about Paris and the Louvre, the Place de la Concorde, the Champs Elysées and the Bois de Boulogne is the magnificent perspective and the majestic wideness that strengthens one's feeling of being in a city while creating a sense of beauty and serenity that captivates the foreigner with a thousand bonds."

Where it proved too difficult to insert parkways into the dense urban tissue, other solutions had to be found. To the northeast of Rotterdam, Witteveen designed a large new park dominated by a lake, 'the Kralingse Bos'. Here, too, a plan by Granpré Molière, Verhagen and Kok preceded this proposal, along with a more traditional plan by the landscape architect L. A. Springer. These plans had been the result of a disagreement about the design and function of a large park for the people of Rotterdam. Whereas Springer was thinking of introducing a landscape park in the nineteenth century fashion, Granpré Molière wanted to create a kind of Volkspark, providing possibilities for gardening, sports and sailing. As a result of these conflicting opinions, the planning of this park became almost impossible. The deadlock was cleared by Witteveen, who succeed-

und unauffällig in einem gut proportionierten Raum manifestiert. Wir empfinden die Größe einer Stadt nur, wenn die Freiräume auf sie hinweisen, wenn ihre Größe sichtbar wird in ruhiger und würdiger Umgebung. Was uns in Paris beeindruckt, im weltberühmten Louvre, der Place de la Concorde, den Champs Elysées, dem Bois de Boulogne sind die großartigen Perspektiven, die majestätische Weite, die einem das Gefühl gibt, in einer Metropole zu sein, während sie die Schönheit und Heiterkeit preisgibt, die den Fremden mit tausend Banden festhält.«

Wo es sich als zu schwierig erwies, Grünzüge in das dichte städtische Netz einzufügen, mußten andere Lösungen gefunden werden. Im Nordosten Rotterdams entwarf Witteveen einen großflächigen neuen Park, mit einem See als Anziehungspunkt, den Kralingse Bos. Auch hier war ein Plan von Granpré Molière, Verhagen und Kok dieser Planung vorausgegangen, ebenso ein eher traditionell gehaltener Plan des Landschaftsarchitekten L. A. Springer. Dies war das Ergebnis der Zwistigkeiten über die Frage von Funktion und Gestaltung eines großen Parks für die Bewohner von Rotterdam. Während Springer sich für einen Park in der Manier des 19. Jahrhunderts einsetzte, wollte Granpré Molière eine Art Volkspark schaffen, der Möglichkeiten fürs Gärtnern, für Sport zu Wasser und zu Lande vorsah. Durch dieses Hin und Her wurde die Planung dieses Parks so gut wie ganz verhindert. Die Pattsituation löste schließlich Witteveen auf, der eine überzeugende Alternative vorschlug. Bevor der Park landschaftlich gestaltet werden konnte, waren umfangreiche Bodenarbeiten nötig. Tonnenweise wurde Aushub aus den neuen Hafenbecken herangeschafft. Wegen der zentralen Lage des Sees war eine Manipulation der Blickbeziehung schwierig. Dennoch weisen die Zeichnungen Witteveens darauf hin, daß er dem Besucher selbst hier eine visuelle Führung geben wollte. Die Baumreihen in seinen Abbildungen erscheinen fast wie feste Wände, mit einer Abfolge »harter« Kurven, die den Blick nach vorne lenken. Durch die Zerstörung des historischen Zentrums von Rotterdam im Mai 1940 ergab sich die Möglichkeit, diesen Park mit dem übrigen Grünflächensystem durch einen langen und sorgfältig gestalteten Grünzug zu verbinden. Zu diesem Zeitpunkt jedoch trat eine entscheidende Wende ein. In den früheren Plänen war der motorisierte Verkehr in die Grünzüge integriert gewesen, waren die Hauptverkehrsstraßen in den Grünzügen gelegen. In den dreißiger Jahren erwies sich dies zunehmend als problematisch, und in seinem Wiederaufbau für Rotterdam entschied sich

Die enge, belebte Straße in der Stadt, einst das Schreckbild moderner Stadtplaner, wird in den 50er Jahren unter besseren Lebensbedingungen zum neuen Ideal. Die Lijnbaan in Rotterdam, 1948 von Van den Broek und Bakema entworfen, war das erste Einkaufszentrum der Niederlande. Konsum in der Fußgängerzone – eine neue, »alte« Freiraumnutzung.

Narrow bustling city streets, once a nightmare for modern town planners, became kind of an ideal of urban development in the fifties when living conditions improved. The Lijnbaan in Rotterdam, designed by Van den Broek and Bakema in 1948, was the first shopping-centre in the Netherlands. Pedestrian precincts had an effect on green spaces.

Witteveen, die zwei Systeme zu trennen, zumindest dort, wo die Grünzüge schmal und der Verkehr dicht waren.

Grünflächensysteme in der Nachkriegszeit. Von den zwei Planungsstrategien im Umgang mit Grünflächen überdauerte in den Niederlanden nur eine den Zweiten Weltkrieg. Die enge Verbindung zwischen den sorgfältig ermittelten Bedürfnissen nach öffentlichem Grün und der Hierarchisierung des Grünflächensystems führten zur Übernahme des in Amsterdam praktizierten neuen Ansatzes in der Stadtplanung. Diese wissenschaftlich etablierte enge Verbindung – eng auch im räumlichen Sinne, da ein Park nur nahegelegene Wohnquartiere versorgte – sollte ein Markenzeichen der Moderne in der Nachkriegszeit werden. Witteveens Methode, die die Doppelfunktion der Grünzüge als Verbindungsglied und einigendes Moment innerhalb der Stadt hervorhob, also eine rein ästhetische, visuelle Sichtweise, wurde als überholt betrachtet – so wie alle Ansätze, in denen die dreidimensionale, visuelle Form Vorrang hatte. Was endgültig das Ende von Witteveens Sicht der Freiflächenfrage bedeutete, war die Einführung der Nachbarschaftseinheit. Nicht die Stadt als große, organische Einheit, sondern das Wohnquartier wurde zur wichtigsten Größe in der Stadtplanung. Anstelle einer visuellen Einheit war die Stadt nach dem Kriege nahe daran, in ein Patchwork aus nachbarschaftlichen Einheiten zu zerfallen, deren Mittelpunkt das Nachbarschaftszentrum sein sollte. Somit endete eine der interessanten Phasen der Freiraumplanung in Holland. Van Eesterens Methode der Integration von Parks in das Stadtgefüge verlor andererseits in dem Maße an Prägnanz, wie es sich auf breiter Linie durchsetzte, da den meisten Planern die Fähigkeiten des Meisters fehlten.

Heute sind die Parks teilweise mit Nachbarschaftszentren überbaut, mit Altenheimen, Schulen und anderen Einrichtungen. Veränderungen im Gebrauch des öffentlichen Grüns reduzieren viele Parks zu ästhetischen Versatzstücken, da die ursprünglichen Sportangebote heute kaum noch benutzt werden. In Rotterdam sind diese Freiräume heute zu Gegenständen groß angelegter Untersuchungen geworden, da sie durch ihre Lage in monotonen Wohnquartieren mit einer überalternden Bevölkerung neue städtische Problemgebiete geworden sind.

Wenn nichts gegen den fortschreitenden Verfall getan wird, wird der alte Traum von glücklichen Leuten, welche die Vorzüge städtischer Parks genießen, schnell verblassen, und desolate Grünflächen werden die einzigen Zeugen der großartigen Visionen von Van Eesteren und Witteveen sein.

ed in making a convincing alternative. Before the park could be "landscaped", however, it was necessary to improve the soil, and for this purpose many tons of mud from the newly dug harbour basins were used. Due to the central position of the lake, manipulation of perspective was rather difficult, however. Nevertheless, the drawings suggest that Witteveen tried to give the visitor visual guidance even here: the way in which he depicts lines of trees makes them appear like walls, with a succession of "hard" bends that induce the eye to "leap" forward. It was first the destruction of the historical city of Rotterdam in May 1940 which provided the possibility of connecting this park with the park system, using a long and meticulously shaped parkway as the link. However, by now an important change had occurred. In Witteveen's previous plans, motorized traffic had been integrated into the park system, the main traffic routes coinciding with the parkways. In the thirties this method had already become increasingly problematic and in his reconstruction plan for Rotterdam, Witteveen decided to separate the two systems in cases where the parkways were narrow and the traffic was expected to be dense.

Park systems in post-war Modernism. Of the two park system strategies developed in Dutch town planning, only one survived the Second World War. The close connection between the carefully calculated needs for public greenery and the separate parts of the park system, adapted to the approach taken in Amsterdam, was the one that came to dominate the post-war era; indeed, this scientifically established link between individual parks and local needs was to become one of the signposts of post-war Modernism. Witteveen's method, which greatly stressed the function of park systems as a means of lending coherence and unity to a city, his purely aesthetic, visual approach, was discarded as obsolete – as were all forms of town planning in which the importance of three-dimensional, visual form had been emphasized. What definitively marked the end of Witteveen's use of open space was the introduction of the neighbourhood unit. Not the city as a large, organic unity, but the living quarter became the most important entity in town planning. Instead of representing visual unity, the post-war city threatened to disintegrate into a patchwork of neighbourhood units, the focus of post-war life being the neighbourhood community centre. In this way, one of the most interesting phases in the use of parks in Holland was discarded. Van Eesteren's method of integrating parks into the urban tissue, on the other hand, lost most of its fervour when it became widely copied, most of his colleagues lacking his consummate skill.

Today, neighbourhood centres, institutions for the elderly, schools, etc. have been built on the grounds of many of the parks, and changes in the use of public greenery have reduced many parks to mere visual assets because the outdoor sports facilities they offer are hardly ever used. In Rotterdam, these open spaces have become the subject of large-scale surveys, since, being located in monotonous living quarters with an aging population, they have now become the city's new problem areas. If nothing is done to stop further decay, the dream of happy people enjoying the benefits of urban parks will soon fade away, leaving desolate spots of greenery to be the only testimony of the great visions of Van Eesteren and Witteveen.

Niederlande: Landschaftsarchitektur – ein Prozeß

The Netherlands: processes versus static states

Michiel den Ruijter

Die zunehmend prozeßhafte Sichtweise der Landschaftsplanung färbt auf die Freiraumgestaltung ab: Schwerpunkt Wassermanagement. The increasingly process-related approach of landscape planning influences the design, particularly with regard to water management.

Was bedeuteten die 90er Jahre für die niederländische Landschaftsarchitektur? Eine Tendenz, die auch in zwei lesenswerten Ausgaben des Jahrbuchs »Landscape Architecture and Town Planning in the Netherlands« beschrieben wird, ist die zunehmende Zusammenarbeit zwischen Landschaftsarchitektur und Städtebau: zweifellos eine starke Allianz. Weniger beachtet, aber vielleicht ebenso bedeutsam, sind Entwicklungen in der niederländischen Landschaftsplanung. Die stärkere Zusammenarbeit mit ökologischen Disziplinen ließ die prozeßhaften Aspekte in der Landschaftsplanung deutlicher hervortreten: weg vom konservierenden Naturschutz hin zur Naturentwicklung.

Dieser Übergang begann in den 80er Jahren mit dem Schlagwort »Cascolandschap«. Gemeint ist damit eine Landschaft mit wenig dynamischen Grundstrukturen, aber hochdynamischem Geschehen. Auftrieb gab der neuen dynamischen Sichtweise in der Landschaftsarchitektur auch die zunehmende Ausweisung von Naturentwicklungsgebieten, die ein Endbild ausschließen und einen prozeßhaften Planungsansatz geradezu herausfordern. Ein vielbeachteter Vorreiter dieser Entwicklung war das Projekt »Ooievaar/Storch«, bei dem es um die Wiederherstellung einer Auenlandschaft ging. Momentan werden in den Niederlanden zahlreiche Agrarflächen zu solchen Naturentwicklungsgebieten umgewandelt, oft allerdings nur in der Rolle von Trittsteinbiotopen, weil die isolierte Lage angeblich nichts anderes zuläßt. Kritiker wenden ein, hier werde mangels Alternativen eine Reservatspolitik betrieben, die lediglich versucht, bestimmte Gegenden frei von menschlichem Einfluß zu halten. Natur bedeute jedoch in den Niederlanden immer auch Kulturlandschaft und Wassermanagement. Hinter der Kritik verbirgt sich ein neuer Ansatz, der Naturentwicklung, Wasserhaushalt und Landschaftsarchitektur als Einheit betrachtet. Obwohl sich dieser integrative Planungsansatz bereits in diversen Projekten niederschlug, wird er noch immer nicht öffentlich diskutiert. Deshalb soll er im folgenden exemplarisch an drei Projekten illustriert werden: Sie alle sind prozeßhaft angelegt, tragen den Charakter einer Naturentwicklung und stützen sich auf die verbindende Rolle des Wassers. Neben den räumlichen Aspekten berücksichtigen sie auch kulturelle und architektonische Komponenten. Die Projekte liegen in Gebieten mit den drei für die

What effects have the nineties had on Dutch landscape architecture? One has been to increase collaboration between landscape architecture and urban development, an undoubtedly powerful alliance, as described in two recent issues of the regular publication *Landscape Architecture and Town Planning in the Netherlands*, both well worth reading. Less attention has been paid to another effect, namely developments in landscape planning, although they are doubtlessly of equal significance, having led to a growing partnership with planning and ecological disciplines. This is proved by the process-related character that landscape planning has taken on, moving away from purely conservational efforts towards a form of management that allows a fair degree of natural development, and known in the Netherlands as 'nature development'.

This transition began in the eighties, when the term *cascolandschap* first emerged in reference to landscapes characterised more by dynamic processes than dynamic structures. This new direction in landscape architecture was able to gather momentum thanks to the increasing designation of 'nature development' areas, in which the object is not to achieve a final state and which thus make a process-oriented planning approach a necessity. The "Ooievaar/Storch" alluvial landscape restoration project was a trailblazer in this respect, and one that met with much acclaim.

At the present, numerous agricultural areas in the Netherlands are being turned into such nature development terrains, mainly as insular biotopes due to their isolated locations. Critics, however, point out that this policy of trying to keep certain areas free of anthropogenic influences is probably because the authorities do not

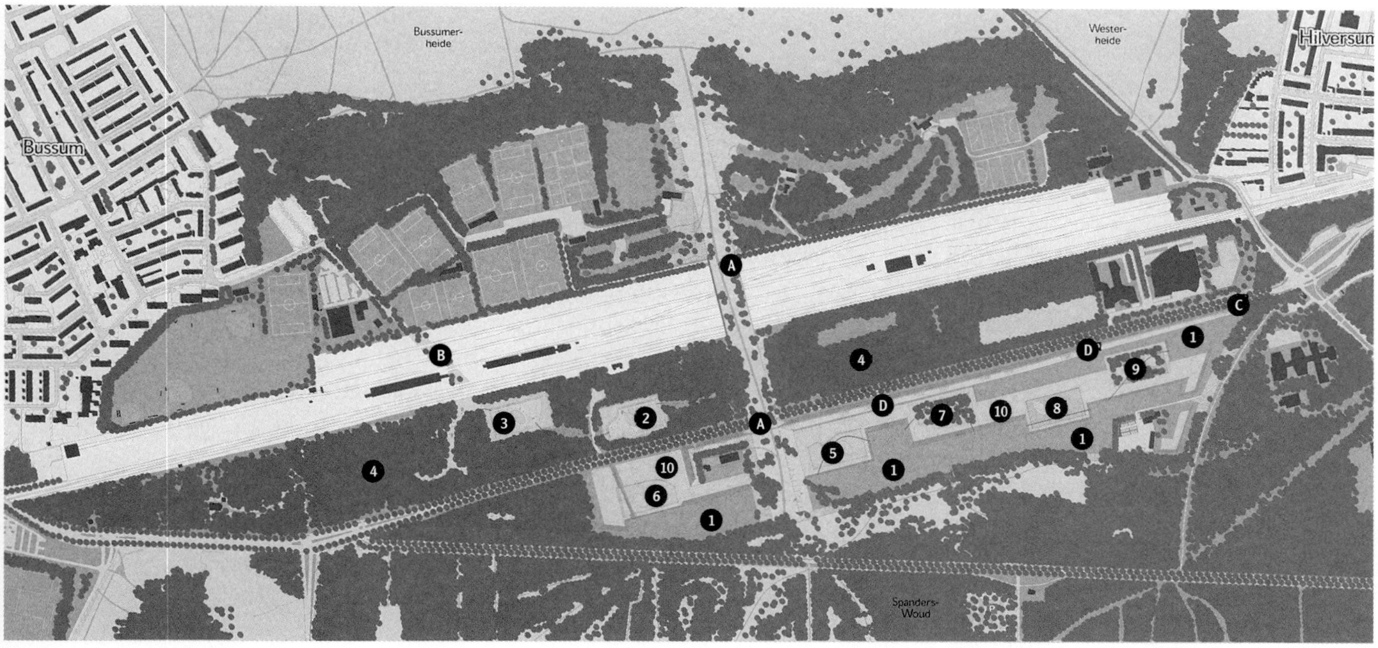

Zanderij-Crailo
Location: Hilversum
Planners: VISTA
office for environmental planning, landscape architecture and ecology, Amsterdam

Sandige Böden prägen das Sandabbaugebiet Crailo bei Hilversum. Es liegt mitten in einer monotonen Agrarlandschaft und weist zwei naturnahe Areale auf, die jedoch durch eine Straße und eine Bahnlinie voneinander getrennt sind. Der Landschaftsentwurf (oben) sieht drei ökologische Korridore vor sowie ein Naturausstellungsgelände.
Ein Aussichtsplatz bietet einen Überblick über die verschiedenen Landschaftstypen, die sich aus Unterschieden in Grundwasserstand und Pflege ergeben.
Das Grundwasser wird nicht technisch reguliert.
A »Ecoduct« für Tiere, B nördlicher Korridor, C südlicher Tunnel für Wild, D ginsterbepflanzter Deich.

Sandy soils characterise the sand quarrying area of Crailo, near Hilversum. Located in a monotonous agricultural landscape, the site in question features two near-natural areas divided by a road and a railway line. The landscape design (above) will now be connecting them with three ecological corridors, and also includes a natural exhibition site. A viewing platform is to provide an overview of the different landscape types that are to develop as a result of differences in management and ground water levels, whereby the water levels will be allowed to fluctuate naturally. A The "Ecoduct" for animals, B The northern corridor, C The southern tunnel for game, D Dyke planted with gorse.

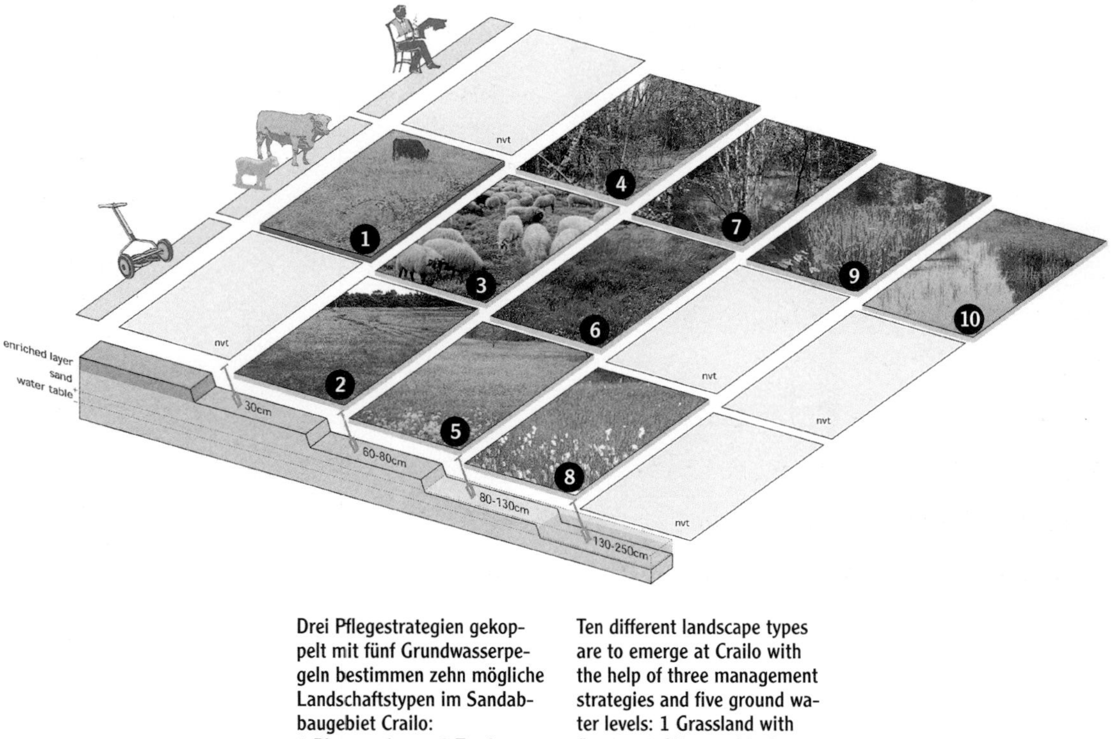

Drei Pflegestrategien gekoppelt mit fünf Grundwasserpegeln bestimmen zehn mögliche Landschaftstypen im Sandabbaugebiet Crailo:
1 Blumenwiesen, 2 Trockenrasen, 3 Heide (trocken), 4 Birken- und Eichenwald, 5 Feuchtwiesen, 6 Heide (feucht), 7 Birkenwald (feucht), 8 Sumpfwiesen, 9 Erlen- und Birkenwald/-gebüsch, 10 Wasserbecken.

Ten different landscape types are to emerge at Crailo with the help of three management strategies and five ground water levels: 1 Grassland with flowers, 2 Oligotrophic dry grassland, 3 Dry heath, 4 Forest of birch and oak, 5 Humid oligotrophic grassland, 6 Humid heath, 7 Humid birch forest, 8 Wet oligotrophic grassland, 9 Forest and shrubbery of alder and birch, 10 Pool.

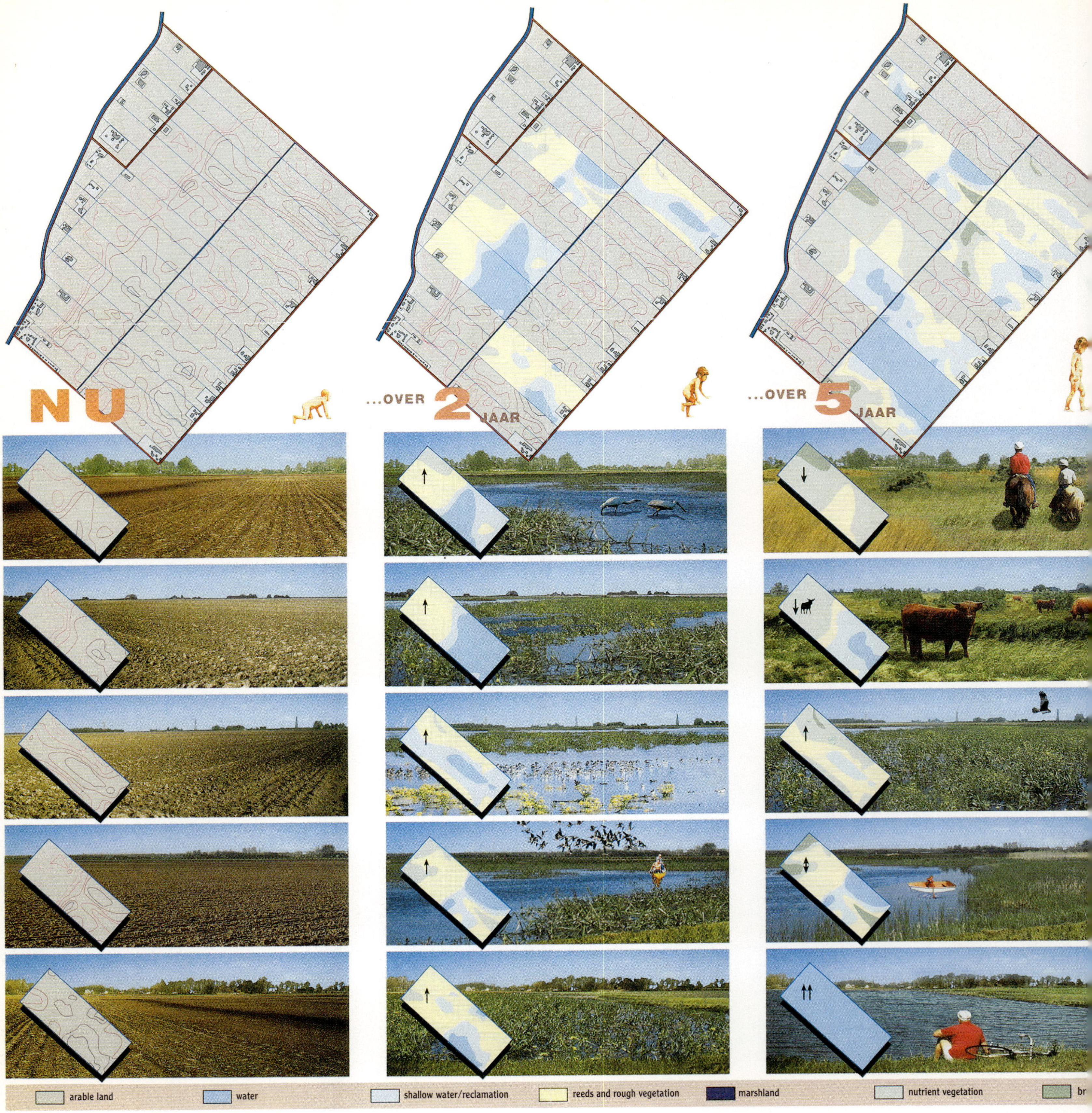

Uit de klei getrokken (Drawn from the Clay)
Location: Nature development area of Haarlemmermeer
Planners: VISTA office for environmental planning, landscape architecture and ecology, Amsterdam

In Haarlemmermeer sollen fünf Pflegekonzepte und das Regulieren der Wasserpegel maximale Biodiversität schaffen. Das Schema (oben) zeigt die Entwicklung im Laufe von 80 Jahren hin zu Wald, Parklandschaft, Torfmarschen, Schilfmarschen, Wasserlandschaft. Nebenstehende Grafik verdeutlicht das Wassermanagement: 1 Ackerland, 2 natürliches Land, 3 Wohngebiet, 4 Wasserstand im Winter, 5 Wasserstand im Sommer, 6 Wasserzufluß für Ackerland, 7 Wasserstand im Sammelbecken (Winter), 8 Wasserstand im Sammelbecken (Sommer), 9 verschließbare Leitung zwischen Sammelbecken, 10 Ausfluß für sauberes Wasser, 11 Abwasserröhre zur Kläranlage, 12 Drainagekanal zu Wasserbecken, 13 Pumpe zu Wasserbecken

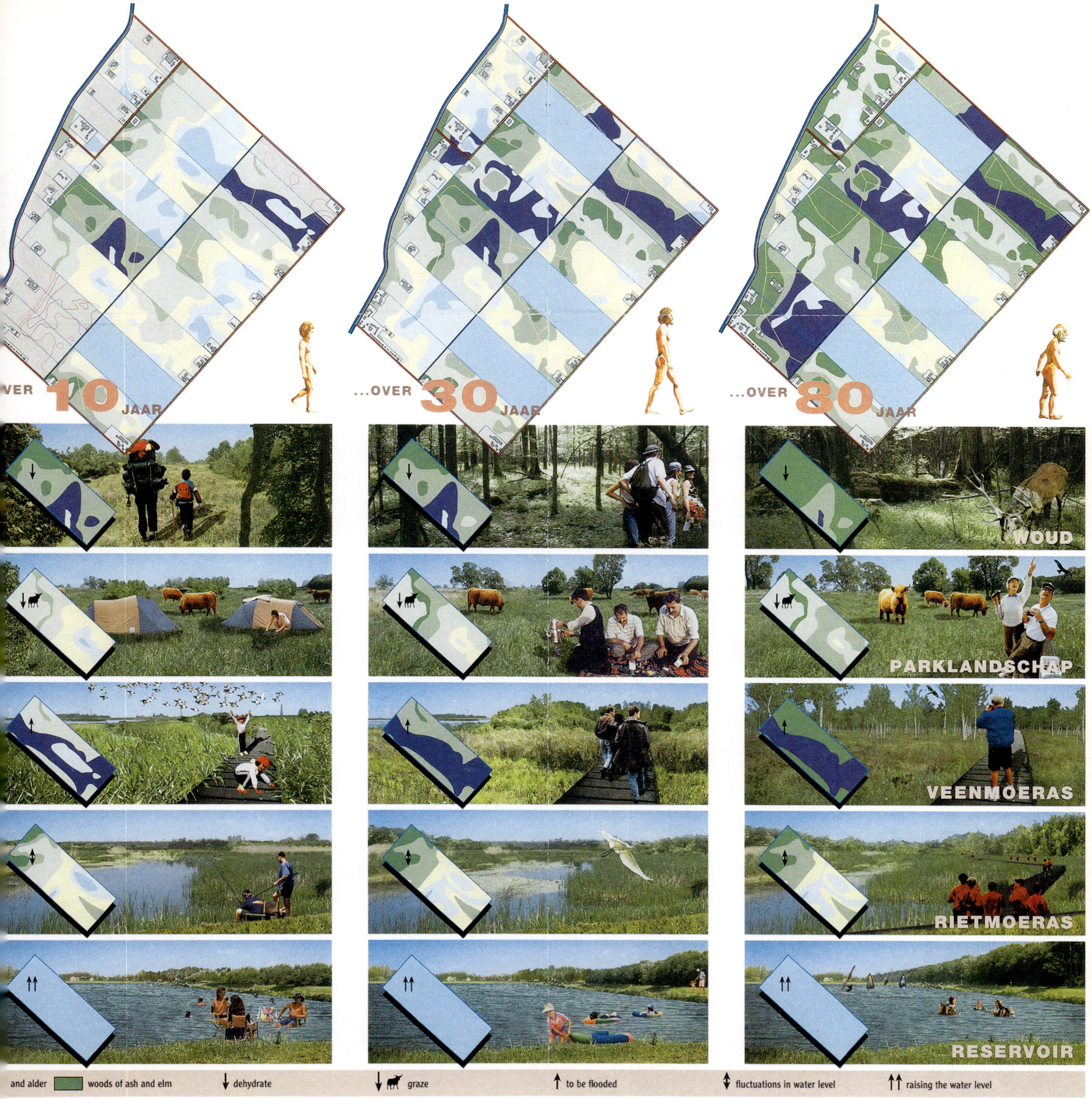

In Haarlemmermeer, five management concepts and regulation of water levels are to enable maximum biodiversity. The diagram (above) shows how forest, parklike landscape, peat-marsh, reed-marsh, water-containing landscape are to develop over the next 80 years.
1 Agricultural area, 2 Nature area, 3 Residential area, 4 Level of water in winter, 5 Level of water in summer, 6 Water intake for agricultural area, 7 Level of water in water-container (winter), 8 Level of water in water-container (summer), 9 Lockable culvert between water-containers, 10 Outlet for clean water, 11 Sewer to water treatment facility, 12 Canal for draining the water to the water-containing facilities, 13 Pumping

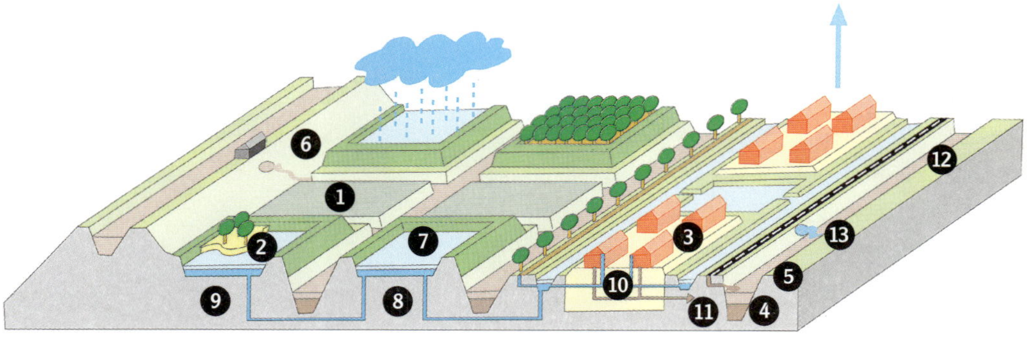

Niederlande charakteristischen Bodentypen: sandig, tonig und schluffig. Darüber hinaus unterscheiden sie sich in den wichtigsten Aspekten der Naturentwicklung und des Wasserhaushalts.

Aus dem Ton gezogen. Das erste Projekt mit dem Titel »Aus dem Ton gezogen« in Haarlemmermeer legt seinen Schwerpunkt auf die großräumige Anpassung eines Wassersystems mit dem Ziel, sauberes Wasser für ein Naturentwicklungsprojekt zu erhalten. Jedem Nicht-Niederländer muß ein derartig komplexes und großangelegtes Wassersystem unterhalb des Meeresspiegels wie ein Wunder vorkommen. Fünf Pflegekonzepte, die sich vor allem auf die Regulierung der Wasserpegel stützen, sollen maximale Biodiversität und ein abwechslungsreiches Landschaftsbild schaffen. Die natürlichen Gegebenheiten der Landschaft sind Bodenfluktuationen und kleine Höhenunterschiede, die typisch für die ehemalige Wattlandschaft sind. Anthropomorph sind geradlinige Strukturen wie Wasserläufe, Straßen und Parzellierungen, die nach der Trockenlegung entstanden. Sie werden beibehalten und bilden den selbstverständlichen architektonischen Rahmen für die weitere Entwicklung. Ein Teil des Areals wird nicht zum Entwicklungsgebiet, sondern bleibt an Wasserläufe und Straßen angeschlossen und dient der Agrarproduktion. Die Wasserläufe sind zu nährstoffreich für die Areale der Naturentwicklung. Deshalb wird das nötige Wasser überwiegend aus Rückhaltebecken herangeführt, die sich aus dem Oberflächenwasser versiegelter Flächen speisen. Während der ersten zwei Jahre wird der Grundwasserstand in allen Naturentwicklungsgebieten bis auf Geländeniveau erhöht, so daß sich zahlreiche Wasserflächen bilden. Dies verhindert zu starkes Wachstum von Pioniervegetation. Später läßt sich dann das Erscheinungsbild der Landschaft durch gezielte Regulation der Wasserpegel und durch Beweidung mit Schottischen Hochlandrindern in gewissen Grenzen manipulieren.

Das Besondere an dieser Methode ist die Tatsache, daß kein Endstadium erstrebt wird. Die Planung gibt vor allem Rahmenparameter vor, innerhalb derer sich die Naturgebiete auf Grundlage der natürlichen und antropomorphen Gegebenheiten entwickeln können. Es entsteht hierdurch eine Art selbstverständlicher Ordnung sowie ein Kontrast zwischen geradlinigen und spontanen Formen. Der landschaftsarchitektonische Entwurf macht – abstrahiert durch den kleinen Maßstab – keine Aussage zu gestalterischen Elementen oder Artefakten wie Stegen, Windmühlen oder sonstigen Bauten. Diese bilden eine zusätzliche Schicht in der Landschaft, eine Schicht in zeitgemäßer Formensprache. Wie der Besucher die neue Land-

know what else to do with them. The criticisms take their basis from a new approach that regards nature development, water regimes and landscape architecture as a single unity. Although this integrative planning approach has found expression in various projects, it is still not publicly discussed, and is therefore now described in the case of the following three projects. All three have one thing in common in that they all entail a process-oriented, 'nature development' approach, and feature water as a coherent element. Moreover, they all take cultural and architectural components into consideration, but differ in terms of soil (variously featuring sandy, argillaceous and silty ground, all typical of the Netherlands), and in the way that nature development and water regime aspects are interpreted.

Drawn from the Clay. The first project, which has the name "Drawn from the Clay", is located in Haarlemmermeer and is mainly concerned with the massive adaptation of a water system in order to obtain clean water for a nature development project. Anyone but a Dutchman would regard the creation of such a complex and large-scale water system below sea level as close to a miracle. The project involves five management concepts, all concerned with water level regulation and designed to enable maximum biodiversity and a varied visual landscape, since the present topography is characterised by little more than slight fluctuations in level, as typical of former tidal flats. Anthropomorphic structures also exist, in the form of the rectilinear water courses, roads and field boundaries that came about after the area had been won from the sea, and are to be retained as the architectonic frame within which further development will be able to unfold. Part of the area will not be devoted to nature development, however, but to agricultural production, and thus remain connected to the watercourses and roads. Since the watercourses are too nutrient-rich for nature development, the areas in question will mainly be provided with water from retention ponds fed with sealed-surface runoff. During the first two years, the ground water level in all the nature development areas is to be kept at surface level to enable the formation of numerous pools and ponds in an effort to stem excessive pioneer growth. Later on, the appearance of the landscape will be influenced by regulating the water level and having it grazed by Scottish highland cattle.

The special aspect of this method is that it does not seek to achieve a final ideal state. Rather, the planning sets out the natural and anthropomorphic parameters within which nature will be allowed to develop. The result is to be a kind of self-evident order, marked by a contrast of rectilinear and organic forms. The plan, which is highly abstract due to the tiny scale, does not show the design elements and artefacts such as boardwalks, windmills and other structures that form an additional layer in a contemporary idiom. The boardwalks, which will be installed at the beginning of the project to enable monitoring of the landscape's development, will play an important role in that their placement and alignment will determine the perception that visitors will have of the landscape. Moreover, they will also make it possible to perceive and recognise the spatial design, and the encounter of ecological planning with classical landscape architecture.

Zanderij-Crailo. The second project is embedded in a landscape with sandy soils, and concerns

schaft erlebt, hängt weitgehend vom Verlauf der Holzstege ab. Sie müssen bereits zu Beginn der Eingriffe gebaut werden, damit eine ständige Beobachtung der landschaftlichen Entwicklung möglich ist. Darüber hinaus machen sie die räumliche Gestaltung erfahrbar: eine Begegnung ökologischer Planung mit klassischer Landschaftsarchitektur.

Zanderij-Crailo. Das zweite Projekt, »Zanderij-Crailo«, liegt in einer Landschaft mit Sandböden – und befaßt sich mit einem Sandabbaugebiet. Das Gebiet inmitten einer monotonen Agrarlandschaft birgt zwei naturnahe Areale auf der West- und Ostseite, die jedoch durch eine Straße und eine Bahnlinie voneinander isoliert sind. Der Entwurf sieht drei ökologische Korridore vor. Einer davon ist der sogenannte »Ecoduct«, der mitten im Planungsgebiet die Bahnlinie und Straße überquert. Zwei weitere Verbindungen – eine trockene und eine relativ feuchte – sind im nördlichen und südlichen Teil geplant. Wegen des zu erwartenden hohen Publikumsverkehrs und weil das Büro der Schutzgebietsverwaltung sehr nahe liegt, entschied man sich für die Einrichtung eines Naturausstellungsgeländes. Ein Aussichtsplatz bietet einen Überblick über die verschiedenen Landschaftstypen, die sich dem Entwurf zufolge aus Unterschieden in den Wachstumsgrundlagen und im Pflegekonzept ergeben. Anders als beim ersten Projektbeispiel wird das Wasserniveau hier jedoch nicht technisch reguliert. Unterschiedliche Grundwasserpegel ergeben sich vielmehr aus der Art des weiteren Sandabbaus. Die hohe Qualität des Grundwassers und der nährstoffarme Boden ermöglichen eine abwechslungsreiche Landschaft: Drei Erhaltungsstrategien in Verbindung mit fünf Grundwasserpegeln bestimmen zehn mögliche Landschaftstypen. Die Tagebaulandschaft läßt zwar die Spuren der natürlichen Landschaft und die nutzungsbedingte Überformung noch erkennen, etwa in Form der durch neue Grabetechniken entstandenen Topographie. Der Prozeß der weiteren Naturentwicklung stützt sich jedoch weniger auf diese Gegebenheiten, sondern auf eine räumlich-plastische Modellierung des Geländes.

Auf den ersten Blick scheint die Entwurfsmethodik beider Projekte gleich zu sein. Die Rolle der Landschaftsarchitektur ist aber sehr unterschiedlich. Im Beispiel Haarlemmermeer werden die landschaftsarchitektonischen Elemente oder Artefakte als eigenständige zeitgemäße Schicht der vorhandenen Landschaft zugefügt und die Wasserstände reguliert. In Crailo dagegen wird der Boden selbst zum Gegenstand landschaftsarchitektonischer Komposition.

1

2

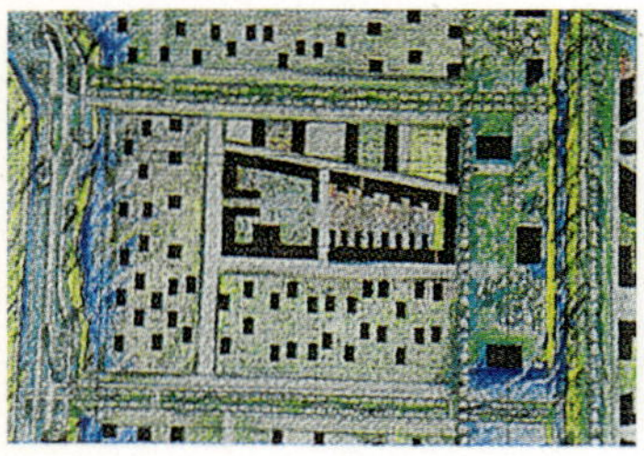

3

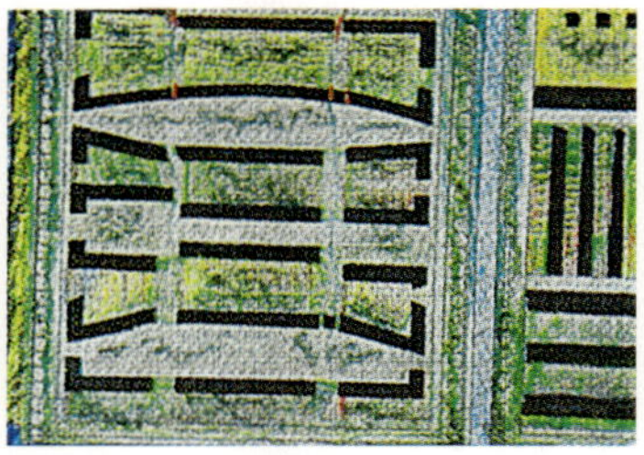

4

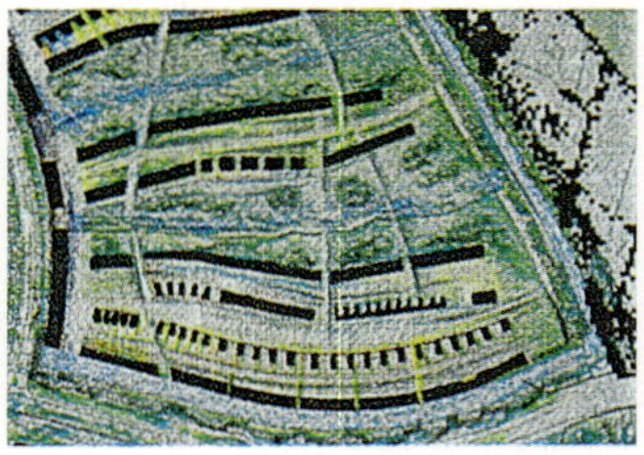

Masterplan Vleuten-De Meern (Leidse Rijn)
Planners: VHP urban designers, architects, landscape architects, Rotterdam

a sand quarrying area. Located in a monotonous agricultural landscape, the site in question features two near-natural areas divided by a road and a railway line. These are now to be connected by three ecological corridors. One of these consists of a so-called ecoduct, which will cross the road and railway line in the heart of the planning area. Two further links – one of them dry, the other relatively wet – are planned in the north and south of the site. Due to the expected high visitor levels and the proximity of the Reserve Management Office, it was decided to turn parts of the area into a natural exhibition site. A viewing platform is to provide an overview of the different landscape types that are to develop as a result of the differing growth conditions and the management concept envisaged by the plan.

In contrast to the first project, the water levels will not be regulated by technical means, but will fluctuate with the continued quarrying of the sand. At the same time, ten different landscape types are to emerge with the help of the low-nutrient soil and the pure quality of the ground water, as well as three preservation strategies and five ground water levels. The quarried landscape still bears traces of original formations and past uses, such as topographies resulting from new excavation techniques, but will nevertheless be subjected to sculpted, spatial modelling as a basis for the desired development processes.

At first glance, the design methodology of the two projects seems to be the same, but the role played by landscape architecture differs considerably. In the Haarlemmermeer project, landscape architectural elements and artefacts form a separate, contemporary layer of the landscape, and water levels will be consciously regulated. In

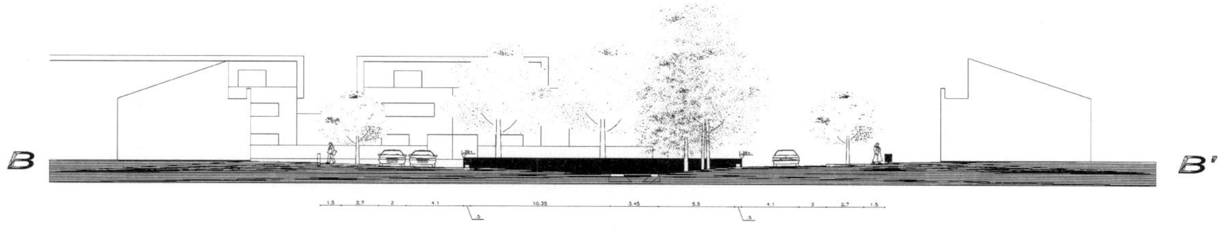

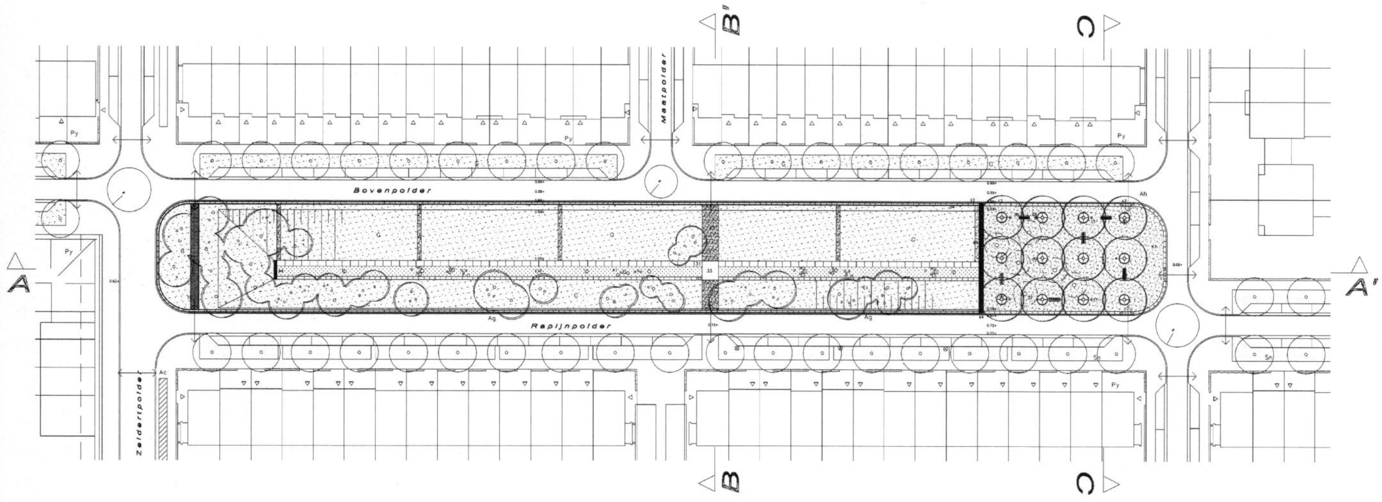

Das Stadterweiterungprojekt »Leidse Rijn« in der Peripherie der Städte Utrecht, Vleuten und De Meern ist in seiner Größenordnung das eindrucksvollste Beispiel der Niederlande, wie in Wohngebieten auf Schluff-Böden der Umgang mit Niederschlagswasser gestalterisch anspruchsvoll integriert werden kann. Im Masterplan läßt sich die unterschiedliche Freiraumgestaltung der Quartiere erkennen, in den Vignetten mögliche Bebauungstypen: 1 Feld, 2 grüne Kammer, 3 Hof, 4 Wasserstraßen.
Wenn unter dem Ton sandige Böden in geringer Tiefe vorkommen, werden Versickerungssysteme in die Freiräume eingefügt, wie bei nebenstehendem Entwurf für einen Wohnhof.

In terms of size, the "Leidse Rijn" urban extension project being realised on the periphery of the cities of Utrecht, Vleuten and De Meern is probably the Netherlands' most impressive example of integration of precipitation management and high design standards at a housing estate built on silty soil. While the vignettes depict possible building types, the master plan shows the differing open space design solutions in the various areas of the estate: 1 Field, 2 Green room, 3 Estate, 4 Water courses.
Seepage elements, as shown in the adjacent design for a residential court, are to be installed at places where sandy layers lie close to the clay surface.

Crailo, on the other hand, the ground itself is part of the landscape architectural composition.

Leidse Rijn. The third project, concerning the water management system for "Leidse Rijn", a housing estate built on silty soil near Utrecht, demonstrates that the new water management approaches are reaching the cities. In the case in question, 30,000 flats are being built over an area of 2,560 hectares, and are accompanied by a concept that involves complete rainwater management. In other words, wherever possible, 175 hectares of retention and infiltration areas are to be created in strata with a high clay and silt content, while seepage elements are to be installed at sandy layers closer to the surface, the idea being to underscore soil-related moisture differences by design and functional means: Water will be visible in areas with silty soil, and its presence minimised in sandy ones.

In terms of size, the project is probably the Netherlands' most impressive example of integration of precipitation management into a housing

Leidse Rijn. Das dritte Projektbeipiel stammt aus einer Gegend mit Schluff-Böden: Das Wassermanagement-System in »Leidse Rijn«, einem Wohngebiet bei Utrecht. Es zeigt, daß die neuen Ansätze im Wassermanagement mittlerweile auch die Städte erreicht haben: Auf einem Areal von 2560 Hektar entstehen 30 000 Wohnungen – und das komplette Niederschlagswasser soll bewirtschaftet werden. Wo sich der Untergrund mit hohen Ton-Schluff-Anteilen dafür eignet, werden insgeamt 175 Hektar Retentions- und Infiltrationsflächen angelegt. An Stellen, die in geringer Tiefe unter dem Ton sandige Schichten aufweisen, werden Versickerungsanlagen gebaut. Die Idee dabei ist, die bodenphysikalisch bedingten Feuchtigkeitsunterschiede gestalterisch und funktional zu unterstreichen: In feuchten Bereichen wird das Wasser sichtbar und erfahrbar, in den trockenen seine Anwesenheit minimiert.

Das Projekt ist in seiner Größenordnung wohl das eindrucksvollste Beispiel der Niederlande, wie in Wohngebieten der Umgang mit Niederschlagswasser gestalterisch anspruchsvoll integriert werden kann. Der Flächenbedarf dafür ist jedoch erheblich: Wasserrückhaltung und -versickerung nehmen rund 15 Prozent des öffentlichen Raumes ein. Auf jede Wohnung kommen für Wasserhaltung und für öffentliches Grün jeweils etwa sechs Quadratmeter Flächenbedarf.

Der Entwurf unterscheidet drei gestalterische Grundzüge. Erstens die Einheit des Systems: Dachflächen, Transportsystem, Versickerung, Rück-

Design for an environment with water infiltration areas
Location: Utrecht, De Meern, Vleuten (Leidse Rijn)
Planners: Quadrat urban design, landscape and architecture, Rotterdam

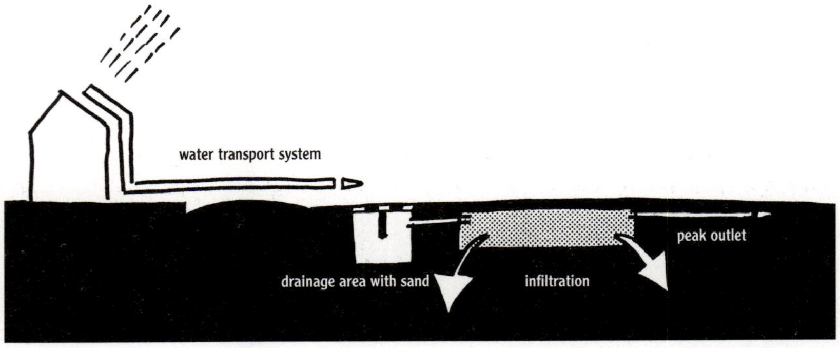

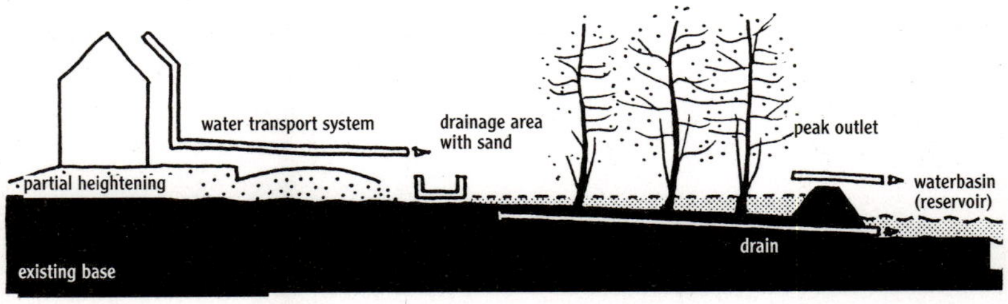

Im Projekt »Leidse Rijn« sollen die bodenphysikalisch bedingten Feuchtigkeitsunterschiede gestalterisch und funktional sichtbar werden. An Stellen, die in geringer Tiefe unter dem Ton Sand aufweisen, werden Versickerungsanlagen gebaut, das Wasser verschwindet schnell (Grafik oben). Wo der Untergrund hingegen hohe Ton-Schluff-Anteile besitzt, werden Retentions- und Infiltrationsflächen angelegt. Hier prägen Wasserflächen die Freiräume. Grafiken: H+N+S landscape architects, Utrecht

At the "Leidse Rijn" project, soil-related moisture differences are to be made visible by design and functional means. Seepage elements are to be installed in clay soil featuring sandy layers below, meaning that water will drain away quickly (drawing above). Retention and infiltration areas, on the other hand, are to be created in strata with a high clay and silt content, resulting in pools and sheets of water. Drawings: H+N+S landscape architects, Utrecht

haltung, Notüberlauf und Wasserflächen bilden dank einheitlicher Materialien und durch die Art der Plazierung im Raum eine Einheit. Zweitens die visuellen Akzente: Verschiedene Komponenten der Regenwasserführung werden visuell hervorgehoben. Drittens die gestalterische Integration: Die Wasserführung übernimmt die Charakteristika angrenzender Gestaltungselemente und fügt sich in das Gesamterscheinungsbild.

Es zeigt sich, daß das Konzept der integralen Wasserhaltung und eine Herangehensweise ähnlich wie bei den Naturentwicklungsgebieten tatsächlich zu markanten und neuartigen Wohnumfeldern führt. Naturgemäß ist dieser Effekt bei den Rückhaltegebieten ausgeprägter als in den Versickerungsgebieten. Weit stärker als bei letzteren gilt für sie das Entwurfsprinzip »aus einem Guß«. Ein Problem: Die Zahl der PKW-Fahrten nimmt mit steigender Verdichtung eines Wohngebiets zu. Regenwasser von Straßen muß aber je nach Verkehrsaufkommen stark gereinigt werden, bevor es in das Wassersystem aufgenommen werden darf; beispielsweise muß das Oberflächenwasser stark befahrener Straßen einer Kläranlage zugeführt werden. Der Grenzwert hierfür wurde kürzlich sogar auf 2000 Fahrten pro Tag halbiert, was Planungen wie in Leidse Rijn nochmals erschwert. Nach allgemeiner Überzeugung gibt es aber keinen Weg zurück. Die Prozeßhaftigkeit von Landschaftsarchitektur, wie sie in der Naturentwicklung angewandt wird, hat die Stadt erreicht.

estate at high design standards. The costs, however, are high in that the retention and seepage facilities consume about 15 percent of open space: Six square metres per flat are required for water management and public green.

The design is characterised by three principle design features: coherence, accentuation and integration. In this, the roofs, the seepage, retention and emergency overflow elements, the water movement system and the water bodies display unity in terms of materials and means of placement; various components of the rainwater system are visually highlighted, and other parts of the system adopt the characteristics of neighbouring design elements, making them seem a self-evident part of the overall picture.

The project proves that integrative urban water management concepts and an approach similar to that used in nature development areas can indeed lead to striking and novel residential environments. At Leidse Rijn, this applies more to the silty retention areas than the sandy seepage ones in that the former are naturally better able to bear the mark of a single signature. However, the concept has an Achilles' heel in that a change has been made in the legislation governing the treatment of surface runoff, halving the threshold levels at which road runoff requires sewage-plant treatment to 2,000 journeys a day. Since the prevalence of roads in a housing estate encourages the use of cars, this poses the Leidse Rijn water management project with a considerable problem. Despite this difficulty it is generally agreed that there is no way back. In other words, the process-related nature of landscape architecture, as applied in the nature development model, has come to stay – both in town and country.

Architektur als öffentliches Ereignis

Architecture as a public event

Tjerk Ruimschotel

Unparalleled by any standards, the new residential district Kattenbroek, a modest extension of the Dutch town of Amersfoort (110,000 inhabitants), has become a major tourist attraction for both the architectural profession and the general public. The project consists of some 5,000 dwellings, built in five years and thus contributing a mere one percent of the yearly housing production in The Netherlands of about 100,000 new dwellings. Included in the project are a shopping centre and offices with a total net floor area of 30,000 square metres and public park leading from the commercial centre to the Schothorst park, which lies in-between the four neighbourhoods making up the Amersfoort-North district. As a result of the public housing policy of the national government, local authorities today are playing an important role in encouraging private investors to realize the part of the national housing production assigned to them.

The Kattenbroek project was triggered off by the negative reply given by alderman Fons Asselbergs, responsible for housing and urban design, to the question whether he himself would like to live in one of the new built-up areas around this, or for that matter any Dutch city. After careful examination of recent plans and projects carried out in Holland and after a thorough search for an urban planner to design "something completely different", Ashok Bhalotra of KuiperCompagnons got the job.

The person and work of Ashok Bhalotra stand out in the anonymous tradition of town planning. Speaking perfect Dutch with an oriental accent, Ashok Bhalotra has an overwhelming impact in the rousing way he talks about his ideas and his work. He adds spice to the trade. He

Die Niederlande sind um eine Attraktion reicher: Bei der Erweiterung der 110 000-Einwohner-Stadt Amersfoort ist ein in jeder Hinsicht beispielloses neues Wohngebiet entstanden, das sowohl in Architektur-Fachkreisen, als auch bei der breiten Öffentlichkeit auf großes Interesse stößt. Kattenbroek besteht aus rund 5 000 Wohnungen, die in etwas mehr als fünf Jahren gebaut wurden, was rund ein Prozent des jährlichen niederländischen Wohnungsbaus von insgesamt rund 100 000 Wohnungen ausmachte. Bestandteil des Projektes sind ein Einkaufszentrum und Büros mit insgesamt 30 000 Quadratmeter Einzelhandelsfläche sowie ein öffentlicher Park. Er führt vom Zentrum aus zur Grünzone Schothorst, die zwischen den vier Nachbarsiedlungen liegt, aus denen sich der Distrikt Amersfoort-Nord zusammensetzt.

Als Folge der nationalen Wohnungsbaupolitik ist es heute eine wesentliche Aufgabe der Kommunen, es privaten Investoren, Unternehmen und Baufirmen schmackhaft zu machen, den festgesetzten Teil des nationalen Wohnungsbaus zu realisieren. Das Kattenbroek-Projekt wurde ausgelöst durch den Stadtrat Fons Asselbergs, dem Verantwortlichen für Wohnungsbau und Stadtgestaltung in Amersfoort. Er stellte sich nämlich die Frage, ob er selber gerne in einer der Neubausiedlungen seiner oder jeder beliebigen anderen niederländischen Stadt wohnen wollte, und mußte dies mit nein beantworten. Nach sorgfältiger Analyse bestehender Pläne und realisierter Projekte in Holland machte man sich eingehend auf die Suche nach einem Stadtplaner für eine »völlig andere« Planung. Ashok Bhalotra von KuiperCompagnons bekam den Auftrag. In der anonymen Stadtplanungs-Tradition fallen die Person Ashok Bhalotra und sein Werk auf. Seine mitreißende Art, in perfektem Holländisch mit orientalischem Akzent über seine Arbeit zu sprechen, hat eine überwältigende Wirkung. Er verleiht dem Berufsstand sozusagen Würze. Seine Architekturausbildung erhielt Bhalotra in einer englisch ausgerichteten Universität in seinem Heimatland In-

Der niederländische Stadtplaner Ashok Bhalotra entwarf einen außergewöhnlichen Plan für die Wohnsiedlung Kattenbroek in Amersfoort.
The Dutch town planner Ashok Bhalotra designed an unusual plan for the Kattenbroek settlement in Amersfoort.

Die Planung für das Stadtviertel Kattenbroek ist bemerkenswert, da die Stadt sich stark mit dem individuellen Denkansatz des Gestalters Ashok Bhalotra identifiziert. Der städtebauliche Entwurf überrascht durch seine Schlichtheit, die bisher entstandenen Bauten durch ihre phantasievollen Formen.

The planning for the Kattenbroek district is of interest in that the city identifies itself closely with the individualistic ideas of the town planner Ashok Bhalotra. The urban development proposal is surprising in its simplicity, the imaginative design of the buildings no less so.

dien. Er arbeitete bei Candilis, Josaic und Woods in Paris, bevor er in die Niederlande ging.

Seit der jüngsten Umstrukturierung bei KuiperCompagnons mit Sitz in Rotterdam ist Ashok Bhalotra dort zusammen mit Wytze Patijn Direktor. Mit rund 110 Angestellten ist dies die größte niederländische Planungsfirma und eine Brutstätte für Universitätsprofessoren. Die Firma wurde 1916 von Granpré Moliere und Verhagen gegründet, als sie in Zusammenarbeit mit Hendrik Petrus Berlage die Gartenstadt Vreewijk in Rotterdam planten. Heute erweisen sich die nonkonformistischen, manchmal künstlerischen Entwürfe von Bhalotra und seinen Gestalter-Teams als sehr erfolgreich in der gegenwärtigen Phase der niederländischen Wohnungsbaupolitik.

Seit dem Stadtplanungsgesetz von 1902 dienten in Holland viele Wohnungsbauprojekte nicht nur dazu, die Nachfrage nach neuem Wohnraum zu befriedigen. Vielmehr waren sie in erster Linie Teile von Entwicklungsprogrammen für Stadt und Wirtschaft oder für angewandte Sozial- und Politikwissenschaft.

Holländischer Wohnungsbau ist demnach das Ergebnis einer kontinuierlichen Reihe von Experimenten – das Land fungiert als Labor, Bauplatz und Testgebiet, und die Bevölkerung nimmt die Rolle von Gestaltern, Bewohnern und Entscheidungsträgern ein.

Die ersten Jahre nach dem Zweiten Weltkrieg waren dem Wiederaufbau gewidmet, der in eine weitgehende Standardisierung und Industrialisierung des Bauens mündete. Stadtgestaltung war in diesem Zeitraum, trotz anderer Ansätze von Lotte Stam-Beese, Gerrit Rietveld und Jaap Bakema, in jeder Hinsicht kantig. In den 70er Jahren entwickelte sich die Stadtplanung unter dem Einfluß der holländischen »Forum-groep« und des niederländischen Strukturalismus zum Typ »Blumenkohl«: Jede Wohnsiedlung bestand vorwiegend aus kleinen Reihenhäusern mit Sozialwohnungen, an engen, verkehrsberuhigten Straßen, zum Teil Sackgassen. Die Ränder benachbarter Wohngebiete folgten den gewundenen inneren Strukturen, so daß sich ein Muster ähnlich den Blumenkohl-Röschen ergab. In der zweiten Hälfte der 80er Jahre kamen neue Entwurfs-Methoden auf, in denen die Wechselbeziehungen zwischen Wohnungstypologie und Stadtgrundriß nicht so streng waren; ein einfaches, oft geometrisches Grundmuster erlaubte auf einem großen Grundstück den Bau unterschiedlicher Haustypen. Dies war notwendig, seit sich die Regierung mit ihrer Politik zunehmend aus dem Wohnungsbau zurückzog: Alles dem Markt überlassen lautete die neue Devise.

received his architectural training at an English orientated university in his native India and worked for Candilis, Josaic and Woods in Paris before moving to The Netherlands. Ashok Bhalotra is now together with Wytze Patijn managing-director of KuiperCompagnons, which is based in Rotterdam. With around 110 employees, this company is the biggest Dutch planning firm and a breeding ground for university professors and honorary members of the BNS (Dutch Association of Urban Planners).
The company was founded in 1916 by Granpré Molière and Verhagen, when they collaborated with Hendrik Petrus Berlage in designing the Vreewijk Garden City in Rotterdam. The nonconformist, sometimes arty designs of Bhalotra and his design teams proved to work well in the latest stage of housing policy in The Netherlands.

Following the Town Planning Act of 1902 in Holland, many housing schemes did not merely serve to meet the demand for new housing, but were primarily part of a wider scheme of urban and economic development or social and political engineering. Dutch housing is thus the outcome of a continuous series of experiments – in which Holland acts as a laboratory, building site and testing field at the same time, with the Dutch people in simultaneous roles of designers, occupants and decision-makers. The first years after World War II were devoted to Reconstruction, cumulating in the far-reaching standardization and industrialization of the building process. The urban design of that period was, despite attempts by Lotte Stam-Beese, Gerrit Rietveld and Jaap Bakema, primarily square in every sense.

In the Seventies, under the influence of the Dutch Forum-groep, Dutch structuralism and advocacy-planning, the urban designs were of the "cauliflower-type". This meant that every neighbourhood consisted mostly of small social housing terraces, with narrow, even dead-end streets to slow down the motor-traffic. The borders of the adjacent neighbourhoods followed the twisted internal structures, thus forming a pattern much like the rosettes of a cauliflower.

In the second half of the Eighties, new design methods emerged in which the interrelations of housing typology and urban pattern were not so rigidly combined; a straightforward layout (often geometrical) of the plan allowed several types of houses to the built. This was necessary

Heute planen und bauen die nationalen und kommunalen Planungsämter nicht mehr selbst, sondern sie produzieren lediglich Richtlinien über die Anzahl der zu bauenden Wohnungen. Gesetzliche Absicherung und finanzielle Unterstützung ist lediglich für die notwendige Infrastruktur, vorzugsweise für öffentliche Verkehrsmittel, vorgesehen. Dies läßt Lokalpolitiker zu Mittlern zwischen großen Immobilienunternehmen und Kommunen werden.

Das Gestaltungskonzept von Kattenbroek. Das Projekt Kattenbroek ist bemerkenswert, da die Stadt sich mit dem sehr individuellen Denkansatz des Gestalters identifiziert. Dieses Denken war das Fundament sowohl für den Entwurfsprozeß selbst als auch für die Art und Weise, wie dieser Prozeß fortwährend mit allen Beteiligten diskutiert und vollendet wurde. Die Gestaltungsphilosophie von Ashok Bhalotra basiert auf drei Prinzipien: Text, Kontext und Pretext. Der Text bezeichnet die Art und Weise, wie Men-

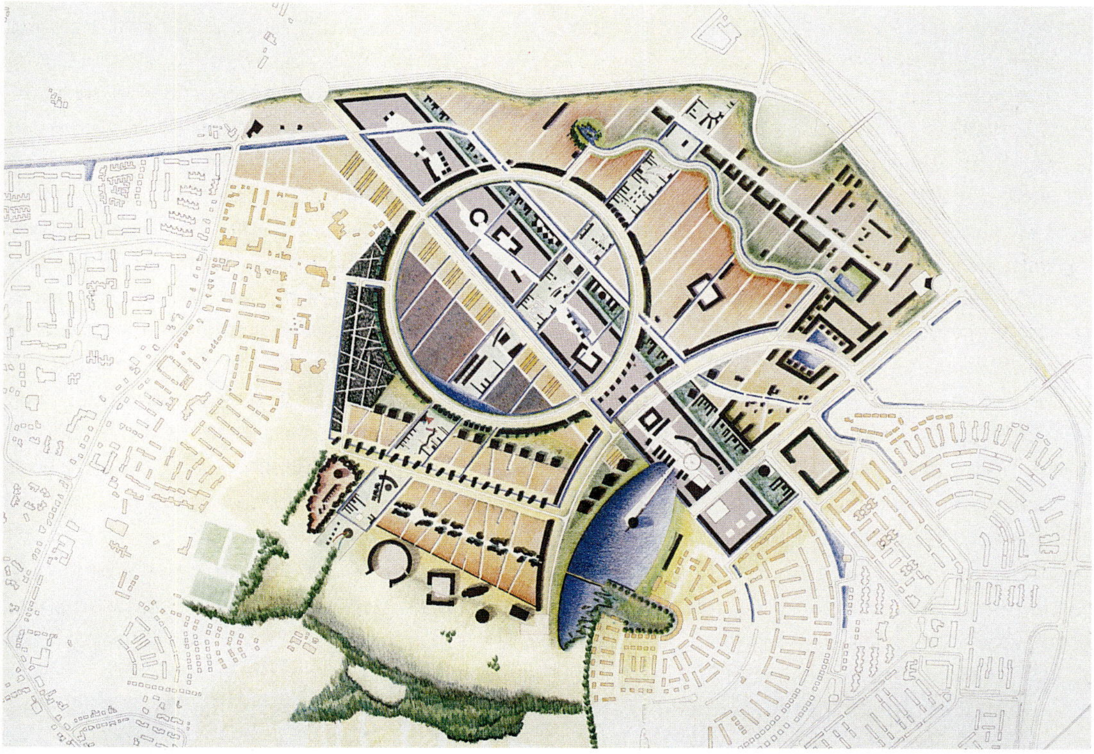

Der Masterplan für Kattenbroek kombiniert fünf urbane Elemente, die sowohl symbolische wie auch räumliche Qualitäten besitzen. Zwei breite Linien durchkreuzen einen Kreis; eine Kurve und eine flatternde Linie flankieren ihn. Den Kreis bildet eine Ringstraße, die das Geschlossene, das Zuhausesein symbolisiert. Aus den beiden Linien leiten sich die breite Straße der Höfe und die Verborgene Zone – ein Park – ab. Im Gegensatz zum Ring steht die Kurve, Maske genannt, für das Anonyme. Die geschwungene Linie schließlich, ein Bach, symbolisiert das Romantische.

The Kattenbroek master plan combines five urban elements that unite spatial ideas and symbolical meaning in the form of two broad lines that traverse a circle flanked by a curve and a wavy line. The circle consists of a circular road and symbolizes a feeling of seclusion and home, while the broad lines form the Avenue of Courtyards and the Hidden Zone. In contrast to the circle, the curve, otherwise called the Mask, stands for anonymity. Finally, the wavy line, a stream, symbolizes Romanticism.

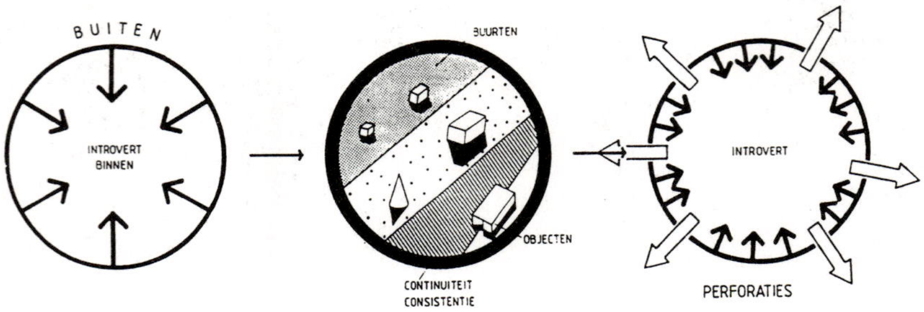

schen über ihre Ziele, Bedürfnisse und Gefühle denken und reden. Das Konzept für die Planung ist daher eher in Worten als raumbezogen formuliert und basiert auf Metaphern, die vom Verreisen und Heimkommen abgeleitet sind. Der Kontext ist die Landschaft, das Programm, der Auftrag, der genius loci – die Landschaft selbst und das Bild der Landschaft in den Köpfen der Beteiligten. Die auf die Landschaft projizierten Metaphern führen zum Entwurf. Dieser Plan bildet die Grundlage für die Gestaltung der verschiedenen Teilbereiche des Projekts. Die Wohnsiedlung, wie sie sich heute darstellt, ist das Resultat eines Gestaltungsprozesses und nicht ein vorgefaßtes Ergebnis, das nur materiell umgesetzt werden mußte.

Paradox, aber auf der anderen Seite eine Notwendigkeit für die nachfolgende Fülle an architektonischen Ausdrucksformen ist die visuelle Schlichtheit des städtebaulichen Entwurfs: Ein voller Kreis, durchkreuzt von zwei breiten Linien, die durch eine Kurve und eine flatternde Linie verbunden sind, um die Komposition auszubalancieren. Er erscheint nun als Logo für die Wohnsiedlung auf den extra gefertigten Schildern mit den Straßennamen.

Der Masterplan ist eine Komposition urbaner Elemente, Wohnungstypologien, Landschaften und Stadtmorphologien. Manchmal sind diese Komponenten eindeutig festgelegt, manchmal sind sie in der Zeichnung nicht ablesbar, sind dem gebauten Projekt selbst überlassen. Die wichtigsten Komponenten sind dabei die fünf urbanen Elemente. Sie besitzen sowohl symbolische als auch räumliche Qualitäten und können als die wesentlichen Eingriffe in die ursprüngliche Landschaft verstanden werden:

1. De Ring – eine Ringstraße, die das Zuhause symbolisiert
2. Laan der Hoven – die Straße der Höfe
3. De Verborgen Zone – die Verborgene Zone, ein Landschaftspark
4. Het Mask – die Maske als das Symbol der Anonymität
5. De Kreek – der Bach, ein romantisches Symbol.

Die bisherige Fachkritik bemängelt, daß die Metaphern und Komponenten des Entwurfs sich in der gebauten Realität nicht deutlich genug unterscheiden lassen. Doch Bhalotra bemüht sich gar nicht darum, die Bewohner in der Weise zu beeinflussen, daß sie die gleichen Assoziationen wahrnehmen wie der Gestalter während des Entwurfsprozesses. Diese Elemente dienten lediglich dazu, die Diskussion zwischen Stadtplanern, Architekten, Geldgebern, Politikern und dergleichen zu bestimmen, um den Bau eines sehr realen Teilstücks einer Stadt voranzutreiben.

since the national government adopted a policy of withdrawing from the housing sector: let the market do its own job, became the slogan. Nowadays national and local governmental planning agencies no longer plan and build themselves, but merely produce memoranda about numbers of houses to be built, giving only legal and financial support for the necessary infrastructure, particularly public transport. This leaves local politicians to act as middlemen between large real estate developers and the local community.

The design concept of Kattenbroek. The Kattenbroek project is notable for the way the town responds to and identifies itself with the very individual thinking of the designer. This thinking was the foundation of both the design process itself and the way in which this process is constantly discussed and elaborated with all those involved. The design philosophy of Ashok Bhalotra is based on three principles: text, context and pretext. The first factor in Bhalotra's design philosophy is the text – the way people think and talk about their needs, their emotions. The concept of the plan is therefore formulated more literally than spatially and based on metaphors derived from the themes of travelling and home-coming. The second element is the context: the landscape, the programme, the brief, the genius loci; both the landscape itself and the image of the landscape by the participants.

The metaphors projected onto the landscape lead to the design of the project. This plan forms the basis for the layout of the various parts of the project. The actual neighbourhood is the result of the design process, not a preconceived outcome which only has to materialize.

Paradoxical, but on the other hand a necessity for the subsequent abundance of architectural expression is the visual simplicity of the urban scheme itself: a full circle crossed by two broad lines coupled with a curve and a wobbly line to balance the composition. It figures now as the logo of the neighbourhood on the custom-made nameplates of the streets.

The Kattenbroek scheme of the 1989 Masterplan is a composition of urban elements, housing themes, landscapes and urban morphologies. The most important components are the five urban elements. They have both symbolic and spatial qualities and can be understood as major spatial interventions in the original landscape:

1. De Ring – the Ring, a circular road
2. Laan der Hoven – Avenue of Courtyards
3. De Verborgen Zone – the Hidden Zone
4. Het Masker – the Mask
5. De Kreek – the Creek

Comments which have been made by other architects are that the metaphors of the scheme are not clearly distinguishable in the built-up reality. However, Bhalotra does not strive to manipulate the inhabitant into experiencing the same associations or metaphors which the designer experienced in the design process. These elements merely served to articulate the debate between urban planners, architects, financers and politicians in the building of a very real piece of a city.

To Bhalotra it was unthinkable to leave the project unfinished to provide "room for the inhabitants" to express their ideas. Instead, Bhalotra wanted to articulate his ideas as clearly as possible, using every pretext (his third element) he can think of and afterwards leaving his finished products in the hands of the occupant, who then

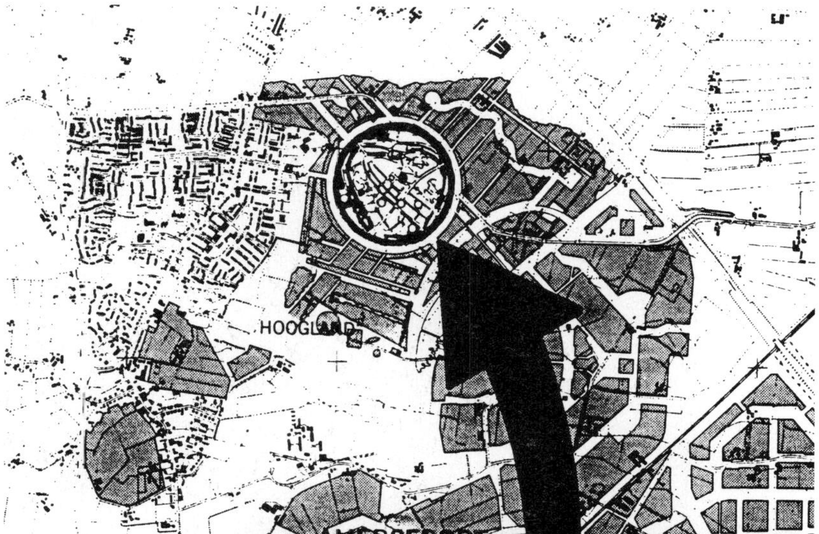

Der Kattenbroek-Ring ist ebenso groß wie die ringförmigen Mauern der Innenstadt von Amersfoort. Doch anders als der Stadtwall mit seinen nach außen gerichteten Ausblicken gewährt der neue Ring Blicke nach innen in das Wohnviertel. An manchen Stellen öffnet sich der Kreis der Landschaft, der Kirchturm von Hoogland wird durch eine Schneise sichtbar.

The Kattenbroek circular road is as large in circumference as the walls surrounding the old part of Amersfoort. Unlike the walls with their lookouts and orientation towards the outside world, the new ring road looks inward to the new residential estate and occasionally opens up to views of the landscape. A long axis permits a view towards the old church spine of Hoogland.

Für Ashok war es undenkbar, solch ein Projekt unvollendet zu lassen, um »Raum für die Bewohner« zum Ausdruck ihrer eigenen Ideen bereitzustellen. Statt dessen will er seine Ideen so klar wie möglich darstellen, indem er jeden denkbaren Pretext (sein drittes Element) nutzt und danach sein fertiges Produkt in die Hände der Bewohner legt, die es sich aneignen und ihrem Geschmack anpassen.

Work in progress. Der Planungsprozeß begann 1988 mit dem Entwurf des Masterplans, der im Januar 1989 genehmigt wurde. Im März 1990 begann man zu bauen, und die Übergabe der letzten Häuser war schließlich 1996. Stadtrat Asselbergs achtete darauf, daß Ashok Bhalotra als Stadtplaner und Leiter des Entwurfsprozesses von Hochbauten und Landschaftsarchitektur in die Arbeit der Verwaltung, der Wohnungsgesellschaften, der Privatkunden und Vertragspartner einbezogen wurde, um so sicherzustellen, daß alle beteiligten Parteien zusammenarbeiten.

Rund 40 Architekten wurden beauftragt; einige kamen aus der Gegend, einige waren traditionell und mittelmäßig, einige waren junge Städter und sehr professionell, mit internationaler Reputation – aber keiner kam aus dem Ausland. Dies steht im Gegensatz zu vergleichbaren Projekten in Amsterdam, Den Haag oder Groningen, wo man sich von ausländischen Architekten die entscheidenden neuen Qualitäten versprach. Die Architektur ist erfreulich – offensichtlich wirkten die städtebaulichen Gestaltungsvorgaben Wunder. Man kann zu Recht von einer außergewöhnlichen Stadtplanung sprechen. In Kattenbroek haben die Architekten sich selbst übertroffen und eine unerwartete Fülle experimenteller Architektur produziert, was von der Bevölkerung herzlich begrüßt wurde, die all die zweckmäßigen, aber unbewohnbaren oder langweiligen Wohnungen satt hat, die man üblicherweise baut.

Trotz der hohen Dichte, die auch auf den Plänen sichtbar wird, erscheint Kattenbroek bemerkenswert offen und geräumig. Die Landschaftsgestaltung rund um die Häuser stand unter der Aufsicht von Bhalotra. Mit seinem Team gestaltete er die Freiräume und sah eine ziemlich informelle Umwelt vor, wo weder Verkehr noch parkende Autos den öffentlichen Raum stören. Städtische Freiräume sind zumeist Teil des Straßen- und Wegenetzes – die Bewegung ist ein bedeutendes Thema der Planung. Die große Vielfalt der Lösungen für die städtischen Freiräume wird geordnet durch die linearen Strukturen der Baumalleen, die uniforme Gestaltung der Bürgersteige und der Straßenmöblierung.

has to appropriate the design product and adapt the product to his liking.

Work in progress. The planning process started in 1988 with the drafting of the Masterplan, approved by the Municipality in January 1989. Actual building started in March 1990 and delivery of the last houses finally was in 1996. Alderman Asselbergs made sure that Ashok Bhalotra, as the urban designer and supervisor of the ongoing process of designing building and landscape architecture, was given a clearly defined role in the professional services.

Some forty architects were commissioned, some were local, some traditional and mediocre, some young urbanite and very professional and with an international reputation, but none was foreign. This stands in contrast to similar projects in Amsterdam or The Hague where well-known architects from abroad were employed.

At Kattenbroek the architects surpassed themselves and produced an unknown and unexpected abundance of experimental architecture, which was heartily welcomed by the people who were sick and tired of all the proper, but uninhabitable or boring housing they were used to.

The landscaping around the houses was part of the supervising role of Bhalotra, who designed a rather informal, oversized environment in which automobiles do not break up the public space. Urban spaces were mostly part of the public network of streets and paths. The very diverse solutions for the urban spaces are tempered by the structural alignments of trees along the main routes, the uniform character of the pavements and of the street furniture.

The Ring has the same size as the walls of the city of Amersfoort but, unlike this wall with

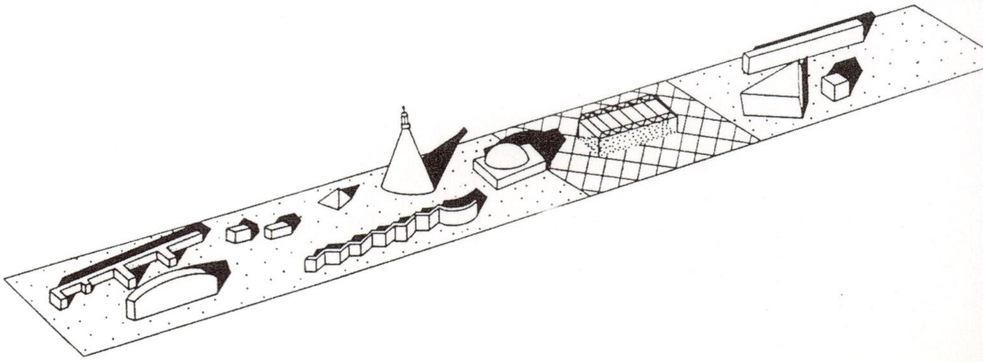

views towards the outside of the city, the Ring offers views to the inside of the circle. The Avenue of Courtyards runs through the entire project in a straight line, adjacent to a canal bordering the urban blocks containing the various forms of the courtyards. Green areas which are traditionally required such as play grounds and pocket parks did not form the backbone of the plan – the parks of Amersfoort-North are close by. These parks outside the housing area are beautifully integrated into the urban layout: long axes permit views towards the slightly elevated green area with the mediaeval church spine peaking over the treetops of an age-old wood.

The Hidden Zone has now been completed too. This zone, walled in from the rest of the scheme is a specific zone in contrast to the rest of the urban tissue. Although planned as a monument to the existing landscape, this zone is also very much built-up, thus offering no striking contrast in that respect to the rest of the urban fabric. However, the assignment of some 15 artists to the task of filling up the treasure chest which the Hidden Zone surely was a promising sign, and it was worth to wait another couple of years to experience in full the richness of Bhalotra's project.

In the meantime, the state of the art of the project bears witness to an outstanding achievement. Fortunately, the Kattenbroek area is easy to find, close to the motorway from Amsterdam to Amersfoort, the dual carriageway leading to Kattenbroek proper has a wide, grassy central reservation to accommodate the cars and couches of all the architecural tourists who are bound to come.

Der Ring ist ebenso groß wie die Stadtmauern von Amersfoort, doch anders als diese Mauern mit ihren nach außen gerichteten Ausblicken gewährt der Kattenbroek-Ring Blicke nach innen. Der Kreis öffnet sich und gibt eine dramatische Blickbeziehung zu der Kirche von Hoogland frei. Die Straße der Höfe verläuft durch das gesamte Gebiet in einer geraden Linie, angrenzend an einen Kanal, der die Wohnblöcke mit ihren unterschiedlich gestalteten Höfen verbindet. Die Hofräume erhielten vielsagende Namen wie »Erinnerung« oder »Kontemplation« und sind sorgfältig gestaltet worden, um entsprechende Assoziationen zu unterstützen. Traditionell erforderliche Grünflächen wie Spielplätze und Pocketparks bildeten nicht, wie sonst in den Niederlanden üblich, das Rückgrat des Plans, so daß das Fehlen dieser Flächen in Kattenbroek kaum auffällt; das Parkgebiet des Amersfoort-Nord-Bezirkes ist von überall schnell erreichbar. Diese Zone außerhalb der Wohnquartiere ist wunderbar in das städtische Konzept integriert: Lange Achsen erlauben Durchblicke zur leicht erhöhten Grünfläche mit der mittelalterlichen Kirchturmspitze, die über die Baumwipfel eines alten Waldbestandes herausragt.

Auch die verborgene Zone ist jetzt fertiggestellt. Diese vom übrigen Teil durch eine Mauer abgetrennte Zone ist ein spezifischer Bereich im Zusammenhang mit dem übrigen städtischen Netz. Obwohl als ein Denkmal für die bestehende Landschaft geplant, ist diese Zone doch sehr stark verbaut und bietet somit keinen eindrucksvollen Kontrast zur übrigen Stadtstruktur. Dennoch erschien der Auftrag an rund 15 Künstler vielversprechend, jene Schatztruhe zu füllen, zu welcher sich die verborgene Zone entwickeln soll. Man wird einige Jahre abwarten müssen, um den Reichtum an Ideen, den Bhalotra in dieses Projekt eingebracht hat, gänzlich erfassen und würdigen zu können.

Mittlerweile gibt das Projekt einen guten Eindruck des hervorragenden Werks. Glücklicherweise ist das Gebiet leicht zu finden. Es liegt nahe der Autobahn von Amsterdam nach Amersfoort, und die mehrspurige Fahrbahn, die nach Kattenbroek führt, hat eine breite, rasenbedeckte Reservefläche für die Autos und Busse der Architekturtouristen.

Mitten durch die Bebauung verläuft die Verborgene Zone, ein 80 Meter breiter, von einer Mauer umgebener Bereich. Als Denkmal für die umgebende Landschaft geplant, soll diese parkartige Zone im Kontrast zur übrigen Stadtstruktur stehen. 15 Künstler wurden beauftragt, sie zu gestalten.

The Hidden Zone, a wall-enclosed, park-like area 80 metres wide, runs through the whole project. As a monument to the surrounding countryside, it is to stand in contrast to the rest of the urban fabric. 15 artists contributed their ideas.

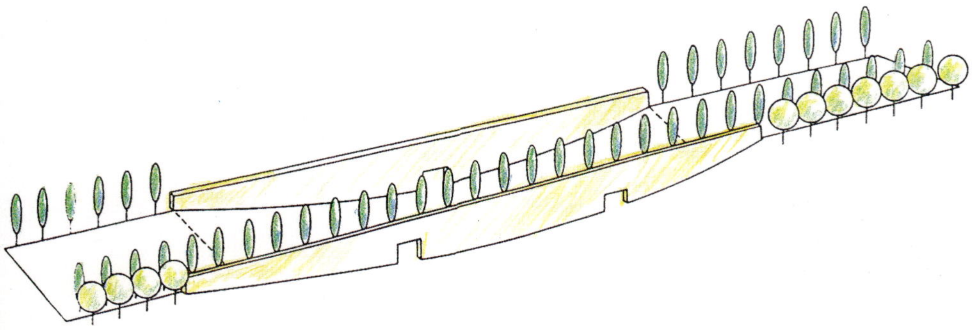

PostHuman – PostNature

PostHuman – PostNature

Bart Lootsma

In einem sozial schwachen Rotterdamer Wohnviertel gestaltete das Büro West 8 den Visserijplein. Highlight: Bäume aus Edelstahl.

West 8 designed the Visserijplein in a socially challenged Rotterdam residential district. Its highlight: stainless steel trees.

Die Platzgestaltung des Visserijplein in Rotterdam entwickelte sich aus einem der ersten großen Aufträge, die West 8 bekam: einer Studie zur Nutzung, Verwaltung und Gestaltung des öffentlichen Raums in Rotterdam-West. Das Stadtbauamt beauftragte die Landschaftsarchitekten, wahrscheinlich nicht nur mit dem Hintergedanken, daß der öffentliche Raum in diesem Teil der Stadt reif für eine Verschönerungskur war, sondern auch, um zu sehen ob analog zu Vorbildern aus Barcelona durch gezielte Freiraumplanung ein Rehabilitationsprozeß in Gang zu setzen wäre. Eine Reihe von Vierteln in Rotterdam-West, wie das berühmte Spangen mit Mietshäusern von Jacobus Johannes Pieter Oud und Michel Brinkmann aus der Zeit zwischen 1910 und 1930, ist stark verarmt und leidet unter zahlreichen typischen Großstadtproblemen wie Drogen, Straßenprostitution und sonstiger Kriminalität.

In ihrem Gutachten aus dem Jahr 1990 kombinierten die Landschaftsarchitekten deshalb eine Analyse mit einer Reihe von prototypischen Entwürfen für den Stadtteil. Es zeigte sich, daß ein Ansatz à la Barcelona in Rotterdam – und wahrscheinlich ganz allgemein in den Niederlanden – nicht funktioniert, weil die Verwaltung des öffentlichen Raums wesentlich komplizierter strukturiert ist. Es genügt in den Niederlanden nicht, einen schönen Entwurf zu machen und dann zu hoffen, daß er auch schön ausgeführt und unterhalten wird.

West 8 entdeckte, daß nicht weniger als 17 Gemeindebehörden beim öffentlichen Raum mitreden können, und daß diese verschiedenen Dienststellen auch noch unterschiedlichen Ressorts zugeordnet sind. Beratungen und Entscheidungsfindung sind sehr komplex, schwer umkehrbar und nicht transparent. Auch unter diesen Tatsachen leidet die Qualität des öffentlichen Raums. West 8 stellte zwar Ansätze fest, übergreifend zu planen, verstärkt über den Zusammenhang der verschiedenen Dienststellen zu diskutieren und die Diskussion über Qualität in die Öffentlichkeit zu tragen, doch bestimmen noch immer entgegengesetzte Kräfte das ungeschriebene Szenario, nach dem der öffentliche Raum in den Niederlanden gestaltet wird. Die eine Kraft führt zu einer Verflachung, die alles einander angleicht, und die andere zu einer Ad-hoc-Entwicklung an bestimmten Orten, die auf anwohnerspezifische Ansprüche, Proteste und Aktio-

The design for the Visserijplein, a square in Rotterdam, evolved from one of the first big commissions that West 8 had: a study of the use, administration and design of public space in Rotterdam West. The municipal architecture department had commissioned the landscape architects, probably with the ulterior motive not only of the fact that the public space in this part of town was ripe for a beauty treatment but also to see whether a rehabilitation process could be brought about by the purposeful planning of free spaces, as in exemplary cases in Barcelona. A series of districts in Rotterdam West, such as the famous Spangen with blocks of flats by J. J. P. Oud and Michel Brinkmann from between 1910 and 1930, are utterly impoverished and suffer from numerous typical urban problems such as drugs, street prostitution and crime. The landscape architects' report dating from 1990 therefore combined an analysis with a series of prototypical designs. It turned out that an approach à la Barcelona would not work in Rotterdam, and probably not anywhere in The Netherlands, because the administration of public space is structured in a considerably more complicated manner. In The Netherlands it does not suffice to make a beautiful design and hope it will be beautifully executed and maintained. West 8 discovered that no less than 17 municipal authorities had a say in matters of public space, and that these various offices are even subject to different jurisdictions. Consultations and decision-making are very complex, hard to reverse and not transparent. The quality of the public space also suffers under these circumstances. West 8 did encounter attempts to plan comprehensively, to discuss connections between various offices more, and to

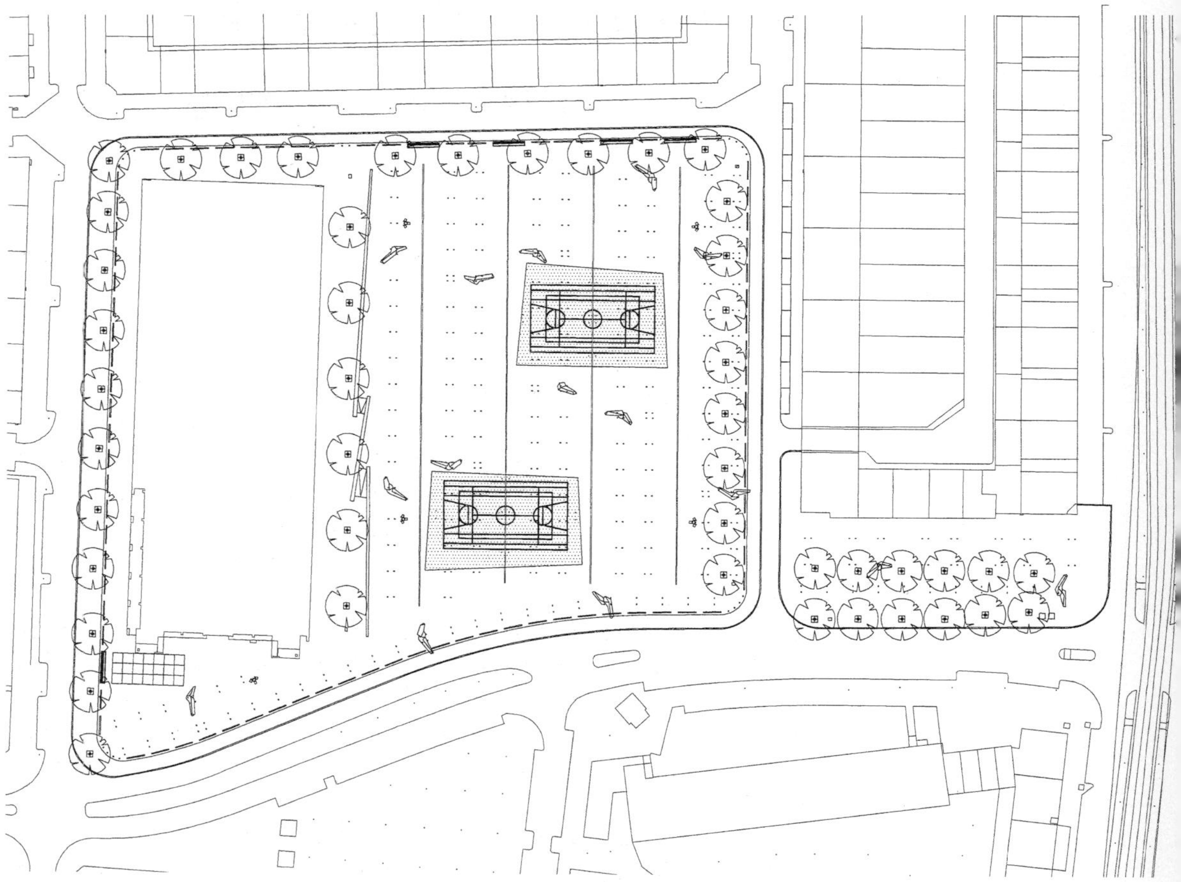

carry on public discussions about quality. Nevertheless, opposing forces continue to determine the unwritten scenario according to which public space is designed. The one force leads to a levelling, making everything like everything else, and the other to an ad hoc development in certain places, in response to residents' demands, protests and action, social injustice and emergencies, or to the need for political eye-catchers. On this basis, West 8 developed a varied strategy which takes into account the local citizens' initiatives, politics and the parties involved in the market. Furthermore, they differentiated the various categories of public space: spaces in residential districts, strategically located places, city squares, traffic squares, shopping streets and long street axes. Some of these sites were worked out as case studies in more detail in designs. Visserijplein was one of them. Now, six years later, it was executed in a much changed outer form. The requirements stayed approximately the same.

Visserijplein is a typical square in the residential district of Bospolder Tussendijken. Twice a week, Thursdays and Saturdays, there is a market here; the rest of the week it is used for recreation. Local youth plays football here, and the community centre Pier 80, closing off one side of the square, has a terrace on it. Pier 80 would like to extend its activities to the square as well, especially in the summer. These programme points and requirements determine the disposal of the Visserijplein to a large extent and take up most of the available space. But even when there is no market and the regular users are at school or work, the square should still look good. This is not easy because the architecture of the fifties, sixties and seventies surrounding the square is extraordinar-

nen, soziale Mißstände und Notlagen, oder auf das Bedürfnis nach politischen Blickfängen reagiert. Auf dieser Basis entwickelte West 8 eine differenzierte Strategie, die die lokalen Bewohnerinitiativen, die Politik und die Marktparteien einbezieht. Die Differenzierung geht außerdem von verschiedenen Kategorien des öffentlichen Raums aus: Plätze in Wohnvierteln, strategisch gelegene Plätze, Stadtplätze, Verkehrsplätze, Einkaufsstraßen und lange Straßenachsen. Einige dieser Plätze wurden in Fallstudien als Entwurfsskizze weiter ausgearbeitet, wozu auch der Visserijplein gehört, der nun, sechs Jahre später, in einer äußerlich stark veränderten Form ausgeführt wurde. Die Anforderungen sind in etwa gleich geblieben.

Der Visserijplein ist ein typischer Platz im Wohnviertel Bospolder Tussendijken. Zweimal wöchentlich, donnerstags und samstags, ist hier Markt. An den übrigen Wochentagen dient er der Erholung: Die Jugend des Viertels spielt hier Fußball, und das Nachbarschaftszentrum Pier 80, das den Platz an einer Seite abschließt, hat hier seine Terrasse. Gerade im Sommer will Pier 80 seine Aktivitäten auch einmal auf den Platz ausweiten. Diese Programmpunkte und Bedürfnisse bestimmen zum Großteil die Einrichtung des Visserijplein und nehmen den größten Teil der verfügbaren Fläche in Beschlag. Doch auch wenn kein Markt ist und die ständigen Nutzer in der Schule oder bei der Arbeit sind, sollte der Platz noch gut aussehen. Letzteres ist nicht einfach, denn die Architektur der fünfziger, sechziger und

Auf dem Visserijplein in Rotterdam erhielt das Zentrum »Pier 80« eine erhöhte Terrasse. Eine Baumreihe und eine Mauer mit Bank trennt sie von der Platzfläche mit zwei horizontalen Sportfeldern. Die mediokren Bauten rundum werden von Bäumen verdeckt. Anker im Boden markieren die Anordnung der Marktstände, Bäume aus Edelstahl enthalten Stromanschlüsse.

On Visserijplein in Rotterdam, the "Pier 80" community centre was given a raised terrace. A row of trees and a wall separate it from the square, including two horizontal playing fields. The mediocre surrounding buildings will be covered by trees. Anchors in the ground mark the locations of the market stands. Trees made of stainless steel contain connections to the electric mains.

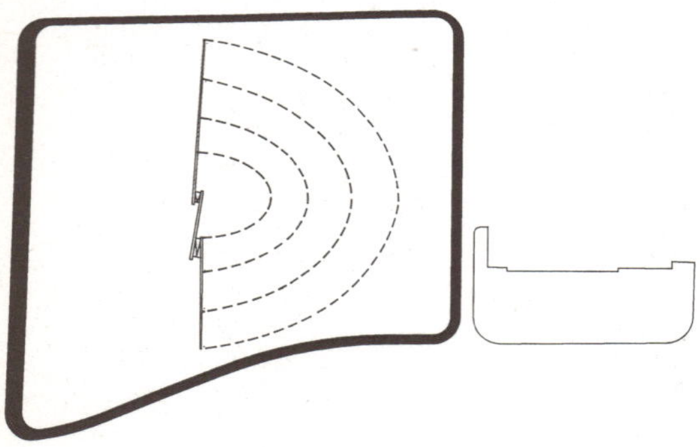

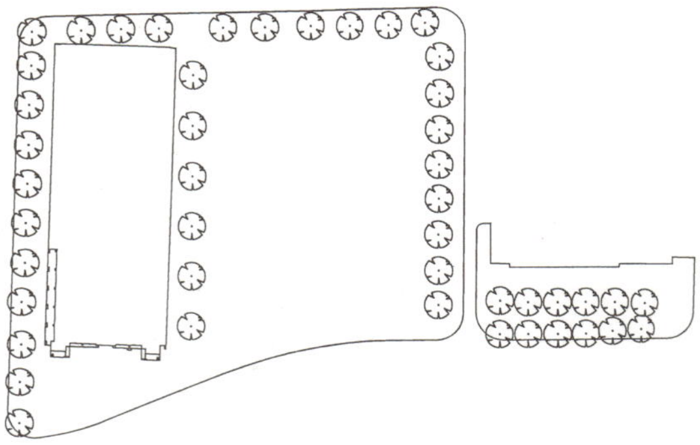

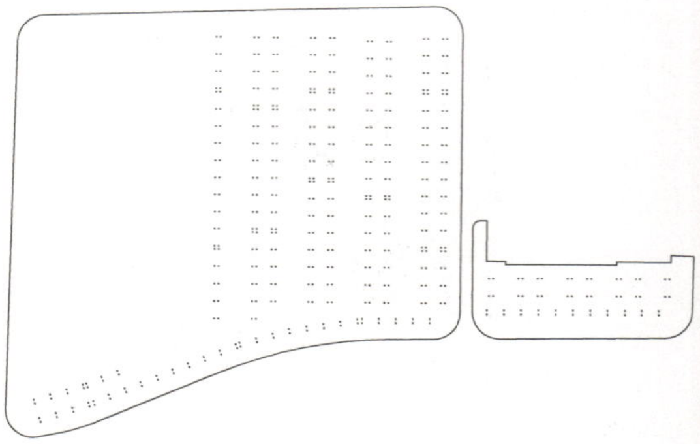

An Markttagen fügen sich die künstlichen Edelstahlbäume als Infrastruktursäulen zwischen die Stände des Visserijplein. Bei Nacht wirken sie auf dem leeren Platz wie expressionistische Skulpturen. Die Skizzen zeigen die landschaftsarchitektonischen Maßnahmen von West 8 (von links nach rechts): Rahmen und Bodenmodellierung, Bäume und Einbauten, Anker für die Marktstände, Sportfelder und Mauer mit Bank, Elektroanschlüsse.

On market days, the artificial stainless steel trees fit between the stands on the Visserijplein as infrastructures. At night they look like Expressionist sculptures on the empty square. The drawings show the landscape architectural measures taken by West 8 (from left to right): relief of the edges and grounds, trees and built-in structures, anchors for market stands, playing fields and wall with a bench, electric outlets.

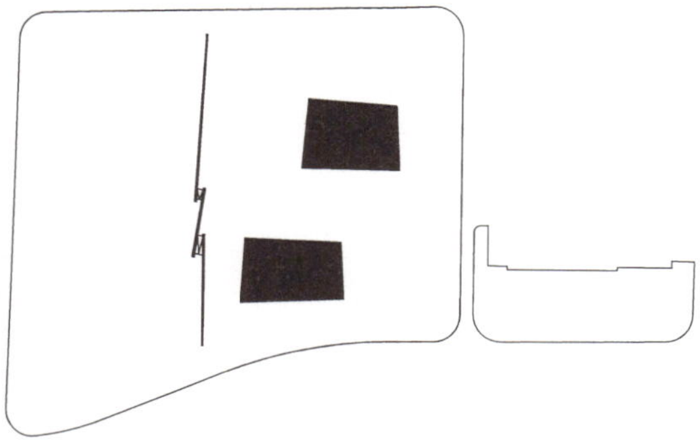

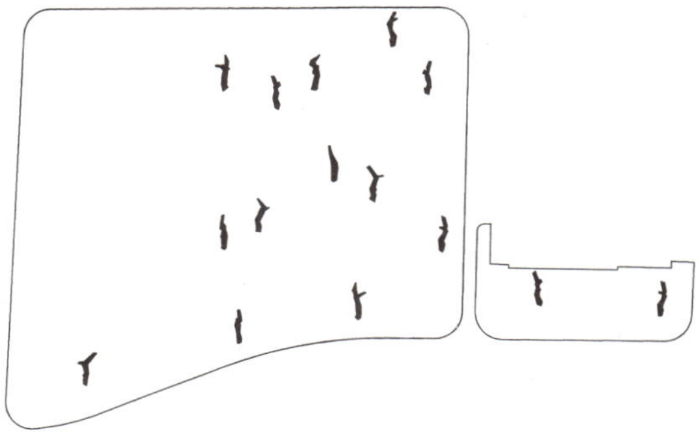

Visserijplein, Rotterdam
Client: Dienst Gemeentewerken Rotterdam
Landscape architects: Adriaan Geuze, Erik Overdiep, Dirry de Bruin, Leon Emmen (West 8); Eric Nijhuis (DS+V)
Project architect: Hetty de Jong (Dienst Stedebouwen Volkshuisvesting Rotterdam)
Size. 9,450 square metres
Planning: 1992–1995
Construction: July 1995–December 1995
Costs: Hfl 2,450,000

siebziger Jahre, die den Platz umgibt, ist außergewöhnlich mittelmäßig und häßlich renoviert, und die Art der Nutzung ist rauh und kümmert sich nicht um Ästhetik. Dazu kommt, daß der Platz von Straßen umgeben ist, auf denen die Anwohner ihre Wagen am liebsten direkt vor der Tür parken wollen. Ein Entwurf, der sich ausschließlich mit Schönheit und Freundlichkeit befassen wollte, hielte dieser harten Umgebung nicht lange stand und wäre wahrscheinlich noch vor seiner Fertigstellung zerstört. Dazu kam ein Budget, das teure Materialien oder etwas größere Eingriffe ausschloß.

Der Entwurf der Landschaftsarchitekten von West 8 besteht aus einigen einfachen Maßnahmen. Zunächst wurde für das Nachbarschaftszentrum Pier 80 mit Hilfe einfacher Mauern, die auch zum Teil als Platzbänke dienen, eine Terrassenzone markiert. Zu den Mauern hin wurde der Platz kreisförmig leicht angehoben, so daß die Terrasse eine gewisse Intimität bekam, deutlich vom Rest des Platzes unterschieden. An den Platzrändern wurden Bäume gepflanzt, die auf Dauer einen Großteil der häßlichen Architektur verdecken sollen. Ein Absperrgeländer um den Platz sorgt dafür, daß keine Autos hereinkommen – nur für den Markt können Teile des Geländers heruntergeklappt werden. Schutzstangen um die Bäume und weitere Details sorgen dafür, daß die empfindlicheren Einbauten vor Fahrzeugen geschützt werden. Eine gute Einteilung der Marktstände war wesentlich für die Zustimmung der Händler, die ihre ganz spezifischen Wünsche und ihre eigene Rangordnung haben. Anker im Boden legen die Plätze fest. Auf einer leicht geneigten Fläche sind zwei horizontale Sportfelder entstanden, die auch die Möglichkeit bieten, Volleyballnetze aufzuhängen. Große Straßenlaternen leuchten den gesamten Platz gut aus.

Als letzte und dominanteste Maßnahme errichteten die Landschaftsarchitekten einige künstliche Bäume auf dem Platz. Ging es bei den meisten anderen Eingriffen um das Neuordnen, Bepflanzen und Einrichten von Parkplätzen, so ist diese Maßnahme eine echte Addition, die eine gewisse Investition verlangt, wenn auch eine verhältnismäßig geringe. Doch selbst die künstlichen Bäume sind in Wirklichkeit notwendige Infrastruktur, da sie die Elektroanschlüsse für die Marktbuden enthalten. Als kubistische oder expressionistische Skulpturen bestehen die Bäume aus Edelstahl. In einem der Äste, quasi als dekoratives Element, befinden sich einige Steckdosen. Die Bäume erinnern an einen Vorschlag von Archigram aus den sechziger Jahren, den Zukunftstraum einer Gesellschaft von maximaler Mobilität, deren Nomaden überall auf der Welt, etwa an Bäumen, An-

ily mediocre, the subject of ugly renovations, and the treatment it gets is rough and not concerned with aesthetics. Above and beyond this, the square is surrounded by streets where the residents prefer to park their cars right in front of their doors. A design exclusively concerned with beauty and friendliness would not last long in these surroundings and would probably be destroyed even before it was completed. On top of that, the budget precluded expensive materials or any major interventions.

The design consists of a few simple measures. First a terrace area was marked off for the community centre Pier 80 by means of plain walls that also serve in part as benches. Trees were planted on the edges of the square to eventually cover up most of the ugly architecture. A locked fence around the square makes sure cars cannot enter. Only for the market can parts of the fence be let down. Anchors in the ground mark the places for the market stands. On a slightly inclined surface, two horizontal playing fields were made that also provide the opportunity for setting up volleyball nets.

As a final and most prominent measure, the landscape architects set up some artificial trees on the square. While most other interventions were concerned with reorganizing, planting and setting up parking spaces, this one is a true new addition calling for a certain investment, albeit a relatively minor one. Yet even these artificial trees are actually an essential part of the infrastructure as they contain the connection to the electric mains for the market stands. Cubist or Expressionist sculptures, these trees are made of stainless steel. In one of their branches, almost as a decorative element, there are a few electric outlets.

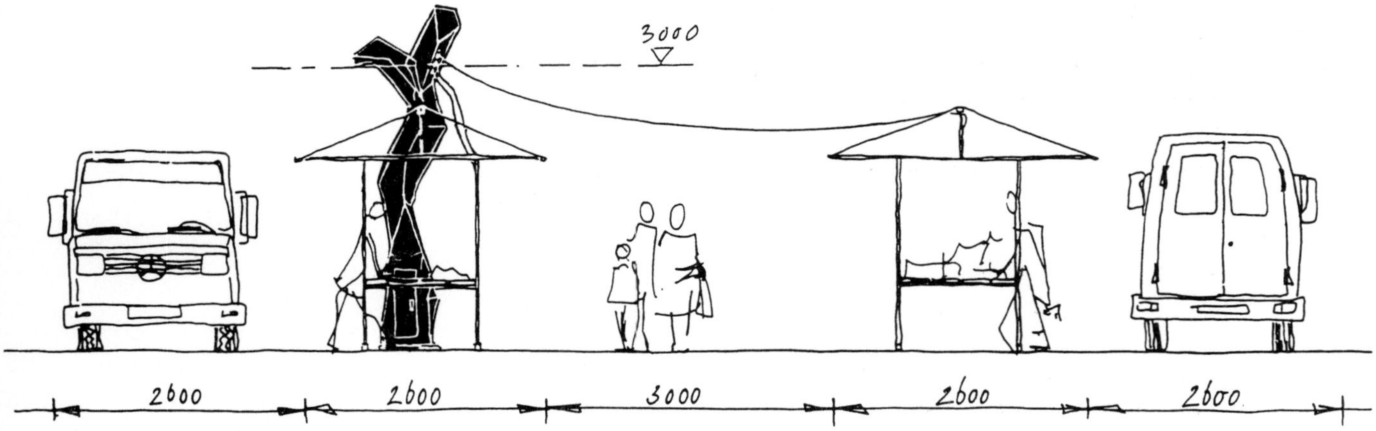

The trees recall a proposal by Archigram in the sixties, a vision of a future society with maximal mobility, whose nomads can find outlets all over the world in, for instance, trees for electric power, water and communication media.

This image fits perfectly into the ideology of West 8, in which nature and the city are no longer separate entities but blend into each other. Nature gradually becomes something that is kept intact artificially by technology, and the city in its uncontrollable spread as an urban jungle is like a natural event.

The stainless steel trees were intentionally not made too perfect, so that it will not show when cars make dents in them or when people find it fun to kick or chop at them In one way or another they fit into the Rotterdam jargon of famous works of art in public spaces that accumulated in the forties, fifties and sixties: the Cubist figure by Picasso beside the building information centre on Weena Street, the Constructivist sculpture by Gabo in front of Bijenkorf department store, the Cubist-Expressionist war monument by Zadkine at the Maritime Museum. Each is a sculpture that imagines the end of humanism: Gabo shows the secret laws of nature in mathematical formulae, Picasso splits up the portrait, and Zadkine shows the postwar city, or rather the postwar human, whose heart has disappeared. A few years ago the art critic Jeffrey Deitch organized the "PostHuman" exhibition on the image of mankind after humanism. The trees by West 8 are the first object for a potential exhibition on "PostNature".

Die Technik-Bäume des Visserijplein passen zur Philosophie des Büros West 8, Natur und Stadt nicht als verschiedene Größen aufzufassen, sondern miteinander verschmelzen zu lassen. In der Stadt wird Natur durch Technik künstlich intakt gehalten. Die Stadt hingegen wuchert unkontrollierbar wie ein Dschungel.

The techno-trees of Visserijplein fit in with West 8's approach of not considering nature and the city as separate entities but letting them blend into each other. Nature in the city is maintained artificially through technology. The city, however, spreads as uncontrollably as a jungle.

schlüsse für Strom, Wasser und Kommunikationsmedien finden. Dieses Bild paßt perfekt zur Ideologie von West 8, in der die Natur und die Stadt keine verschiedenen Größen mehr sind, sondern nahtlos ineinander übergehen. Natur wird allmählich zu etwas, das durch die Technik künstlich intakt gehalten wird, und die Stadt ähnelt in ihrer unkontrollierbaren Wucherung und als Stadtdschungel einem Naturereignis. Die Vision von Archigram sah zwar etwas gewagter und nach »sixties mellow« aus, doch es kommt aufs gleiche heraus: Die Natur läßt sich um so mehr genießen, als überall an unsichtbaren Stellen eine technische Infrastruktur vorhanden ist, die einem ein praktisches und angenehmes Leben ermöglicht.

Bei West 8 ist die Natur jedoch keine Kompensation mehr für das Stadtleben – auch nicht, wenn sie eine Steckdose enthält. Die Edelstahlbäume von West 8 sind eine Art pflanzliche Variante des Cyborg. Sie wurden bewußt nicht allzu perfekt ausgeführt, damit es nicht auffällt, wenn Autos Dellen hineinfahren, oder wenn Leute Spaß daran haben, dagegenzutreten oder hineinzuhacken – die Bäume überleben, so wie Arnold Schwarzenegger, der in den Terminator-Filmen immer wieder aufsteht und weiterläuft. Sie dominieren als glitzernde, futuristische Objekte die glatte, maschinell verlegte Oberfläche aus grauen Betonsteinen.

Auf die eine oder andere Weise passen sie in den Rotterdamer Jargon der berühmten Kunstwerke im öffentlichen Raum, die sich während der vierziger, fünfziger und sechziger Jahre in der Stadt angesammelt haben: die kubistische Figur von Picasso beim Bauzentrum an der Straße Weena, die konstruktivistische Skulptur von Gabo vor dem Kaufhaus Bijenkorf, das kubistisch-expressionistische Kriegsmonument von Zadkine am Seefahrts-Museum. Jedes für sich ist eine Skulptur, die das Ende des Humanismus imaginiert: Gabo zeigt die geheimen Gesetze der Natur in mathematischen Formeln, Picasso fragmentiert das Porträt, und Zadkine zeigt die Nachkriegsstadt, nein, den Nachkriegsmenschen, dessen Herz verschwunden ist. Vor einigen Jahren organisierte der Kunstkritiker Jeffrey Deitch die Ausstellung »PostHuman« über das Menschenbild nach dem Humanismus – die Bäume von West 8 sind die ersten Objekte einer denkbaren Ausstellung mit dem Titel »PostNature«.

Rotterdam: Zentrum und Peripherie

Rotterdam: centre and periphery reconsidered

Frits Palmboom

Jeder Besucher Rotterdams kennt sie, die verwirrende Suche nach dem Stadtzentrum. Die Frage lautet: Wie wirkt sich diese Irritation schließlich auf das Erleben der Peripherie aus?

Im Bereich der Stadtplanung hat Rotterdam ein breites Spektrum exemplarischer Projekte verwirklicht: Wiederaufbau der kriegszerstörten Innenstadt, neue Wohnviertel (Pendrecht und Alexanderpolder, entworfen unter anderem von Bakema), Stadterneuerungsprogramme und Projekte zur Nutzung ehemaliger Hafengebiete, wie Kop van Zuid.

Trotz all dieser planmäßigen Interventionen steht die Stadt noch immer im Ruf, extrem komplex und undurchschaubar zu sein. Rotterdam paßt sich nicht dem klassischen Schema einer Stadt an. Durch die Bombardierung des Stadtzentrums gibt es so gut wie nichts aus der Zeit vor dem 19. Jahrhundert. Rotterdam ist eine Industriestadt mit den tiefen Spuren politischer Willkür und kapitalistischer Ausbeutung. Die Beziehung zwischen dem Stadtraum und seinen Gebäuden ist bei weitem nicht eindeutig; sie ist gekennzeichnet von einem labyrinthischen Straßennetz mit einer enormen Vielfalt an Gebäudetypen. Aus diesem Grund wurde die Stadt oftmals als chaotisch beschrieben: eine Stadt ohne Struktur. In gewisser Weise kann man sagen, daß die Stadt als Ganzes die Kriterien erfüllt, die normalerweise für die Peripherie gelten.

Der Zweck dieses Beitrags ist es, die verborgenen Regeln hinter dem Chaos aufzudecken, Licht in die Logik der Komplexität Rotterdams zu bringen. Ein wirkliches Verstehen dieser Logik ist die Grundvoraussetzung für eine effektive Intervention. Dazu werden hier drei Schichten in der Stadtstruktur Rotterdams unterschieden und untersucht.

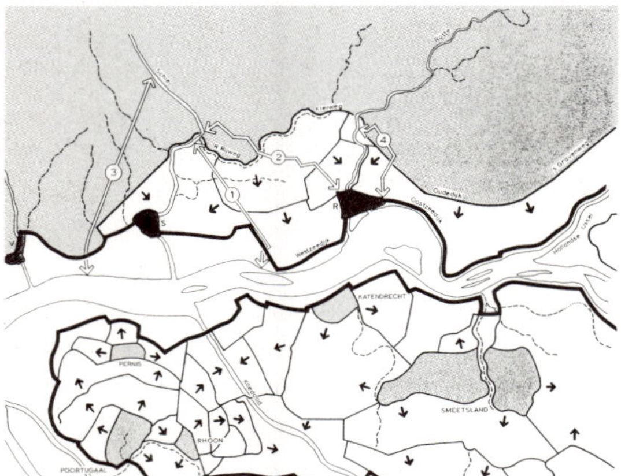

Meer, Fluß und Deiche. Die erste Schicht entsteht durch die Dynamik von Delta und Deichen. Rotterdam wurde am Rand des Rheindeltas erbaut, in einer ganz von Menschen-

Hinter dem Chaos der Rotterdamer Stadtstruktur finden sich Regeln. Drei Schichten lassen sich bei näherem Hinsehen unterscheiden.

There is a hidden coherence to the chaos of Rotterdam's urban structure, a coherence that is based on three constituent layers.

Every visitor to Rotterdam is familiar with the confusion relating to where the city centre actually is. How does this state of confusion influence the way in which the city's periphery is perceived and what implications does it have for the way in which the structure of the city as a whole is understood?

Within the field of town planning and urban design, Rotterdam has accommodated a wide range of examplary projects: postwar reconstruction of its devastated city centre; plans for new housing districts (Pendrecht and Alexanderpolder; designed by Bakema and others), which were discussed in depth by members of the CIAM and Team X; the urban-renewal operation of the last twenty years; recent projects, such as the Kop van Zuid, for the reuse of old harbour areas.

Despite all these planned interventions, the city still has a reputation for being extremely inscrutable and complex. Rotterdam does not conform to the classic model of a city. As a result of the bombardment of the city centre, virtually none of it is pre-nineteenth century. It is an industrial boom town, with deep traces of political arbitrariness and capitalistic exploitation. The relation between urban space and buildings is far from unambiguous, however being characterized by a labyrinthine network of streets and an enormous variety of building typologies. For these reasons, the city has been described many times as being, above all, chaotic: a city lacking in structure. In a sense, it can be said that the city as a whole answers the description that normally applies to urban peripheries.

The purpose of the article is to reveal the hidden coherence behind the chaos; to bring to light the logic of Rotterdam's complexity. A genuine

Die Deiche, die die Dynamik des Flußdeltas bändigten, bilden die erste Schicht der Stadtgestalt Rotterdams. Die zweite Schicht ergibt sich aus der landwirtschaftlichen Parzellenstruktur und den Straßen, die diesem Muster folgen, wie deutlich auf dem Plan von 1850 und dem Foto zu erkennen ist.

The dykes that tamed the dynamics of the delta formed the first layer of Rotterdam. The second is based on the pattern created by the division of agrarian land and the resulting network of streets, as the 1850 plan and the photo clearly show.

understanding of this logic is the primary requirement for the realization of effective intervention. Three constituent layers in Rotterdam's urban structure have to be distinguished.

The sea, the river and the dykes: The first layer is formed by the dynamics of the delta and the dykes. Rotterdam lies at the edge of the delta where the Rhine River flows into the sea within a completely man-made landscape, most of which is below sea level. The northern part of the city originally formed an extended peat marsh, a huge, water-retentive sponge which, albeit with difficulty, has been reclaimed. The southern part, open to the sea, had a highly dynamic nature, influenced as it was by the tidal forces of the sea and the seasonal cycles of the rivers and forming an ever-changing landscape of islands in the midst of creeks and distributaries.

Until the dykes were built, the land that composed this delta or estuary had no definitive

hand gestalteten Landschaft, deren größter Teil unter dem Meeresspiegel liegt. Die nördliche Stadthälfte war ursprünglich ein ausgedehntes Sumpfgebiet, ein riesiger, Wasser speichernder Schwamm, der nur mit Mühe urbar gemacht werden konnte. Der südliche, sich dem Meer öffnende Teil lag in einer sehr dynamischen Natur, von den Gezeiten und den jahreszeitlichen Rhythmen der Flüsse beeinflußt. Es entstanden immer neue Landschaften aus Inseln, umspült von Bächen und Deltaarmen. Bis zum Bau der Deiche hatte dieses Land an der Flußmündung keine bestimmte Form. Erst im dreizehnten Jahrhundert wurden nach vielen Fehlschlägen die Hauptdeiche errichtet, zum größten Teil dort, wo sie heute noch stehen. Um die regelmäßigen Überschwemmungen aufzunehmen, mußten die Deiche in einiger Entfernung vom eigentlichen Fluß errichtet werden. Als Folge davon ist die Stadt heute durch eine ausgesprochene Differenzierung ihrer Bereiche innerhalb und außerhalb der Deiche charakterisiert. Ursprünglich war Rotterdam weit mehr eine Stadt hinter den Deichen als eine Stadt am Fluß.

Parzellen und Straßen. Die zweite Schicht bilden die landwirtschaftliche Parzellenstruktur und die Straßen, die diesem Muster folgen. Die Parzellen wurden durch die langen parallelen Entwässerungsgräben definiert, die meist im rechten Winkel zu den Deichen und anderen relativ festen Landstrichen angelegt waren. Auf diesen Deichen und Landstreifen verliefen die Straßen. In der offenen Landschaft zeichneten sich die Bauernhöfe entlang der Straßen als Siedlungsbänder und Baumgruppen ab. Auf der Karte zeichneten die Straßen und Gräben ein kammartiges Muster.

Auf der Nordseite des Flusses bildeten die Kanäle fächerförmige Strukturen. Manche Fächer ergaben sich aus der Richtung des Hauptflusses, während andere sich an einzelnen Torfbächen oder vorübergehenden Rinnsalen orientierten. An Orten, an denen verschiedene Fächer zusammenkamen, entstanden komplexe Muster, die Brüche innerhalb des Gesamtgewebes bildeten. Das System der Parzellen und Gräben war stark, aber nicht starr, es erfüllte eine ganze Reihe von Aufgaben: Die Gräben entwässerten das Gelände und artikulierten die Trennung der Parzellen; die Parzellen selbst waren gleichzeitig Eigentumsgrenzen und landwirtschaftliche Einheiten; die Kanäle dienten dem Transport zu Wasser, die Straßen dem Transport zu Lande.

Das System war zudem flexibel. Parzellen konnten geteilt oder zusammengelegt werden, um kleinere oder größere Einheiten zu bilden, die alle Teil des Gesamtsystems waren. Solche Einheiten wurden für ein weites Spektrum von Nutzungen gebraucht: von Bauernhöfen über Erholungsgebiete bis hin zu Gaswerken. Auf diese Art diente das Parzellensystem als Grundlage für den Verstädterungsprozeß am Ende des 19. Jahrhunderts. Lange, rechteckige Baublöcke säumten die Straßen zu beiden Seiten und füllten die Parzellen aus. So wurden die Hauptzüge der Landschaft direkt in das Stadtgewebe übernommen. Aus den langen, leicht gebogenen Wegen entstanden die Hauptdurchgangsstraßen, das Rückgrat des städtischen Lebens, und die meisten Nebenwege verwandelten sich in Wohnstraßen. Dieses mehr oder weniger kontinuierliche Straßennetz, unterbrochen von den früheren Bruchzonen, nimmt nur teilweise Bezug auf den Fluß, wie

form. It was not until the thirteenth century, after many attempts and failures, that the main dykes were realized at the location where for the most part they still stand today.

In order to accommodate periodic overflow, the dykes had to be created some distance from the river itself. As a result, Rotterdam is characterized by a pronounced differentiation between the areas lying inside and outside the dykes, and was originally a city behind a dyke.

Parcels and streets: The second layer is formed by the agrarian pattern of land division and the network of streets based on this dyke system. The land parcels were defined by long, parallel ditches that drained water from the marshy land, most of them dug at right angles to the dykes and to other strips of relatively solid land. The dykes and strips accommodated the roads, and in the open landscape, farmhouses situated in close proximity to the roads appeared as ribbons of buildings and groups of trees. On the map, roads and ditches formed patterns resembling a comb.

On the north bank of the river, land-division patterns formed large fans. Some were related to the main river, while others conformed to certain past streams or tidal creeks. At places where various fans converged, complex patterns were treated, and those formed fracture zones within the total fabric of the area.

As a system, the pattern of parcels and ditches was powerful and repetitive, thus fulfilling a number of functions simultaneously: the ditches served as a draining system and articulated the separation of the parcels; the parcels themselves were pieces of property as well as units of agrarian exploitation; the ditches offered a network for transport by water and the roads for transport by land.

The system was flexible as well. Plots could be divided or combined to form smaller or larger units, all of which remained part of the overall system. Such units were used for a wide variety of purposes: from farm to recreational facility, from rope-walk to gasworks. In this way, the parcel system functioned as an underlying element of the process of urbanization that began at the end of the nineteenth century. Long, rectangular building blocks lined both sides of streets laid out within a parcel.

Consequently, the main features of the landscape were incorporated directly into the urban fabric. The long and somewhat winding roads became main thoroughfares, the backbones of city life, and most of the side-roads in the former parcels were transformed into residential streets. This more or less continuous network of city streets, interrupted by the former fracture zones, is related only partially to the main river, as was also the case in the original pattern of lots. Even today these fracture zones form a kind of labyrinth, devoid of any form of hierarchy, that blocks connections between various parts of the growing city.

The traffic machine: The third layer, which influences urban morphology, has been formed by the development of the delta around Rotterdam into a gigantic traffic machine consisting of large clusters of highways, railways, harbours and canals. This traffic machine has a dual affect: on a large scale, it simplifies connections, but for the immediate environment, it creates barriers. This system ignores Rotterdam's fragmented foundation and avoids the complex pattern of streets within the city. At the same time, it causes the city to disintegrate into an agglomeration of

schon das ursprüngliche Parzellenmuster. Bis heute bilden diese Bruchzonen gewissermaßen ein Labyrinth ohne jede Art von Hierarchie – die Verbindung zwischen den Stadtvierteln wird dadurch blockiert.

Die Verkehrsmaschinerie. Die dritte Schicht, die die Stadtform beeinflußt, entsteht durch die Transformation des Rotterdamer Deltas zu einer gigantischen Verkehrsmaschinerie, bestehend aus einer Anhäufung von Schnellstraßen, Schienensträngen, Häfen und Kanälen. Sie hat einen doppelten Effekt: Im großen Maßstab vereinfacht sie die Verbindungen, für die direkte Umgebung dagegen schafft sie Barrieren. Dieses System ignoriert die Fragmentierung Rotterdams und vermeidet das komplexe Straßensystem der Innenstadt. Gleichzeitig führt es dazu, daß sich die Stadt in eine Ansammlung von »Inseln« auflöst, umspült von Hauptverkehrsströmen.

Gegen Mitte des Jahrhunderts, als die Urbanisierung in größerem Maßstab und nach Plänen vorangetrieben wurde, sah man diese Inseln als Einheiten der Urbanisierung an. Das Wachstum Rotterdams sollte nicht länger in einzelnen, aus der Bandstruktur entstandenen Parzellen stattfinden, sondern in Stadtinseln, die es zu vervollständigen galt. Aus diesem Grund richtete man mehr oder weniger autonome Distrikte ein, jeweils konzentrisch

Die dritte Schicht, die die Stadtform beeinflußt, ist die Verkehrsinfrastruktur. Das Rotterdamer Delta bietet sich heute als gigantische Verkehrsmaschinerie dar.

The third layer of the urban morphology has been formed by the conversion of the Rotterdam delta into a gigantic traffic machine.

und nach innen hin orientiert, mit einer Typologie von freistehenden Gebäuden in grüner Umgebung. Das Erscheinungsbild fast der gesamten Peripherie von Rotterdam, einschließlich der Planungen für Pendrecht und den Alexanderpolder, wurde von diesem Ansatz bestimmt.

Rotterdam, eine urbanisierte Landschaft. Diese Analyse von Rotterdam, die auf einer Reihe von Konstruktionsschichten basiert, ist nicht einzigartig; viele Städte können auf diese Weise charakterisiert werden. Was jedoch ziemlich prägnant ist, ist die Art, wie die verschiedenen Schichten miteinander in Verbindung stehen. Die drei Schichten – die Dynamik des Deltas, das Netzwerk der Parzellen und Straßen sowie die Verkehrsmaschinerie – sind einander überlagert. Es gibt keine festgefügte Verbindung zwischen den Lagen und keine Hierarchie. Keines der Muster dominiert die anderen, alle drei existieren und funktionieren gleichzeitig.

Als Folge aus dieser Situation treten zwei Merkmale auf, die einen starken Einfluß auf die Identität der Stadt haben: Das erste ist die unglaubliche Menge überraschender Kombinationen und Kontraste, die aus der lose geschichteten urbanen Struktur entstehen. Völlig gegensätzliche Welten stehen sich plötzlich gegenüber, wie etwa die kurze, unerwartete Konfron-

Rotterdams Landschaft ist durch und durch urbanisiert. Das Bild zeigt einen ehemaligen Torfstich und die neue Stadtsilhouette.

"islands" or "compartments" surrounded by main traffic lines.

Around mid-century, when urbanization began to be realized on a larger scale and according to plans, these islands or compartments were seen as units for urbanization. No longer would Rotterdam's growth take place within individual parcels developed from ribbon construction but within compartments that were to be filled to completion. The latter assumed the form of autonomous districts, each with a concentric and inwardly oriented layout and a typology of freestanding buildings within a green setting. The appearance of virtually the entire periphery of Rotterdam, including plans for Pendrecht and Alexanderpolder, has been determined by this approach.

Rotterdam, an urbanized landscape. This analysis of Rotterdam, based on a number of constituent layers, is not unique; many cities can be characterized in the same manner. What is relatively distinctive, however, is the way in which the various layers relate to one another. The three layers – the dynamics of the delta, the network of parcels and streets, and the traffic machine – are superimposed on one another. There is no established relationship between the layers, however, and no hierarchy. One pattern does not dominate the others; all three exist and function simultaneously. As a result of this situation, two features emerge that have a powerful influence on the city's identity. The first consists of the incredible amount of surprising combinations and contrasts offered by the loosely layered urban structure. Totally different worlds stand face to face, such as the brief and unexpected confrontation of ocean-going vessel and city street.

The second feature is the city's manifestation

The landscape around Rotterdam is totally urbanized, as the photo of a former peat dig and the new skyline prove.

as an urbanized landscape rather than as an architectonic unity. Traces of age-old "natural" Dutch landscape coexist with images of the utmost artificiality and modernity. This multiplicity of themes is the direct result of the pragmatic way in which the complex geomorphologic situation has been utilized.

The Modernists: Aiming for homogeneity. Postwar reconstruction and urban expansion made the city into an experimental laboratory for the Modern Movement. After the bombardment transformed Rotterdam into a "city without a past", the Modern Movement propagated it as a "City of Tomorrow".

Projects for the city centre and the urban periphery were united by the concept of a harmonious city: functionally zoned, with a clear distinction between inner city and suburban districts; spatially homogeneous, and provided with a streamlined traffic network and an unequivocal typology of free-standing buildings.

In the city centre, the tabula rasa formed an opportunity to reshape the city according to the single unifying theme of a city on the river. A network of main thoroughfares was proposed: those parallel to the river would connect the various prewar "fans", and those perpendicular to the river would link the areas inside and outside the dykes and would open the city to the river.

The problem, however, lay in how to impose the same concept upon the remaining nineteenth-century districts. It could not be done without creating a great number of structural "openings" in the urban fabric, many of which proved to be unfeasible as time passed by.

The impossibility to realize this comprehensive plan once again led to a problematic relation-

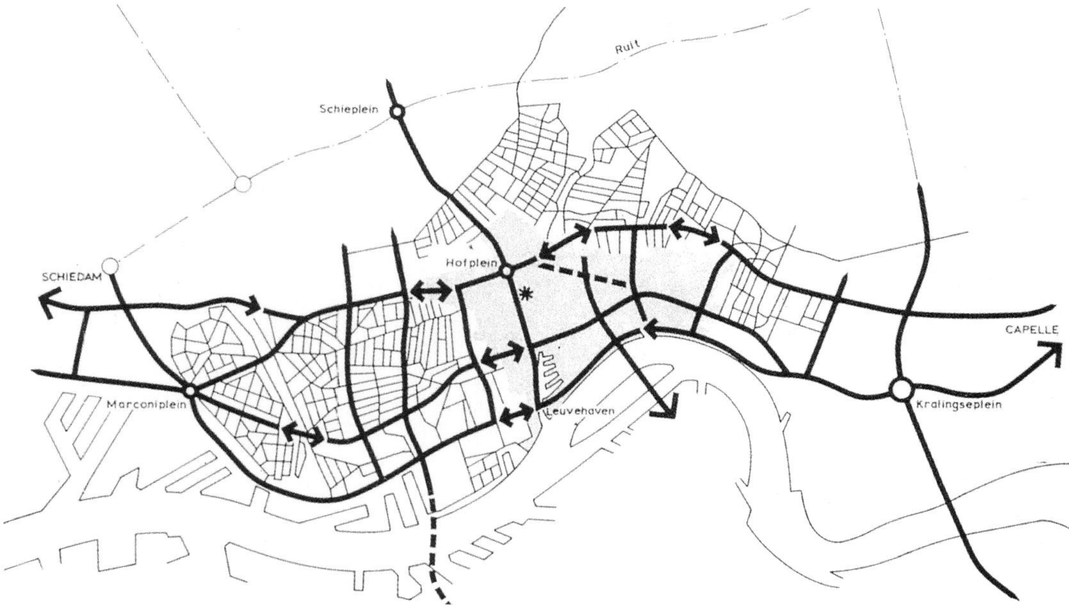

tation von auslaufendem Schiff und Stadtstraße. Das zweite Merkmal ist der Ausdruck der Stadt, die sich eher als urbanisierte Landschaft, denn als architektonische Einheit darstellt. Spuren jahrhundertealter niederländischer »Natur«-Landschaft existieren neben Bildern von äußerster Künstlichkeit und Modernität. Diese Vielfalt von Themen ist das direkte Ergebnis der pragmatischen Art, in der die komplexe geomorphologische Situation genutzt wurde.

Die Moderne: Streben nach Homogenität. Der Wiederaufbau nach dem Krieg und die Erweiterung der Stadt ließen Rotterdam zu einem Experimentierfeld für die Moderne werden. Nach der Bombardierung war die Stadt in eine »Stadt ohne Vergangenheit« verwandelt, die Bewegung der Moderne propagierte sie als »Stadt von morgen«. Projekte für das Stadtzentrum und die Peripherie wurden nach dem Konzept der harmonischen Stadt vereint: funktionell gegliedert, mit klarer Trennung zwischen Innenstadt und Vorstädten; und räumlich homogen, mit stromlinienförmigem Verkehrsnetz und einer klaren Typologie freistehender Gebäude.

Im Stadtzentrum bot die tabula rasa Gelegenheit, die Stadt nach einem einheitlichen Bild zu formen: der Stadt am Fluß. Ein Netzwerk von Haupt-

Die Zerstörungen des Krieges ließen Rotterdam nach 1945 zu einem Experimentierfeld für Ideen der Moderne werden, Pläne für ein stromlinienförmiges Straßennetz wurden entworfen.

The destruction caused by World War II made Rotterdam an experimental laboratory for the Modern Movement. One of the proposals put forward included plans for a streamlined traffic network.

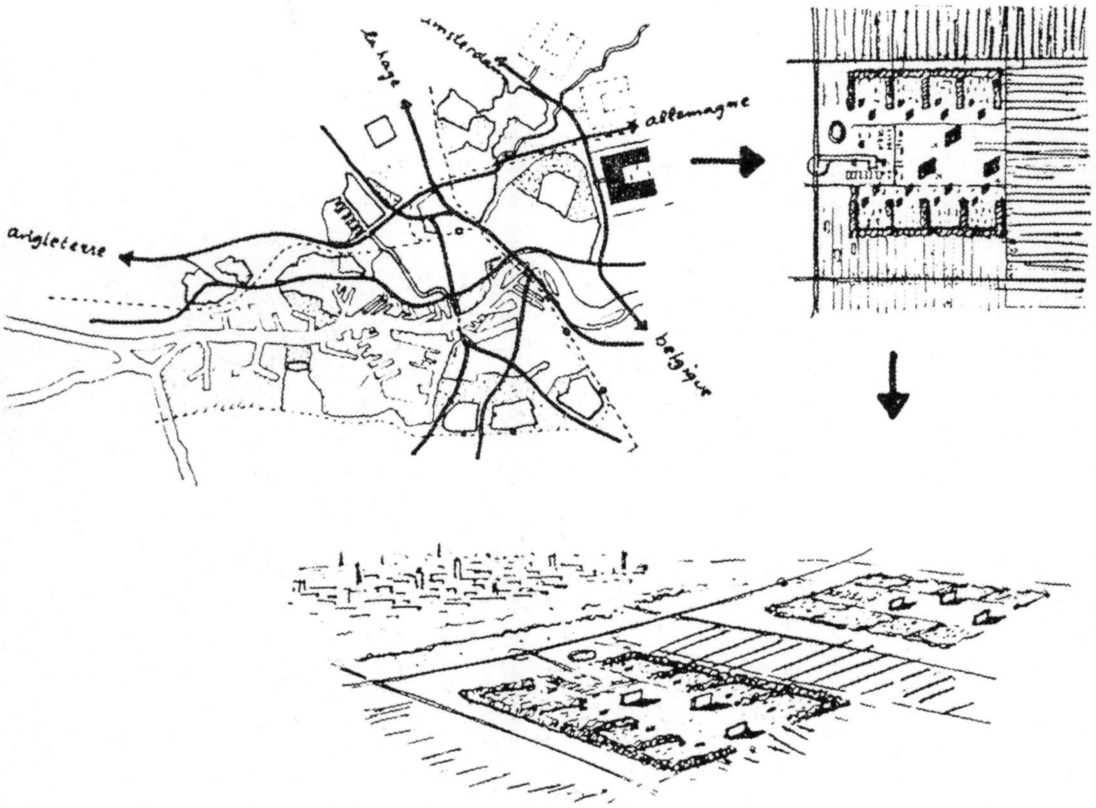

verbindungsachsen wurde angelegt: Diejenigen parallel zum Fluß sollten zwischen den verschiedenen vorkriegszeitlichen »Fächern« verlaufen und die Straßen senkrecht zum Fluß würden die Gebiete innerhalb und außerhalb der Deiche verbinden und die Stadt zum Fluß hin öffnen.

Das Problem bestand nun noch darin, wie man dasselbe Konzept auf die verbleibenden Bezirke aus dem 19. Jahrhundert übertragen könne. Ohne eine große Zahl an strukturellen »Durchbrüchen« im Stadtgewebe wäre dies nicht möglich, viele davon erwiesen sich jedoch im Laufe der Zeit als undurchführbar.

Die Unmöglichkeit der Stadt, diesen umfassenden Plan zu verwirklichen, führte wiederum zu einem problematischen Verhältnis von Stadtzentrum und Peripherie. Statt Teil der stromlinienförmigen, homogenen

ship between the city centre and the urban periphery. Instead of becoming part of a streamlined, homogeneous urban structure, the new city centre was simply a fragmentary addition to a heterogeneous unit. In reality, the city turned out to be more unruly than it had seemed in its conceptual form on paper. In a sense, history took its revenge.

The periphery: the loss of the blueprint. The urban periphery was also regarded as a virtual tabula rasa. In 1950, on the eve of the great urbanization operation, Alexanderpolder was nothing but a vast area of swampy grassland. Nonetheless, this landscape, too, had been the object of human intervention on many occasions and had been transformed, more than once, from land to water and back again. Traces of such projects can be seen in the area's division into two parts: a mediaeval, fan-shaped allotment system in the south and a rationally parcelled polder seven metres below sea level to the north. The boundary between these two sections is formed by a relief line that encompasses the whole area, east to west, in a long, curved line. A certain amount of urbanization had already occurred along a number of ribbon developments.

Completely unrelated to morphology was the division of the area into two municipalities: socialist Rotterdam to the west, with its ambitions of becoming the Dutch Modernist capital; and the village of Capelle to the east, carefully guarding its age-old stability and its orthodox Calvinist culture. At the inception of plan development, a decision was made to ignore any of these unruly interruptions for the benefit of a rational and homogeneous urbanization process. A look at the results, however, shows that it was precisely these

Wie die Stadt faßte man die Peripherie als Brachland auf, und ignorierte bestehende Strukturen. Beispiel Alexanderpolder: Für diese weite sumpfige Graslandschaft entstanden mit der Urbanisierungswelle der 50er Jahre Studien zur Bebauung wie die abgebildete der Gruppe Opbouw.

Not only the city itself but also its periphery was perceived as a virtual tabula rasa, and existing structures were completely ignored. Development studies, as in the case of the Opbouw Group's plan, were drawn up for a vast area of swampy grassland known as Alexanderpolder during the great wave of urbanization in the fifties.

conflicts of interest that proved to be the deciding factor. Tension between the autonomy of development in the peripheral area (a policy advocated by the village) and the coherence of the agglomeration as a whole (a strategy supported by the big city) can be found in two concepts that dominated the discussion.

One concept was the satellite-city model, which showed an autonomous city separated from its surroundings by highways and railway lines. A circle of residential districts was located around a park and a city centre, both of which were situated in the plan's geographic centre. Every trace of existing morphology that did not concur with this idea was eradicated.

The other concept was the finger-city model, in which new urbanization was concentrated along radial public-transport lines extending from the major city's centre to the outer reaches of the periphery, with continuous green zones in between. Any idea of suburban autonomy was abandoned.

This conflict ultimately frustrated every form of integral physical planning. The municipal boundary became a kind of Berlin Wall. The only thing that survived this crisis was the plan for the network of main highways. Within that network, each municipality developed its districts as it saw fit, employing the architectonic expression currently in fashion.

Heterogeneity as inspiration. Both models are based on fixed relationships. The satellite city attempts to create such relationships among housing, green areas and the city centre, an arrangement that by definition occurs within a bordered composition. The finger city's goal is to realize fixed relationships among transport, housing and

Stadtstruktur zu werden, war das neue Stadtzentrum schlicht ein fragmentarischer Anhang an eine heterogene Stadt. In Wirklichkeit erwies sich die Stadt als wesentlich widerspenstiger, als es in der Planungsphase auf dem Papier erschienen war. Die Geschichte rächte sich auf ihre Art.

Die Peripherie: Der Verlust der Blaupause. Die städtische Peripherie wurde ebenfalls als Brachland aufgefaßt. 1950, kurz vor der großen Urbanisierungswelle, war der Alexanderpolder nichts als eine weite sumpfige Graslandschaft. Trotz allem war auch diese Landschaft oftmals vom Menschen bearbeitet, von Land zu Wasser und wieder zurückverwandelt worden. Spuren solcher Projekte finden sich in der Zweiteilung der Fläche: ein mittelalterliches, fächerförmiges Siedlungssystem im Süden und im Norden ein rationell parzellierter Polder sieben Meter unter dem Meeresspiegel. Die Grenze zwischen diesen zwei Abschnitten wird von einem Relief gebildet, das die ganze Fläche von Osten nach Westen in einer langen, gebogenen Linie durchzieht. Entlang einiger Siedlungsbänder hatte schon ein gewisses Maß an Urbanisierung und Konzentration stattgefunden.

Ganz ohne Bezug zur Morphologie wurde das Gebiet in zwei Verwaltungsbezirke aufgeteilt: das sozialistische Rotterdam im Westen, das danach strebte, die niederländische Hauptstadt der Moderne zu werden und das Dorf Capelle im Osten, das mit seiner orthodox-calvinistischen Kultur sorgfältig seine jahrhundertealte Stabilität bewahrte.

Zu Anfang der Planungen wurde der Beschluß gefaßt, diese Einwände nicht zu beachten, um den rationalen und homogenen Urbanisierungsprozeß nicht zu stören. Ein Blick auf das Ergebnis zeigt jedoch, daß genau diese Interessenkonflikte entscheidend waren. Spannungen zwischen der Autonomie bei der Entwicklung der Peripherie, wie sie das Dorf verfolgte, und dem Gesamtzusammenhang des Ballungsraums, wie er von der Stadt propagiert wurde, lassen sich auch in den beiden Konzepten wiederfinden, die die Diskussion dominiert haben.

Ein Konzept war das Modell der Satellitenstadt, das eine autonome Stadt zeigt, die von ihrer Umgebung durch Schnellstraßen und Schienen abgeschnitten ist. Ein Ring von Wohnbezirken legt sich um einen Park und die Innenstadt, die beide im geographischen Zentrum zu finden sind. Jeder Rest von bestehender Morphologie, der nicht mit dieser Idee übereinstimmte, wurde eliminiert.

Das andere Konzept war das Finger-Stadt Modell, in dem die neuen Urbanisierungszonen entlang radialer Verbindungsachsen zwischen Zentrum

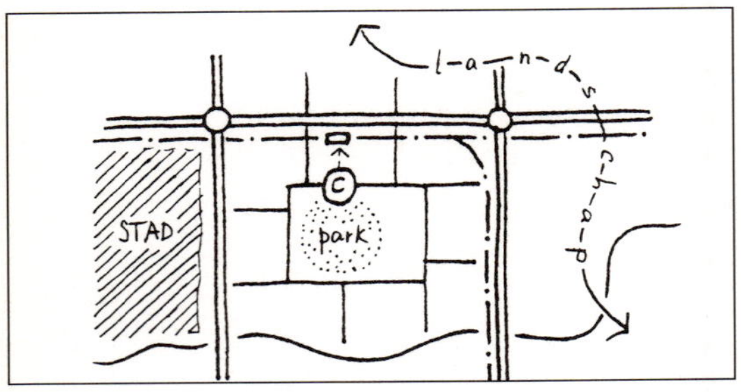

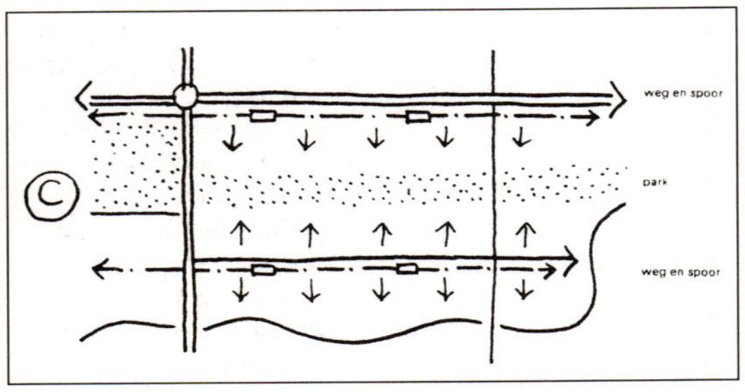

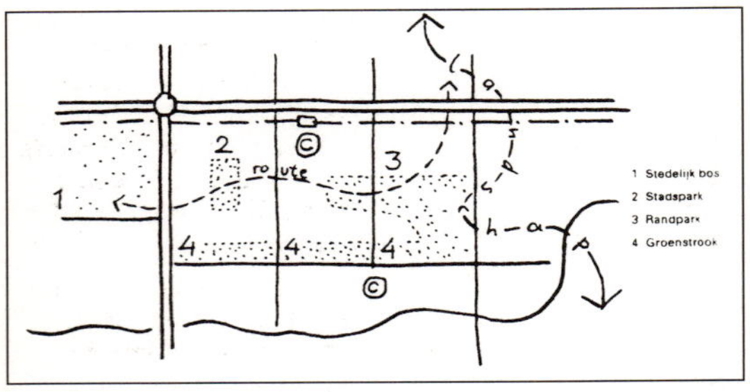

und Außenbezirken angelegt waren. Diese Straßen sollten dem öffentlichen Verkehr dienen, kontinuierliche Grünzonen die Siedlungsbereiche voneinander trennen. Alle Vorschläge zu einer teilweisen Autonomie der Vorstädte wurden verworfen.

Dieser Konflikt vereitelte schließlich eine notwendige gemeinsame Planung. Die Gemeindegrenzen wurden zu einer Art Berliner Mauer. Das einzige, das diese Krise überlebt hat, war der Entwurf für das Netz der Haupt-Schnellstraßen. Innerhalb dieses Netzes entwickelte jede Gemeinde ihre eigenen Stadtteile, wie es ihr passend erschien – der gerade aktuellen Architekturmode entsprechend.

Heterogenität als Inspiration. Beiden Modellen liegen feste Bezüge zugrunde. Die Satellitenstadt versucht, diese Bezüge zwischen den Wohnungen, den Grünbereichen und dem Stadtzentrum aufzubauen, eine Anordnung, die sich in einer per Definition begrenzten Komposition findet. Das Ziel der Finger-Stadt ist es, feste Beziehungen zwischen Transport, Wohnen und einem Grüngebiet herzustellen, wobei die Organisation dieses Modells in einer wiederum per Definition, unbegrenzten Komposition stattfindet. Nach der Realisierung lassen sich im Gebiet keine erkennbaren festen Bezüge zwischen irgendwelchen dieser Elemente mehr erkennen. Das Verkehrssystem funktioniert als autonome Einheit, es teilt das Gebiet in Viertel, in denen Grünzonen und bebaute Flächen auf verschiedenste Weise miteinander in Beziehung stehen. Räumliche Bezüge, die den Maßstab dieser Gebiete überschreiten, sind selten. Diese größere Rolle wird nur von gewissen Elementen erfüllt, die der Planungskontrolle entkommen sind: Flüsse, Bodenreliefs und bereits existierende Siedlungsbänder. Der Alexanderpolder zeigt eine Struktur, die der lose geschichteten Struktur der Gesamtstadt Rotterdam ähnelt. Kann diese Struktur als Inspirationsquelle erfaßt werden, statt nur als Hindernis erfahren zu werden?

a green area, whereby the organization of this model once again by definition takes place within an unbordered composition. Since being realized, the area no longer contains any recognizable fixed relationships between any of these elements. The transport system functions as an autonomous entity, dividing the area into compartments in which green zones and developed areas relate to one another in a variety of ways.

Spatial relationships that exceed the scale of individual developments are few and far between. This greater role is filled only by certain elements that escaped the planning control of the blueprint: rivers, relief lines and pre-existing ribbon development. Alexanderpolder exhibits a structure that resembles that of the loosely layered structure of Rotterdam as a whole. Can it be grasped as a source of inspiration instead of experienced as an impediment?

The Prinsenland experiment: The plan for Prinsenland (1984), a design for a new residential district at Alexanderpolder, is one of the first town-planning projects to break with the Modernist model-like approach.

Instead of adding yet another autonomous district to the city, this plan makes an effort to introduce a conscious interplay of traffic, developed areas, green zones and facilities, all of which are relatively autonomous elements, and takes into consideration the results of previous measures in and around the area. Geomorphologic differences provide welcome opportunities to use various urbanization principles. A larger scale urbanization has been applied in the northern, lowlying polder and a lot by lot urbanization in the southern strip of fan-shaped parcels. The contrast between the two sections is dramatized by the

Heterogenität als Inspiration. Prinsenland als Wohnviertel auf dem Alexanderpolder gilt als erste Planung, die mit der Moderne brach. Modelle der Satellitenstadt oder der Fingerstadt standen zur Debatte. Gewählt wurde ein Experiment, bei dem die unterschiedlichen Bereiche ineinandergreifen und die Freiflächenplanung der Bebauungsplanung vorausgeht.

Heterogeneity as inspiration. The plan for Prinsenland, a residential district at Alexanderpolder, was one of the first projects to break with the Modernist approach. Two concepts, namely the satellite-city model and the finger-city model, were put forward, but in the final analysis what was chosen was an experiment. This features an interplay of various elements.

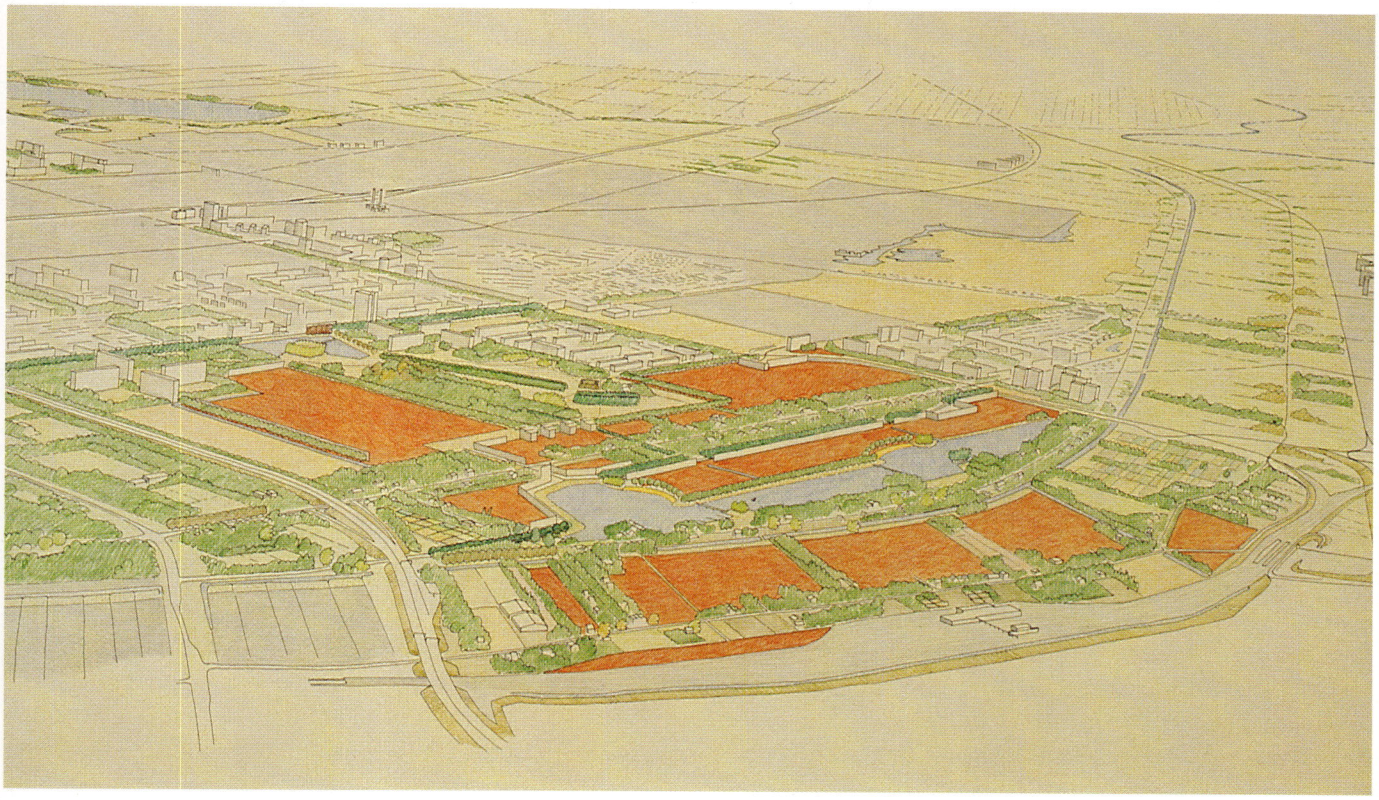

Prinsenland aus der Vogelperspektive: links die regelmäßige Parzellenstruktur des Alexanderpolders, rechts die fächerförmigen Grundstücke, dazwischen die geschwungene Relieflinie. Das Gebiet wird von Straßen mit Reihenbebauung durchschnitten. Strukturskizze von 1984 für das Prinsenland (unten): In den Bogen der Relieflinie wurde ein langgestreckter See gelegt, ein Park flankiert die Hochhaus-Cluster. See, Park und die bandförmige Entwicklung bilden die Hauptelemente der Komposition, innerhalb der die Wohnhäuser entwickelt werden.

Bird's-eye-view of Prinsenland: left, the orderly division of Alexanderpolder; right, the fan-shaped organization of plots; inbetween, the curved relief line. The area is transected by roads flanked by ribbon development. Below: Structural outline of Prinsenland, 1984. An elongated lake is located in the cavity of the curved relief line and a park is situated next to the high-rise clusters. The lake, the park and the ribbon development form the main elements of the composition within which residential buildings are to be developed.

Das Prinsenland-Experiment. Der Plan für Prinsenland von 1984, ein Entwurf für ein neues Wohnviertel im Alexanderpolder, ist eines der ersten Projekte, die mit dem modernistischen, modellhaften Ansatz brechen. Statt der Stadt noch einen weiteren autonomen Distrikt hinzuzufügen, versucht dieser Entwurf bewußt, ein Zusammenspiel zwischen Verkehr, bebauten Flächen, Grünzonen und verschiedensten Versorgungseinrichtungen zu schaffen, die alle für sich relativ autonome Elemente sind.

Geomorphologische Unterschiede bieten willkommene Gelegenheiten, verschiedene Urbanisierungsprinzipien zu verwenden. In den nördlichen, tiefliegenden Poldergebieten wurde eine Stadtentwicklung im großen Maßstab geplant, in der südlichen Zone eine abschnittweise Urbanisierung. Der Gegensatz zwischen den beiden Gebieten wird durch die Planung eines Sees entlang der Grenze verstärkt, einem Element, das die lange gebogene Reliefkante noch betont. Bestehende Siedlungsbänder, die Verbindungen zwischen dem Stadtzentrum und den Außenbezirken schaffen, werden in den Entwurf integriert. Im Entwurf für das Prinsenland geht die Freiflächenplanung der Bebauungsplanung voraus. Der Plan, der weder abstrakt noch modellhaft ist, dramatisiert und artikuliert die bestehende Landschaft, um sie damit sozusagen für die Urbanisierung vorzubereiten. Er fügt der bereits entwickelten Landschaft eine weitere Schicht hinzu und bereitet sie gleichzeitig für zukünftige Transformationen vor. Der Entwurf entspricht der lose geschichteten Struktur, die sowohl die Innenstadt als auch die Peripherie charakterisiert.

Während die Peripheriezonen der niederländischen Städte, über die Jahrhunderte betrachtet, ihre vierte oder fünfte radikale Transformation erleben, ist es für die Stadtzentren etwa die zwanzigste oder dreißigste. In beiden Fällen liegt die Aufgabe darin, die Komplexität zu verstehen und nicht zu ignorieren.

Die AIR Alexanderpolder-Veranstaltung von 1993 bot den betroffenen Vorstädten die Möglichkeit, über eine neue Schicht der Transformation nachzudenken, und zwar vor dem Hintergrund der fortschreitenden Urbanisierung der Randstad. Zum ersten Mal waren verschiedene künstlerische Disziplinen aufgerufen, sich der Herausforderung einer kulturellen Interpretation auf einem Feld zu stellen, das normalerweise der technologisch-rationalen Planung vorbehalten war. Auf lange Sicht können solche Interpretationen eine Humusschicht bilden, in der Ideen Wurzeln schlagen und gedeihen können.

proposal of a lake along their common boundary, an element that will accent the long, curved relief line. Existing ribbon development is integrated into the plan, creating links with the city centre and the outer periphery. In the plan for Prinsenland, the design of open space precedes the organization of the developed area. This design, which is neither abstract nor model-like, dramatizes and articulates the existing landscape in order to prepare it, so to speak, for urbanization. It adds a newly transformed layer to an already urbanized landscape, while at the same time preparing the area for future transformation. The design conforms to the loosely layered structure that characterizes both the city centre and periphery.

In my opinion, the peripheral areas do not require a design approach that differs essentially from that used in central, "historical" areas. While the provincial periphery of Dutch cities, measured in centuries, is undergoing its fourth or fifth radical transformation, the city centre of Rotterdam is experiencing perhaps its twentieth or thirtieth. In both cases, it is crucial to understand the complexity involved and not ignore it. The 1993 AIR Alexander symposium formed an invitation for suburbia to consider a new layer of transformation, set against a background of the continuing urbanization of the Randstad. For the first time, different disciplines and areas of artistic skill were presented with the challenge of developing cultural interpretations within an arena previously reserved for technological-rational planning. In the long term, such interpretations can provide a layer of humus in which ideas pertaining to "the periphery" are able to take root and thrive.

Urbanität light

Urbanization light

Lightness. Our land seems filled up. But filled with what? The suburban mixture of factory-like farms, houses with gardens, and warehouses seems to comprise density without matter. Enormous areas are turning into a sea of planned mediocrity. Must we accept this situation as fixed or can we envisage experimental environments that can be dismantled, allowing us to change our urban goals at any given time? A lighter form of urbanization could be brought about by reducing the economic value of expensive aspects of our ways and means of urbanization: there could be grass roads instead of asphalt, ecological purification pools instead of sewage pipes, electric power lines instead of gas-mains, portable telephones without telecommunication lines, mini-busses or busses on demand instead of costly underground systems. Such economy could create exciting possiblities. Lower densities would become affordable on the same budget. Economy would thus connect with ecology.

Camping land. In an increasingly individualized society, the middle class spreads out widely. More people work fewer hours and relatively many people work at home in numerous different working and living arrangements. Houses, chalets, large and small farms, condominiums could assemble on one big campsite, with a holiday atmosphere built into everyday life.

Permanence. Such a light kind of urbanization questions the permanence of the city. The existing town could dissolve into a changing landscape. Extremely mixed programs would then become imaginable, from living on a farm to farming in the city. Change would claim its rightful place in urbanization. It would describe the space for the unpredictable.

Lightness. Unser Land scheint allmählich voll zu werden. Aber voll womit? Die Vorstadtmischung aus fabrikähnlichen Bauernhöfen, Häusern mit Gärten und Geschäften scheint eine Dichte ohne Substanz zu beinhalten. Enorme Landstriche verwandeln sich in dieses Meer der geplanten Mittelmäßigkeit. Nehmen wir diese Situation als gegeben hin, oder stellen wir uns den experimentellen Stadtlandschaften, die wieder abgerissen werden können, wenn wir unsere städtebaulichen Ziele nach einer gewissen Zeit ändern? Können wir uns eine »light«-Version des Städtebaus vorstellen, die solange genutzt wird, bis wir die politische Courage finden, konkrete Entscheidungen zum Thema Konzentration oder Sprawl zu fällen? Diese »leichtere« Form des Städtebaus kann forciert werden, indem man den ökonomischen Wert der teuren Urbanisierungsmaßnahmen reduziert: Graswege statt Asphalt, ökologische Klärbecken statt Kanalisation, Elektroheizung anstelle von Gasleitungen, keine Telefonleitungen, sondern tragbare Telefone, keine teuren U-Bahnen, sondern Minibusse. Solch eine Sparsamkeit würde interessante Möglichkeiten schaffen: mit dem gleichen vorgegebenen Budget kann man sich eine geringere Dichte leisten. Somit verbindet sich Ökonomie mit Ökologie. Es entsteht das paradoxe Gefühl, daß sich ökologische Nachhaltigkeit in »Lightness« und Vorläufigkeit manifestiert.

Winy Maas

Campingland. In einer sich individualisierenden Gesellschaft kann sich die Mittelschicht enorm ausdehnen: immer mehr Leute arbeiten immer kürzer. Die Mittelschicht wird aus vielen Heimarbeitern bestehen, die sehr differenzierte Arbeits- und Lebensbeziehungen unterhalten. Die Stadt löst sich auf im ländlichen Raum, der durch Netzwerke organisiert ist. Häuser, Landhäuser, kleine und große Bauernhöfe, Wohnheime, Eigentums-Wohnanlagen und Kolonien werden zu einem großen Supercampingplatz, der das Feriengefühl auf den Alltag überträgt.

Permanenz. Diese »light«-Variante des Städtebaus stellt die Dauerhaftigkeit der Stadt in Frage. Die bestehende Stadt könnte sich in eine wechselhafte Landschaft auflösen. Extreme Nutzungsmischungen werden denkbar: vom Wohnen auf dem Bauernhof bis hin zum Ackerbau innerhalb der Stadt. Die Veränderung findet so ihren Platz im Städtebau. Sie definiert den Raum für das »Unvorhersehbare«.

Eine flexible, ökologisch verträgliche Camping-Landschaft mit geringem Finanzbedarf könnte den monumentalen Städtebau ablösen.

A flexible, ecologically compatible camping landscape with minor financial requirements could replace monumental urban architecture.

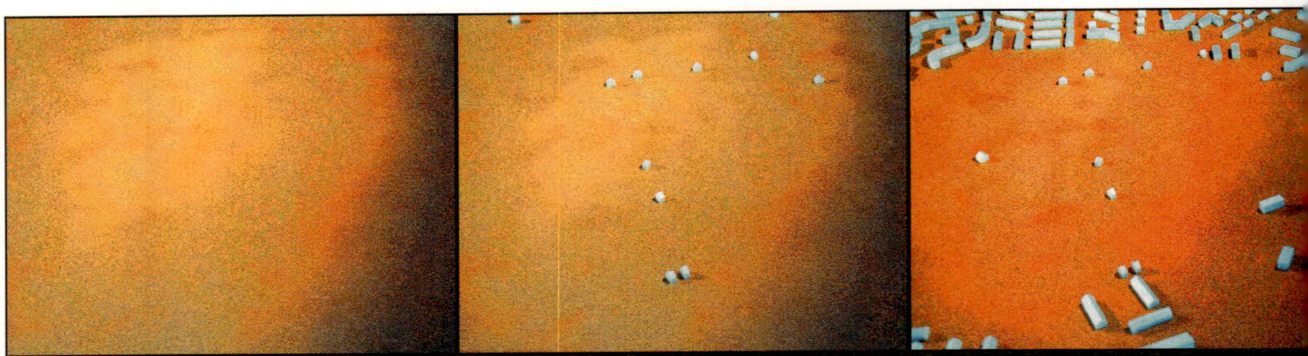

LIGHTNESS. Our lands seem to become full. But full of what? The suburbian mix of factory-like farms, hou

itself into this sea of planned mediocracy. Do we accept this condition as fixed or can we envisage experime

This lighter form of urbanism can be forced by reducing the economical value of expensive parts of our way

cables for heating, no telecomlines but portable phones, no expensive metrolines but minibusses or bus

be afforded. Economy obtains thus a connection with ecology. It delivers the paradoxical feeling that

th gardens, warehouses seem to contain density without matter. Enormous areas of our lands are turning

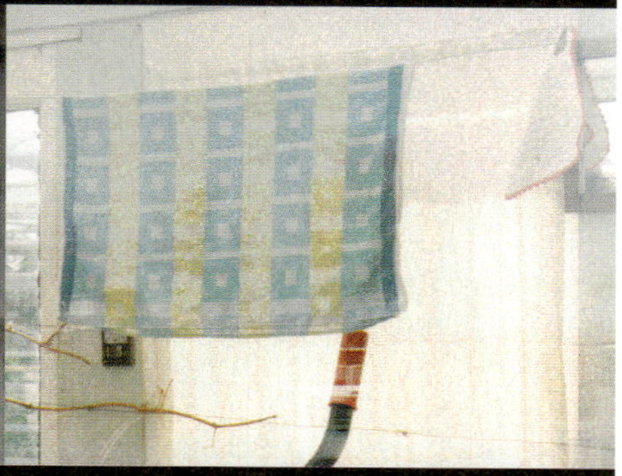

vironments, which can be broken down, so that we can change our urbanistic goals within a certain time?

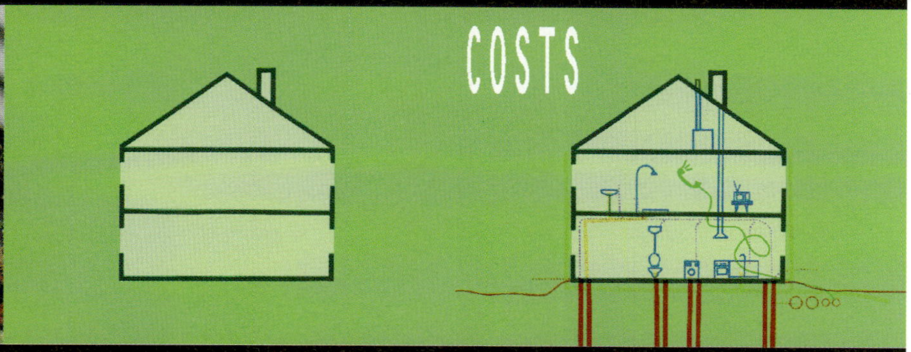

ɔanization: grass roads instead of asphalt, no sewage pipes but ecological pools, no gaspipes but electricity

-demand. This economy can cause exciting possibilities: within the same existing budget, lower densities can

ECOLOGY = ECONOMY

ical sustainability has been translated into lightness and temporariness.

CAMPINGLAND. In a more and more individualizing society the midle class can extend enormously: more pec

working and living relationships. The town dissolves itself into a 'land' of smaller and bigger plots, which are org

are gathered in one big super-camping, where the holiday feeling is included within the day to day life. **VIL**

who have not will organize themselves to protect their acquisitions or to fight for it. It leads to towns that co

groups, the higher the complexity, the intenser the possible need for cohesion. Bordering these villages by 'fi

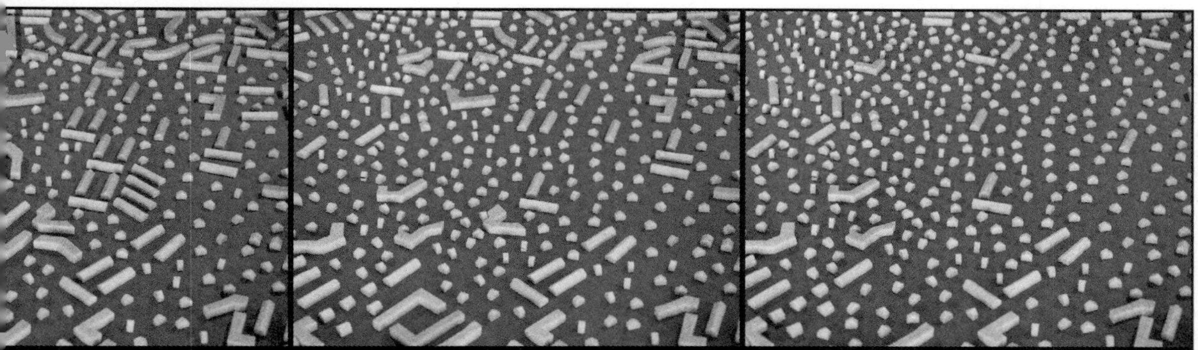

k in fewer hours. It will consist of relatively many homeworkers, who have many and differentiated

y different series of networks. Houses, chalets, fermettes, homes, farms, condominiums and colonies

D. In a society that can be characterized by the 'struggle of the fittest', those who have and those

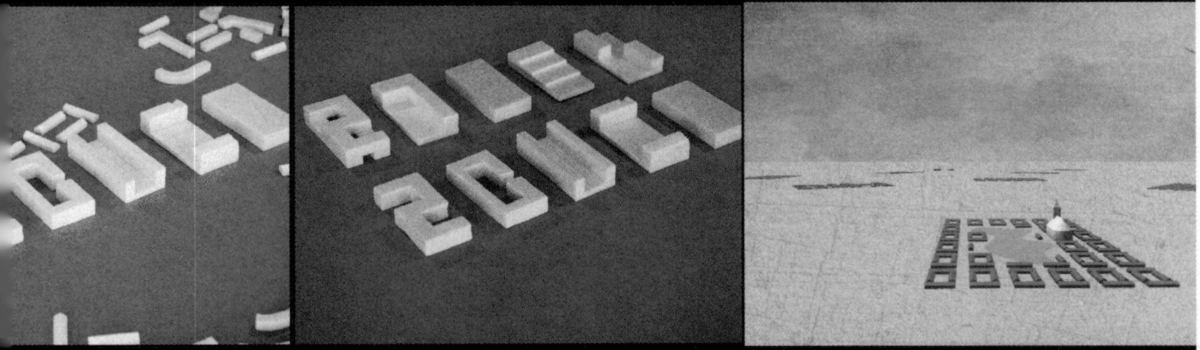

nore or less fenced communities, 'villages' or 'colonies'. The bigger the differences among the

re', their relative autonomy can be assured. It gives space to the required ecological fields.

PERMANENCE. This lighter type of urbanism questions the permanence of the town: should we consider all of the

monuments? Can this heavy and fixed way of urbanistic behaviour be replaced by a lighter one in which we can giv

can revalue its necessity after their functioning. Evaluating the quality of the existing, within 3 years huge 'vo

town finds the opportunity to dissolve itself in a landscape of changes. Extreme melanges of programs become im

It defines space for the 'unpredictable'. M

urban fabric as permanent? Are all our buildings that valuable that they should be considered as

or experiments and imagination? If we consider the economical value of the built environment, we

multiple fantasies can be foreseen, in which monuments appear as 'Mont St. Michel's'. The existing

from living at a farm till farming within the town. 'Change' finds thus its position within urbanism.

5, Winy Maas, Jacob van Rijs, Nathalie de Vries, Tom Mossel, Joost Grootens

Masterplan für Nieuwegeins Zentrum

A master plan for Nieuwegein's centre

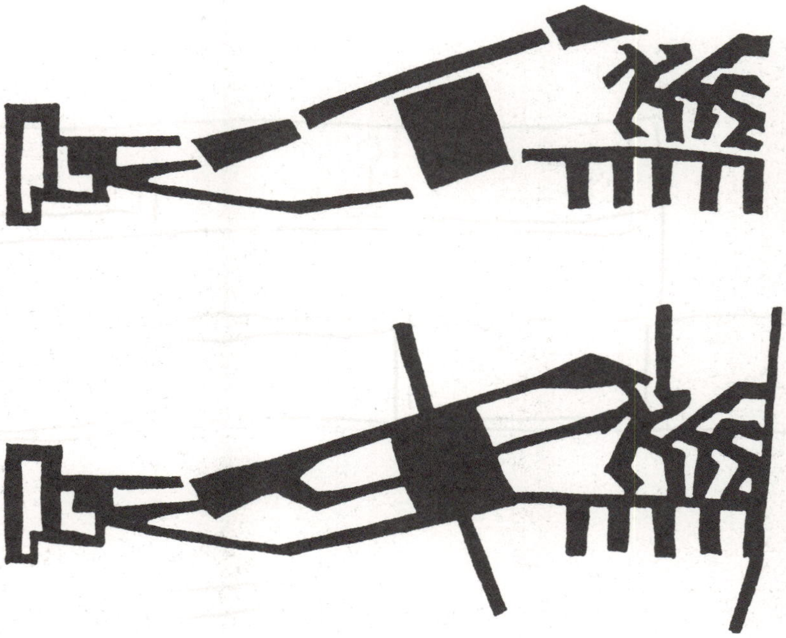

Marieke Timmermans
Martine van Vliet
Harmen van de Wal

Nieuwegein liegt im Zentrum der Niederlande etwas südlich von Utrecht und entstand erst in den 70er Jahren. Rund 60 000 Menschen leben heute in dieser jungen Stadt mit modernem Zentrum, aber eher trister Atmosphäre. Nieuwegeins Funktion als Regionalzentrum droht verlorenzugehen, seit Utrecht in seiner Stadtmitte einige Umbauten vorgenommen hat und nun mit öffentlichen Verkehrsmitteln sehr gut zu erreichen ist. Daher will Nieuwegein sein Zentrum ausbauen und mehr Geschäfte, Wohnungen, Büros, Kultur und vor allem Parkplätze schaffen. Kurz gesagt: Nieuwegein setzt hauptsächlich auf das Auto. Das Büro B+B wurde eingeladen, zusammen mit Michael van Gessel und UN/studio Van Berkel en Bos einen Entwurf für die Entwicklung der Stadtmitte zu konzipieren. Ursprünglich sollte nur ein relativ kleiner Teil des Zentrums umgestaltet werden, doch die Büros konnten die Gemeinde von der Notwendigkeit überzeugen, den gesamten Stadtkern anzugehen. Insgesamt werden 200 000 Quadratmeter Bürofläche, 20 000 Quadratmeter Geschäftsräume,

Drinnen, draußen, oben, unten – eine wogende Ebene zieht sich durch das Stadtzentrum und erklärt alles zum öffentlichen Raum.

Inside, outside, up and down – in the city centre an undulating skin declares everything to public space.

Nieuwegein lies in the heart of the Netherlands, slightly to the south of Utrecht, and came into existence during the seventies. Today around 60,000 people live in this young town, which has a modern centre but a somewhat dreary atmosphere. Nieuwegein is in danger of forfeiting its function as a regional centre now that Utrecht has plans for redeveloping its centre and has become easy to reach by public transport. It is for this reason that Nieuwegein plans to extend its centre and create more shops, apartments, offices, cultural facilities and, above all, parking spaces. In short: Nieuwegein is staking its future on the car. Along with Michael van Gessel and UN/studio Van Berkel en Bos, the B+B office was invited to submit a design proposal for the development of the town centre. The original intention was to redesign only a relatively small part of the centre, but the offices were able to convince the municipality of the necessity of an integrated solution for the centre as a whole. All in all office space of 200,000 square metres, shopping space of 20,000 square metres, 800 apartments and 5,000 covered parking spaces are to be created. The development is to extend between four attracting areas, so-called anchor points.

The street level as a continuous design element. The unifying factor in the design is a continuous, undulating skin which passes through the entire centre like a landscape, linking all buildings and literally incorporating them. This undulating skin constitutes public space over its entire length, no matter whether inside, outside, up or down. It also passes through a number of layers of the project area. Uniform material has been chosen for the surface, material which is to cover the ground and sometimes even walls and ceilings of both the buildings and the outside areas. The skin can be the roof of a building, a small public square between buildings or the lobby of a building. Areas which were previously closed off on account of their private nature are to be opened up and supplement the public area. Elements which once formed barriers such as railway lines are to be integrated into the centre in a natural way. Cycling is permitted everywhere, and a number of paths are set aside for cyclists alone. One of the cycle routes runs through the station concourse, another passes the library and the town hall. These routes contain bicycle stands integrated into buildings that are also especially lit at night. Although cars are only able to use parts of the undulating skin. Vehicles are concentrated on the lowers levels, which are linked to higher levels at numerous points and which represent the most important means of public access to the centre. The parking levels are key public areas and give way to magnificent large, high areas with fountains, giving them the semblance of squares. In order to define the garages as public space they are provided the same material as the undulating skin. The character of the access areas from the parking levels to the upper levels refers to the functions located above. Vertical access is in the form of escalators, lifts and ramps which cut through a spacious concourse. A continuous circular road giving access to the garages links all exits and entrances. A certain number of parking spaces is reserved for the upper levels, whereby care has been taken to ensure that the various uses of these buildings are staggered in terms of time so that the parking area is available for a number of different functions.

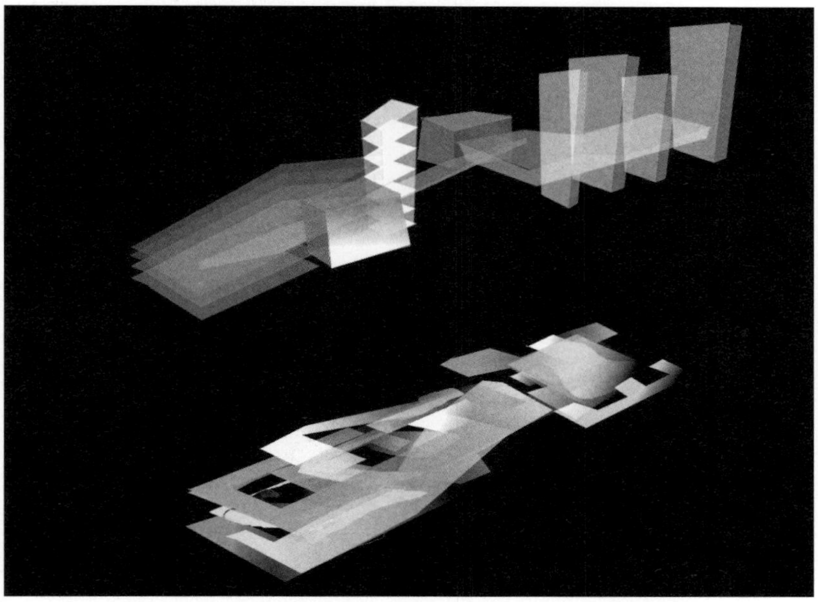

Ein autofreundliches Stadtzentrum wünscht sich Nieuwegein. Die Planer schlagen eine wogende Ebene vor, die alle Gebäude verbindet und in der gesamten Länge einen öffentlichen Raum bildet. Unterschiedliche Raumtypologien sind vorgesehen, die homogene Fläche durch nur ein Material einheitlich gestaltet.

A car-friendly city centre is expressly desired in Nieuwegein. The planners propose an undulating surface linking all the buildings, its full length forming a public space. Different space typologies along it are planned, while the continuous surface is uniform, being of only one material.

800 Wohnungen sowie 5000 überdachte Parkpätze errichtet. Die Erweiterung wird zwischen vier stark frequentierten Plätzen, sogenannten Ankerpunkten, aufgespannt.

Das Straßenniveau als kontinuierliches Gestaltungselement. Der verbindende Faktor in diesem Entwurf ist eine durchgehende wogende Ebene, die sich wie eine Landschaft durch das gesamte Zentrum bewegt, alle Gebäude miteinander verbindet und buchstäblich in sich aufnimmt. Diese gewellte Ebene ist in ihrer gesamten Länge ein öffentlicher Raum, ganz gleich ob drinnen oder draußen, oben oder unten. Sie bewegt sich darüber hinaus durch mehrere Schichten des Projektgebiets. Für die Oberfläche wird ein einheitliches Material gewählt, das Böden, und manchmal sogar Wände und Decken sowohl der Gebäude als auch der Außenräume bedecken soll. Die Ebene kann das Dach eines Gebäudes sein, ein kleiner offener Platz zwischen den Gebäuden, oder auch die Lobby innerhalb eines Gebäudes. Räume, die bisher wegen ihres privaten Charakters geschlossen waren, werden geöffnet und ergänzen den öffentlichen Bereich. Elemente, die früher Barrieren gebildet haben, wie die Bahn- und S-Bahn-Gleise, werden auf ganz selbstverständliche Weise ins Zentrum integriert. Radfahren ist überall

Wohnen, Arbeiten, Einkaufen, Verkehr – die Nutzungen sind gemixt und auf verschiedenen Ebenen anzutreffen. Tiefgaragen werden zu öffentlichen Plätzen, zu prachtvollen hohen Räumen. Durch die Nutzungsmischung werden die Parkplätze optimal ausgelastet. Rollsteige, Rampen und Aufzüge durchschneiden großzügige Hallen, verbinden die Etagen. Der Gang durch das Zentrum wird zu einem Erlebnis, wie der Comic rechts erzählt.

Living, working, shopping, traffic – uses are mixed and can be encountered on different levels. An underground carpark becomes a public space, with magnificently high rooms. Mixed uses cause the parking spots to be used to capacity. Escalators, ramps and lifts cut through expansive halls, linking the storeys. Walking through the centre becomes an experience, as shown in the cartoons on the right.

NEM
CAFE
GRAND CAFÉ
THE
SUPER

erlaubt, einige Wege sind eigens für Fahrradfahrer ausgeschildert. Ein Radweg führt etwa durch die Bahnhofshalle, ein anderer an der Bibliothek und am Rathaus entlang. An diesen Strecken befinden sich in die Gebäude integrierte Fahrradstellplätze, die nachts beleuchtet sind. Für Autos ist die wogende Ebene zwar nur teilweise freigegeben, trotzdem läßt sich das Zentrum gut erreichen. Die Fahrzeuge werden in den unteren Etagen konzentriert, die an vielen Stellen mit den oberen Ebenen verflochten sind und die wichtigsten öffentlichen Zugänge zum Zentrum darstellen. Die Tiefgaragen sind wichtige öffentliche Orte und erweitern sich zu prachtvollen großen und hohen Räumen, die durch Springbrunnen zu Plätzen werden. Um auch die Garagen als öffentliche Räume zu definieren, werden sie mit dem selben Material wie die wogende Ebene ausgestattet. Die Aufgänge von den Parkebenen hin zu den höheren Etagen weisen in ihrem Charakter auf die darüberliegenden Funktionen hin. Es sind vertikale Straßen mit Rollsteigen, Aufzügen und Rampen, die großzügige Hallen durchschneiden. Die Garagen werden von einem durchgehenden Rundweg erschlossen, der alle Ein- und Ausfahrten verbindet. Für die höher liegenden Etagen wird eine bestimmte Zahl

Funktionsmischung auch in den Gebäuden. In der Bahnhofshalle finden sich Läden und Büros. Ein Radweg führt durchs Gebäude. Radfahren ist überall erlaubt. Die Landschaft zieht sich durch die Gebäude.

The anchor points. In the town hall anchor, the wings of the library weave their way through the stories of the town hall, while the transparent volume of the museum extends over the roof of the town hall and uses it as a sculpture garden; as for the roof of the museum, it is part of the undulating skin. In the department store, office floors alternate with shopping floors grouped around an atrium. The theatre anchor is topped by a layer of patio houses with large gardens. They form the roof of a large space containing offices, a theatre,

Master plan and Development plan for Nieuwegein Centre, The Netherlands
Project team: B+B office Michael van Gessel, UN/studio Van Berkel & Bos

Mixed functions are also in the buildings themselves. The railway station houses shops and offices. A bicycle path runs through the building. Cycling is allowed everywhere. Buildings and landscape blend.

a supermarket and shops. All functions share a large concourse, a vast horizontal space, which will be a public lobby at office hours, a theatre foyer in the evening and a large entrance hall for the apartments at all times. Huge areas cut out of the ceiling of the concourse provide a view of the sky. The high office towers of the congress centre and hotel anchor soar above the street like ice floes. Various floors of these office towers house sports and entertainment facilities – both open air and covered – that are accessible to everyone.

von Parkplätzen reserviert, wobei darauf geachtet wurde, daß die verschiedenen Nutzungen dieser Gebäude zeitlich aufeinanderfolgen, so daß die Parkplätze für mehrere Funktionen zur Verfügung stehen.

Die Ankerpunkte. Im Rathausanker flechten sich die Trakte der Bibliothek durch die Geschosse des Rathauses, das Museum zieht sich als gläserner Baukörper über das Rathausdach und nutzt dieses als Skulpturengarten, während das Dach des Museums selbst wiederum Teil der wogenden Ebene ist. Im Kaufhaus schlängeln sich rund um ein Atrium die Bürogeschosse zwischen den Einkaufsetagen hindurch.

Im Theateranker liegen über den Bürogeschossen Patiohäuser mit großen Dachgärten, im Untergeschoß befinden sich das Theater und eine Bühne. Die Erschließung der Büros erfolgt von der Halle aus über Aufzüge, Galerien und Treppen. Riesige Aussparungen in der Decke der Halle geben den Blick in den Himmel frei. Die hohen Bürotürme des Kongreß- und Hotelankers ragen wie Eisschollen aus der Straßenebene heraus. In verschiedenen Stockwerken dieser Bürotürme liegen Ebenen für Sport oder Vergnügen, offen oder überdacht, für jedermann zugänglich.

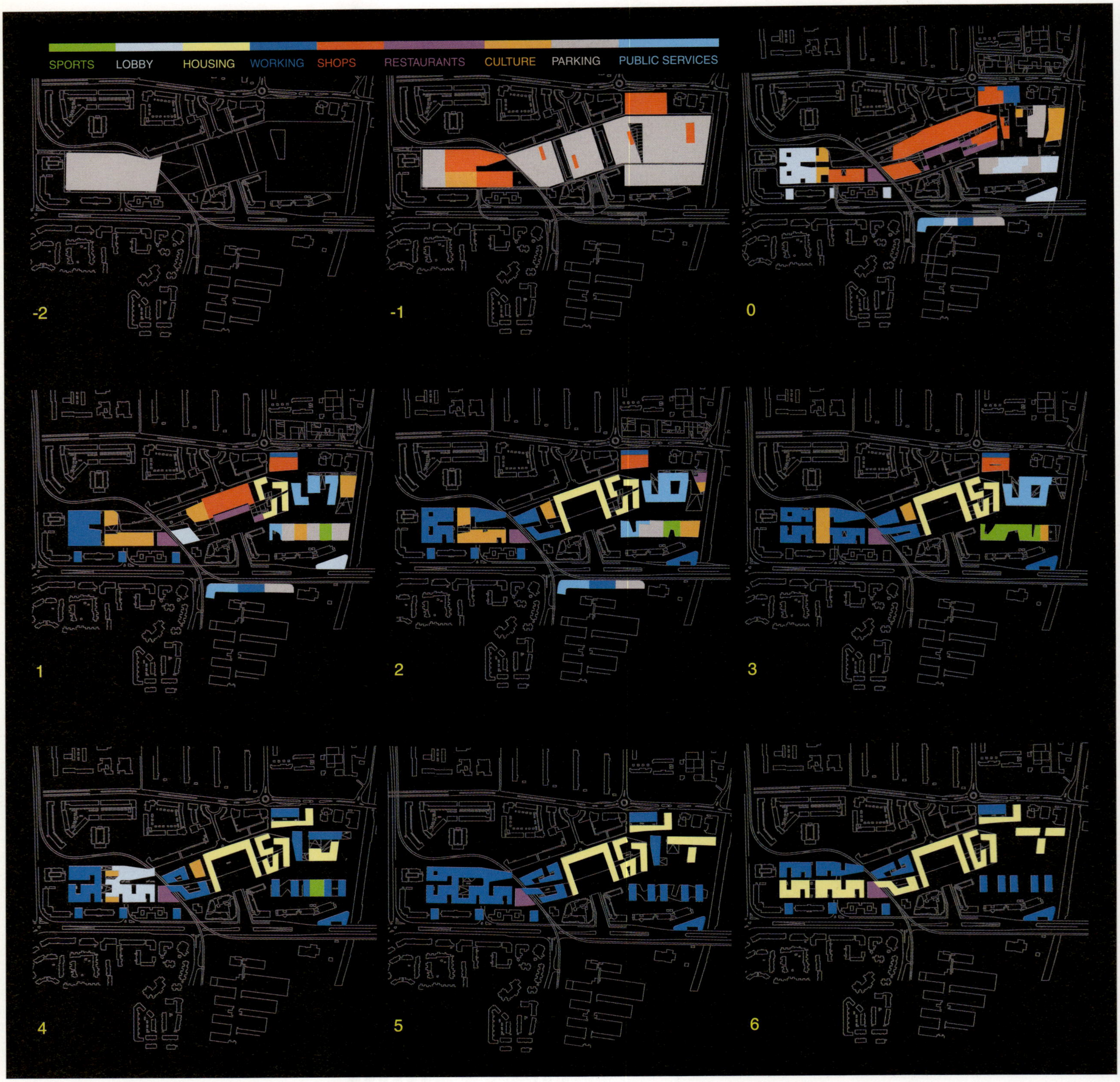
SPORTS
LOBBY
HOUSING
WORKING
SHOPS
RESTAURANTS
CULTURE
PARKING
PUBLIC SERVICES
-2
-1
0
1
2
3
4
5
6

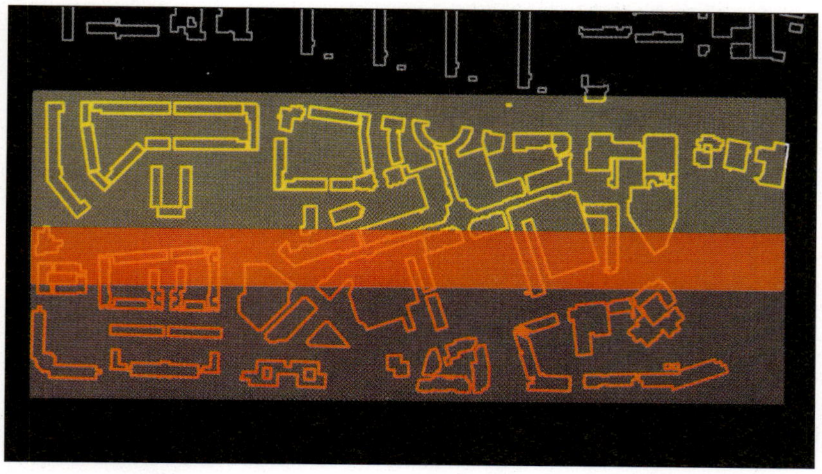

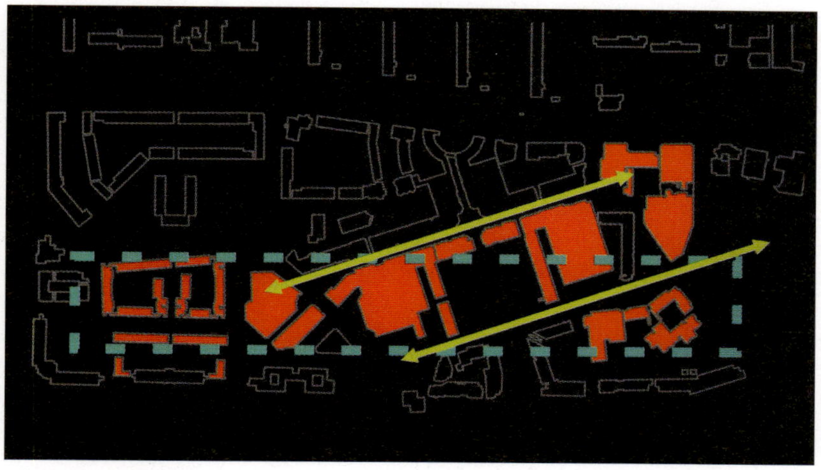

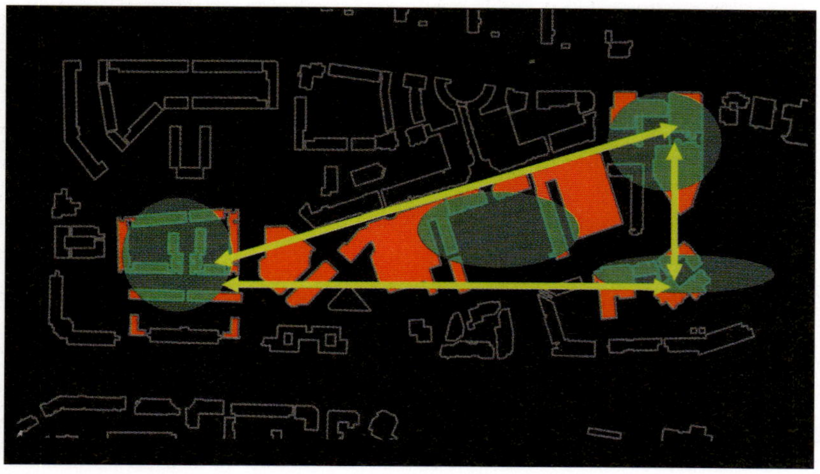

Die Grafik auf Seite 66 zeigt die verschiedenen Nutzungen in einem der Ankergebäude vom zweiten Tiefgeschoß bis zum sechsten Stock.
Vier Ankergebäude sind der Kultur, dem Markt, Büros und dem Rathaus gewidmet (ganz unten). Die mittlere Abbildung zeigt die Strukturlinien (gelb), Gebäude die entfernt werden sollen (rot) und die Entwicklungszone für Büros (blau). Die obere Grafik zeigt den dem Ort dienenden Bereich (gelb) und den Bereich für die regionale Versorgung (orange).

The graphics on page 66 show various uses in one of the "anchor" buildings from the second basement up to the sixth storey. The four "anchor" buildings are devoted to the arts, the market, offices and the city hall, respectively (this page, below). The figure in the middle shows structure lines (yellow), buildings to be demolished (red) and the development zone for offices (blue). The top diagram shows the areas devoted to municipal services (yellow) and regional public utilities (orange).

Amsterdam: Platz frei für die Museen

Amsterdam: A square makes room for museums

Klazien Brummel

Mit einer offenen Rasenfläche hat Sven-Ingvar Andersson dem Museumsplatz skandinavische Gelassenheit und Raum für Events verschafft.

With an open lawn Sven-Ingvar Andersson provided Scandinavian informality and room for events in Museum Square.

Der Amsterdamer Museumsplatz (Museumplein) ist nie ein Platz gewesen, und er ist auch nach der Umgestaltung keiner geworden. Am Ort selbst liegt es nicht, dass dort niemals ein grandioser Platz entstanden ist. Als Amsterdam Mitte des 19. Jahrhunderts aus allen Nähten platzte und seine Stadtmauern überrollte, lag die weite Welt vor den Toren. Rund um die Stadt wurden Wiesen enteignet, um Wohnviertel zu bauen – und das Museumsviertel. Die Museen entstanden, ebenso ein ehrwürdiges Konzertgebäude, das zu jedermanns Ärger nicht direkt dem Reichsmuseum gegenüber steht, sondern etwas aus der Achse gerückt ist. Jedoch gelang es keinem einzigen Architekten, dazwischen einen Traumplatz mit großstädtischem Ambiente zu schaffen. Die Stadt blieb unschlüssig und hielt namhafte Architekten wie Van Niftrik, Cuypers und Berlage immer wieder hin. Erst 1952 entschloss sie sich, das brachliegende Gelände zwischen den Museen und dem Konzertgebäude zu gestalten. Nach dem Entwurf des Stadtplaners Van Eesteren wurde eine breite Allee gepflastert, dazu ein paar Grasflächen angelegt und einige Platanen gesetzt, ordentlich in Reih und Glied. Fortan nannten die Leute den Museumsplatz »die kürzeste Autobahn der Niederlande«, und eine Fahrt über das Kopfsteinpflaster bescherte ihnen ein Gefühl von Südeuropa, oder zumindest von Antwerpen. Wie es sich für Plätze gehört, diente auch dieser als Versammlungsstätte für die Massen, die zu großen Demonstrationen oder Jahrmärkten nach Amsterdam reisten. Doch meistens parkten auf dem Platz Hunderte von Reisebussen, denen jährlich Tausende von Touristen entstiegen, um nebenan Rembrandts »Nachtwache« oder Van Goghs »Schwertlilien« zu bewundern. Kurz, der Platz bot wenig Erheiterndes außer der phantastischen Aussicht über die große, leere Fläche hinweg auf die Fassade des Reichsmuseums, die in der Nachmittagssonne glänzt wie ein Rubin. Dass der Platz niemals das Aussehen eines Platzes bekommen hat, wird als typisch holländischer Flop angesehen. Es heißt nämlich, die Niederländer könnten keine Plätze gestalten. In einem Interview erläuterte der Direktor des Reichsmuseums einmal, wie so etwas in seinem Land vonstatten geht: Ein Platz wie die Place des Vosges oder die Place de la Concorde, meinte er, könne gar nicht zustande kommen, denn es fehle den Niederländern die Tradition der großen königlichen Gesten. In Holland setze vielmehr jemand einen Pumpenschwengel

Amsterdam's Museum Square (Museumplein) was never actually a square, and now that it has been redesigned it has become smaller. The site is not to blame for the fact that there was never a grand square here. When Amsterdam was bursting out of its seams in the middle of the 19th century, spreading beyond the city walls, the whole wide world lay beyond the gates. Meadows were expropriated all around the town in order to develop residential districts – and the museum district. The museums were built, and a respectable concert hall, which to everyone's dismay is not right opposite the Rijksmuseum, but somehow slipped off the axis. Yet not one architect ever got the chance to create a dream square with metropolitan ambience in between. The city remained indecisive and kept putting off renowned architects such as Van Niftrik, Cuypers and Berlage. It was not until 1952 that it decided to landscape the derelict land between the museums and the concert hall. According to designs by the urban planner Van Eesteren, a broad avenue was paved, a few lawns were laid out and a few plane trees planted, nice and orderly in straight rows. From then on people called Museum Square "the shortest motorway in The Netherlands," and driving over the cobblestones gave them a feeling of being in southern Europe, or at least in Antwerp. As is fitting for a square, this one too served as a meeting place for crowds travelling to Amsterdam for big demonstrations or fairs. But usually it was a parking lot for hundreds of parked tourist buses, from which thousands of tourists a year would descend in order to admire Rembrandt's "Night Watch" or Van Gogh's "Irises" next door. In other words, the square provided little that was cheering except for a fabulous view across the big empty space towards the facade of the Rijksmuseum. The fact that the square was never given the look of a square is regarded as a typically Dutch flop. For the story goes that the Dutch are incapable of designing squares. In an interview the Director of the Rijksmuseum once described how this sort of thing happens in his country: a square such as Place des Vosges or Place de la Concorde, he believes, could never come about because the Dutch lack the tradition of grand royal gestures. Instead, in Holland someone would set up a pump handle somewhere, another person would dig a hole beside it, and a third would put up a bench. And then we say: "Hey, that looks like nothing. Shouldn't we pretty that up a little bit?"

To everyone's relief, the Museum Square was not only prettied up but completely rebuilt. Additional impetus also came from the projected renovations of the museums. The city museum wanted a new wing planned by the Portuguese architect Alvaro Siza. The Japanese architect Kisho Kurokawa designed a red annexe for the Van Gogh Museum that has since been completed. And the Rijksmuseum refurbished one of its wings according to designs by the Dutch architect Wim Quist. Still before construction began, it was announced in 1992 that the Swedish-Danish landscape architect Sven-Ingvar Andersson was to be given the commission to plan the Museum Square. Some voices could be heard complaining that it was unfair that no design from The Netherlands had been chosen. But considering the bad reputation of the Dutch when it comes to designing squares, no one really dared to call this a catastrophe. What they found much more catastrophic was that instead of an urban

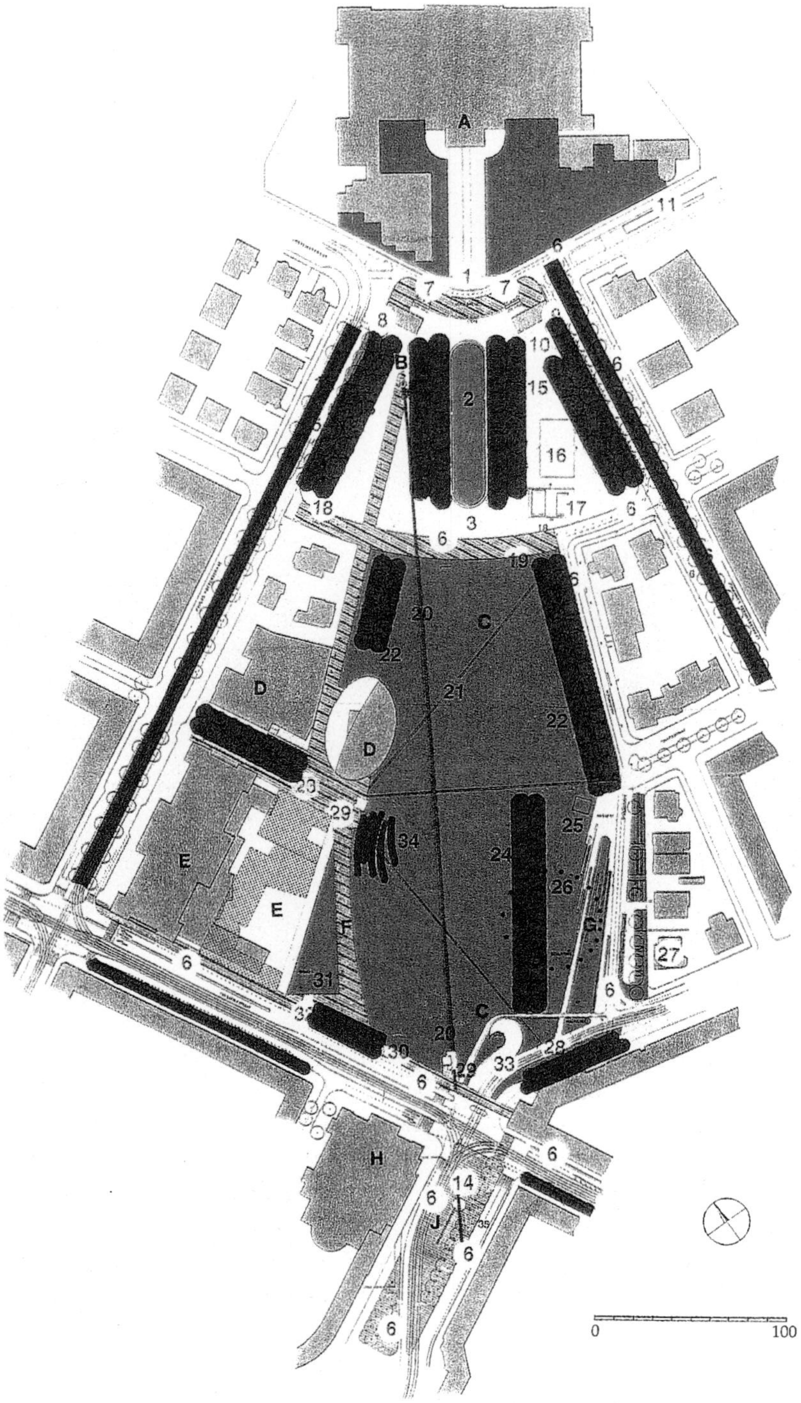

1 terrace paved with brick
2 pool plus skating rink
3 gravel-paved square with plane trees
4 quiet recreation area
5 sports and games area
6 bicycle path
7 light masts
8 pavilion with entrance to underground car park
9 pavilion with café, kiosk, toilets
10 open air café
11 exit ramp of the underground bus park
12 entrance ramp of the underground bus park
13 area for small kiosks
14 fountain
15 "petanque" court
16 basketball court
17 half-pipes for skateboarders
18 stone border framing museum grove
19 pathway paved with brick
20 the line of light
21 narrow path
22 linden avenue
23 chestnut avenue
24 linden 'cathedral'
25 Ravensbrück monument
26 the circle of lights
27 American Consulate
28 tram stop
29 pedestrian entrance and exit to underground car park
30 broad sidewalk
31 grass-covered sloping platform
32 car park entrance
33 car park exit
34 Japanese cherry trees

A Rijksmuseum
B Museum grove
C Great lawn
D Van Gogh Museum with annexe
E Stedelijk Museum with annexe
F Museum path
G Flower garden
H Concert Hall
J Concert Hall Square

irgendwo hin, ein anderer grabe ein Loch daneben, und ein Dritter stelle eine Bank dazu. »Und dann sagen wir: Das sieht ja nach gar nichts aus. Sollen wir das nicht ein bisschen herrichten?«

Zu jedermanns Erleichterung wurde der Museumsplatz nicht nur hergerichtet, sondern komplett umgekrempelt. Anlass dafür waren auch die angekündigten Umbauten der Museen. Das Städtische Museum wünschte einen neuen Trakt nach den Plänen des portugiesischen Architekten Alvaro Siza. Der Japaner Kisho Kurokawa entwarf einen roten Anbau für das

In seinem Entwurf sieht Andersson zwei Bereiche vor: einen symmetrischen Kiesplatz mit Wasserbecken und Baumdach vor dem Reichsmuseum, und eine große Rasenfläche, die sich zwischen Van-Gogh-Museum, Städtischem Museum und dem Konzertgebäude erstreckt. Ein Pflasterweg verbindet die Häuser miteinander. Durch den Rasen verläuft eine Lichtlinie.

In his design Andersson creates two areas: a symmetrical square covered with gravel with a pool and a roof of trees in front of the Rijksmuseum, and a large lawn that extends between the Van Gogh Museum, the municipal museum and the concert hall. A paved pathway links the buildings. A line of light runs across the lawn.

Van-Gogh-Museum, der inzwischen fertig ist. Und das Reichsmuseum baute nach dem Entwurf des Niederländers Wim Quist einen seiner Flügel um. Noch vor dem Bau wurde 1992 bekannt, dass der schwedisch-dänische Landschaftsarchitekt Sven-Ingvar Andersson mit der Planung des Museumsplatzes beauftragt werden sollte. Es gab Stimmen, die fanden es ungerecht, dass kein niederländischer Entwurf den Zuschlag bekommen habe. Doch angesichts des schlechten Rufs der Niederländer, was das Plätzegestalten angeht, wagte niemand wirklich von einer Katastrophe zu sprechen. Für viel gravierender hielten es viele, dass statt eines Stadtplaners nun ein Landschaftsarchitekt zum Zuge kam. Die Leute fürchteten, dass die Chance auf einen harten, städtischen Platz von Format nun endgültig vergeben war. Und sie haben Recht behalten.

Hinter dem Reichsmuseum gelangt man über einen symmetrisch angelegten Platz auf eine Kiesfläche, deren Zentrum ein ovales Wasserbecken bildet. Zu beiden Seiten stehen Pavillons aus Stahl und Glas, ein Kiosk und ein Café-Restaurant. Dieser Teil des Museumsplatzes besitzt eher französisches Flair. Der Kies knirscht unter den Füßen, und die Besucher können sich im Schatten der Platanen auf violetten und rosa Bänken aus perforiertem Stahlblech niederlassen. Bei schönem Wetter planschen die Kinder im Bassin. Dieser Teil des Platzes wird durch einen breiten, steinernen Weg für Fußgänger und Radfahrer von der Rasenfläche getrennt. Rasen bedeckt

planner it was a landscape architect that was being given the opportunity. People feared that the chance to acquire a hard, urban square with a certain status was now lost forever. And they were right. Behind the Rijksmuseum, after crossing a symmetrically arranged square, you come to an area covered with gravel, its centrepiece an oval pool. On either side are glass-and-steel pavilions, a kiosk and a café plus restaurant. This part of Museum Square has a rather French flair. The gravel crunches beneath your feet and you can sit down in the shade of the plane trees on purple and pink benches of perforated steel plate. In warm weather, children splash in the pool. A wide, stone pathway for pedestrians and cyclists separates this part of the square from the lawns. For grass is what covers the rest of the square. A few geometrical elements run through it, such as a long straight line of light, two circles of light, and two narrow footpaths running diagonally. The major focus of attention is the so-called

Einige geometrische Elemente fügen sich in die ausgedehnte Rasenfläche des Museumsplatzes: die Lichtlinie, zwei Lichtkreise, und im Hintergrund das »Eselsohr«, ein schräg gestelltes, rasenbedecktes Dreieck. Das Städtische Museum dahinter soll einen Anbau des Architekten Alvaro Siza erhalten. Bereits fertig ist die Erweiterung des Van-Gogh-Museums des Japaners Kisho Kurokawa.

A few geometrical elements blend in with the broad expanse of the lawn: a line of light, two circles of light, and the "donkey's ear" in the background, a sloping, grass-covered triangle. The municipal museum behind it is to acquire an annexe designed by Alvaro Siza. The annexe of the Van Gogh Museum by Kisho Kurokawa has already been completed.

"donkey's ear" on the south side over the entrance to a supermarket and an underground car park. This is a sloping plane shaped like a triangle, rising up into the air and serving as an open-air platform. There is no question that this attraction could have been at least three times its size. Its details too could have been a size larger and more robust, for their subtlety gets lost where the adjacent lawn makes its grand gesture. A rose garden ducks anonymously down by one side of the lawn. Just as anonymously, a quasi-boulevard runs from the city museum to the Van Gogh Museum, its proportions and design not worth mentioning, in the true sense of the word. Perhaps the garden and the boulevard looked like more on the drawing board but in reality they are overcome by the overwhelming lawn and bite the dust as frayed edges of the square. Clever details only make sense when they can also be maintained with the greatest possible care. But maintenance causes problems for all big cities, as it

nämlich den Rest des Platzes, durchzogen von ein paar geometrischen Elementen wie einer langen, geraden Lichtlinie, zwei Lichtkreisen und zwei diagonal verlaufenden, schmalen Fußwegen. Der wichtigste Blickfang ist das so genannte »Eselsohr« an der Südseite, über dem Eingang eines Supermarkts und einer Tiefgarage. Es handelt sich um eine schräge Ebene, die als Dreieck in die Luft ragt und als Freilufttribüne dient. Ohne Zweifel hätte diese Attraktion mindestens dreimal so groß ausfallen dürfen. Und auch ihren Details wäre eine Nummer größer und robuster gut angestanden, denn das Subtile geht unter, wo die Rasenfläche nebenan die große Geste vollführt. Nichtssagend duckt sich ein Rosengarten an der einen Flanke des Rasens, und ebenso unbedeutend verläuft ein Quasi-Boulevard vom Städtischen Museum zum Van-Gogh-Museum, in Proportion und Gestaltung im wahrsten Sinne des Wortes nicht der Rede wert. Auf dem Zeichentisch mögen Garten und Boulevard vielleicht noch nach etwas ausgesehen haben, doch gebaut erliegen sie der Übermacht des Rasens und geben klein bei als ausgefranste Ränder des Platzes. Zudem: Raffinierte Details machen nur dann Sinn, wenn sie auch mit größtmöglicher Sorgfalt unterhalten werden können. Doch die Pflege bereitet allen großen Städten Probleme, so auch in Amsterdam. Die Stadt ist aufgeteilt in Bezirke mit eigenen Regierungen. Die zentrale Stadtverwaltung greift nur bei grenzüberschreitenden Belangen ein, oder wenn ein Bezirk Hilfe braucht. Der Museumsplatz ist

Das »Eselsohr« dient bei schönem Wetter als Freilufttribüne, von der aus sich das städtische Leben beobachten lässt. Unter der schrägen Ebene liegen die Eingänge zu einem Supermarkt und zur Tiefgarage unter dem Museumsplatz. Die Autos und Busse der vielen Touristen parken nun nicht mehr auf, sondern unter dem Platz.

In fine weather the "donkey's ear" serves as a grandstand without a roof, from which to contemplate urban life. Under its sloping surface are the entrances to a supermarket and the underground car park under Museum Square. The many tourist cars and buses now no longer park on but under the square.

zwar von nationaler Bedeutung, liegt aber mitten in einem Bezirk, Oud Zuid, ohne irgendwelche Grenzen auch nur zu berühren. Befremdlich, dass ein kleiner Bezirk die Planung eines so wichtigen Platzes übernahm. Wenn es aber um den Unterhalt geht, lässt sich kaum erklären, warum der Bezirk allein dafür aufkommen sollte. Schon die Pflege des Rasens bedeutet viel Aufwand, Schäden werden folglich nicht schnell repariert und verleihen dem Ort ein bedauernswertes Aussehen.

Doch selbst wenn die Pflege noch eine offene Frage ist und die ansprechenden Details zu verwahrlosen drohen, gilt der Platz insgesamt als Erfolg. So wie er jetzt ist, zieht er Massen von Besuchern an – zu Zeiten der Miniatur-Autobahn hingegen blieben die Menschen weg. Unablässig strömen die Touristen an, doch ihre Busse und Autos verschwinden nun in der Tiefgarage, und der Platz bleibt vollkommen autofrei. Touristen wie Einheimische lagern gern auf dem Rasen, mit oder ohne Proviant aus dem Supermarkt im Souterrain.

Das Wasserbecken und die schräge Ebene sind zweifelsohne die Highlights des Platzes. Von der Tribüne aus lässt sich vortrefflich das vorbeiziehende Leben betrachten, am besten im Liegen. Das Bassin bietet Erfrischung an heißen Tagen und Eisvergnügen bei Frost. Für Demos taugt der grüne Platz nun weniger, für alle möglichen anderen Kulturevents aber durchaus – sofern es nicht zu stark regnet. Sven-Ingvar Andersson hat erkannt, dass es vor allem den weiten Blick über die Ebene zu bewahren galt. Amsterdams Museumsviertel hat er so keinen Platz geschenkt, sondern einen Garten.

does in Amsterdam. Amsterdam is divided up into districts with their own governments. The central municipal administration only intervenes in issues that concern more than one jurisdiction or if one district needs assistance. While the museum square is of national importance, it lies in the middle of one district, Oud Zuid, nowhere near any other boundaries. Surely it seems odd that such a small district is responsible for the planning of such an important square. As for maintenance, it is almost impossible to understand why that district has to cope single-handedly. The maintenance of the lawns alone is very expensive. Hence damages are not repaired quickly, making the square a lamentable sight. But even if maintenance is still an open question and the attractive details are threatening to become dilapidated, the square as a whole is considered a success. With its present look it draws crowds of visitors. Tourists pour in ceaselessly, but their buses and cars now disappear into the underground car park and the square is completely free of motor vehicles. Both tourists and locals enjoy lying on the lawn with or without food from the supermarket. The pool and the graded platform are doubtless the highlights of the square. The platform is an excellent place from which to watch the passing scene, preferably while lying down. The pool provides cooling water on hot days and fun on the ice when it freezes. The square is not that well suited for demonstrations nowadays but all the more for all kinds of other cultural events – as long as it is not raining too hard. Sven-Ingvar Andersson realised that the main objective should be to retain the broad view across the flat expanse. He gave the museum district not a square but a garden.

Eher französisches Flair besitzt der nördliche Teil des Museumsplatzes vor dem Reichsmuseum. Ein langgestrecktes Wasserbecken teilt die Kiesfläche in zwei Hälften. Bänke aus perforiertem Stahlblech laden zur Rast unter dem Platanendach. Zwei Stahl-Glas-Pavillons beherbergen einen Kiosk und ein Café-Restaurant.

The northern section of Museum Square in front of the Rijksmuseum has a rather French atmosphere. A long pool divides its gravel-paved surface into two parts. Benches of perforated steel plate invite passers-by to rest under the plane trees. Two steel and glass pavilions house a kiosk and a café.

Die Gärten von West 8

The gardens of West 8

Jan de Graaf

Ungewöhnliche Materialien, größtmögliche Nüchternheit und ein Hang zur Übertreibung – drei Gartenentwürfe aus den Niederlanden.

Unusual materials, the greatest possible degree of sobriety and a tendency to exaggerate – three designs for gardens in the Netherlands.

A garden is useless. Or it is about as useful as music or poetry. Three recent designs by the Dutch landscape architecture office West 8 bear out the realization that gardens are far too valuable to be left to fulfil romantic needs or, as has recently been the case, abandoned to the terror of Mediterranean design. What counts today is, according to Adriaan Geuze, the search for ways to minimalize designs. How? The garden of the V.S.B.-Bank in Utrecht, the garden for the Centre of Fine Arts in Dordrecht and the garden at Schiphol, Amsterdam's international airport provide three answers.

The West 8 office is eagerly seeking usable materials and textures. "Local" materials steeped in history top the list of what they would like. When nothing suitable can be found, the office designs something itself. The landscape architects are obsessed with inventing forms, building models and trial pieces. Demolition materials, such as parts of a ship's hull in the Dordrecht garden – Dordrecht was once a proper river port with a tradition of ship-building (today of ship decay) – provide an unexpected source. For Schiphol's enclosed garden the designers discovered broken pieces of clay, material which cost nothing and had an archaeological feeling. As a final step, what has been chosen is arranged in a way which is contrary to every design convention and has a tendency to exaggerate – this is demonstrated by the thirteen-kilometre long box hedge –, the result being effortless beauty which is undeniable, indeed almost timeless. Illusion of any kind has been avoided. Areas and spaces do not appear to be other than what they are. It is for this reason that the special attention which is paid to the edges and boundaries is characterized by the greatest possible degree of sobriety,

Ein Garten ist zu nichts nutze. Oder er nutzt gerade so viel wie Musik oder Poesie. Drei neuere Entwürfe des niederländischen Landschaftsarchitekturbüros West 8 zeugen von der Einsicht, daß Gärten viel zu wertvoll sind, um sie nur den romantischen Bedürfnissen zu überlassen, oder, wie in jüngerer Zeit, dem Terror des mediterran angehauchten Designs. Heute, so Adriaan Geuze, geht es eher um die Suche nach Möglichkeiten, Entwürfe zu minimalisieren. Wie, das zeigen die Gärten der V.S.B.-Bank in Utrecht, der Garten des Zentrums für Bildende Kunst in Dordrecht und den Gartenhof von Schiphol, dem internationalen Flughafen in Amsterdam.

Das Büro West 8 sucht stets nach brauchbaren Materialien und Texturen. »Lokale«, von der Geschichte durchtränkte Materialien stehen ganz oben auf der Wunschliste. Wo sich nichts Geeignetes anbietet, entwirft das Büro selbst etwas. Als besessene Erfinder basteln die Mitarbeiter Formen, bauen Modelle und Probestücke. Abrißmaterial, wie etwa Teile eines Schiffsrumpfs im Dordrechter Garten bieten eine überraschende Grundlage – Dordrecht war eine echte Flußstadt mit einer Schiffsbau-Tradition und unterhält heute eine Schiffsverschrottungs-Industrie. Für den innenliegenden Garten von Schiphol entdeckten die Entwerfer Tonscherben, kostenloses Material mit einer archäologischen Ausstrahlung. Schließlich ordnet man das Auserkorene entgegen aller Entwurfskonvention mit einem großen Hang zur Übertreibung – das zeigt die 13 Kilometer lange Buxushecke – wodurch wie von selbst eine unausweichliche, fast zeitlose Schönheit entsteht. Jede Illusion wird vermieden. Flächen und Räume erscheinen nicht weiter, als sie sind. Mit größtmöglicher Nüchternheit und ebensolcher Sensibilität wird darum den Rändern und Begrenzungen besondere Sorgfalt gewidmet: Der Garten als eingefriedeter, abgeschirmter Ort.

Gartenentwürfe sind innerhalb des Büros ein ziemlich separates Arbeitsfeld, das durch die Herangehensweise, die den Prozeß an den Anfang eines Entwurfs setzt, besonders viel Zeit kostet. So ist der Garten um die V.S.B.-Bank in Utrecht in drei aufeinanderfolgenden Stadien entstanden. Das Gebäude ist eine glatte, unnahbare, aufgeständerte Scheibe, 85 Meter hoch, von der aus gut tausend Mitarbeiter kapitale Geldströme um den Erdball schicken. Erst ruhte die Scheibe auf einem Sockel einer doppelstöckigen Tiefgarage, dazwischen waren die kollektiven Funktionen

Anthrazitfarbene Platten mit dem fossilen Abdruck von Birkenzweigen wurden auf dem Parkdeck der V.S.B.-Bank verlegt. Die Wiese um das Gebäude, üppig mit filigranen Birken bepflanzt, bildet den Gegenpart.

Dark grey tiles with fossilized imprints of birch branches cover the parking deck of the V.S.B. Bank. The meadow around the building, generously planted with filigree birches, forms its counterpart.

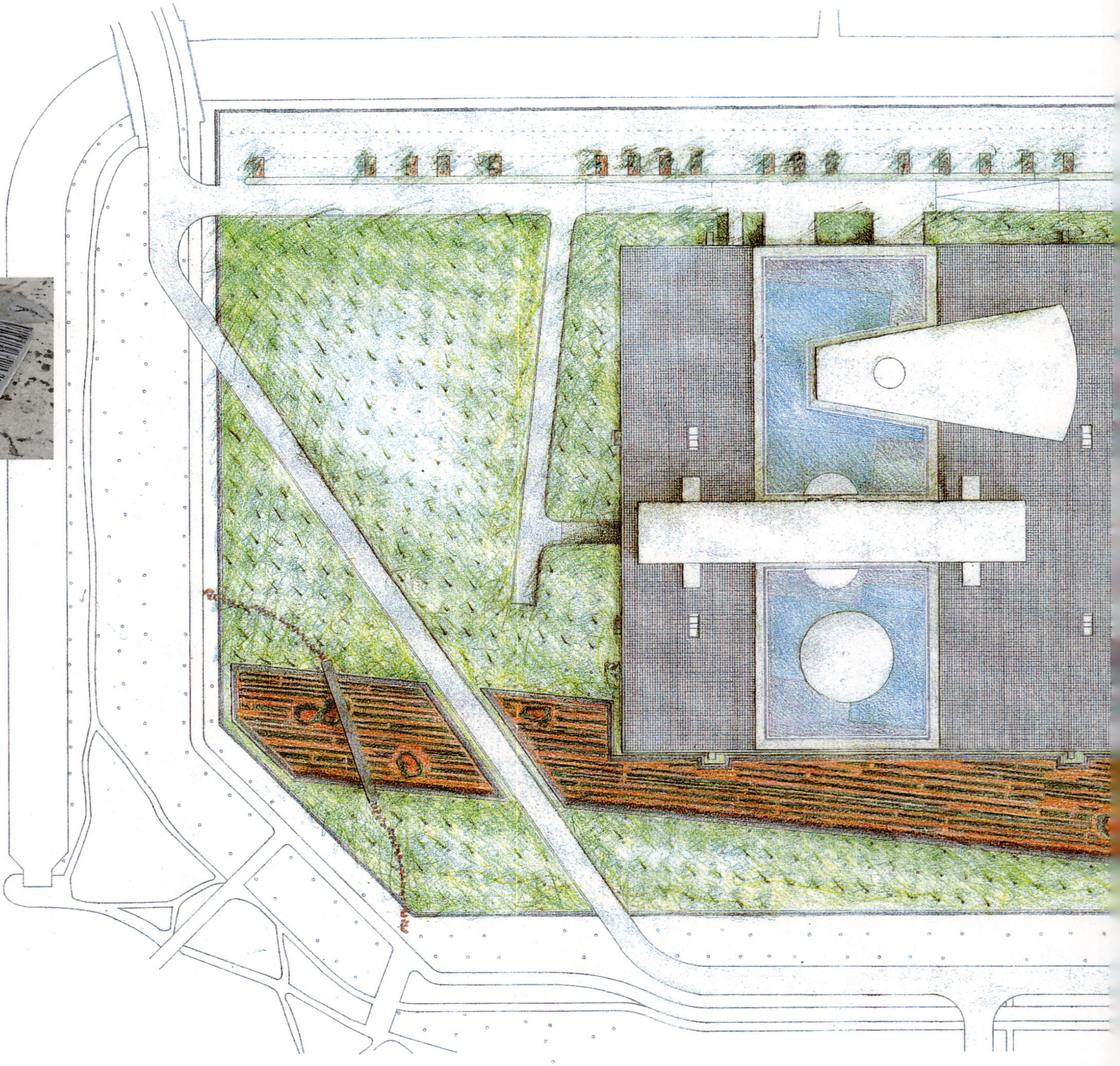

V.S.B.-Bank, Utrecht
Client: AMEV levensverzekering N.V.
Architects: VMV
Landscape architects: Adriaan Geuze, Han Beumer (West 8)
Assistants: Erik Overdiep, Erwin Bot, Dirry de Bruin, Chidi Onwuka, Joost de Natris, Cyrus Clark, Peter Cue
Project management: Aronsohn raadgevende ingenieurs b.v.
Site: 25 000 square metres
Planning: 1993–1994
Construction: January–May 1995
Costs: 2 100 000 Hfl

Das Gebäude der V.S.B.-Bank in Utrecht besteht aus einem quadratischen Flachbau, einem Bürohochhaus und einem Garten. Mit seinem reliefierten Plattenbelag wurde das Dach des Flachbaus zum Parkdeck. Im Garten senkten die Planer einen Teilbereich ab und führten eine Brücke darüber hinweg. Zwischen die Reihen der Buchshecken stellten sie riesige Steinblöcke.

The V.S.B. Bank building in Utrecht consists of a rectangular low structure, an office high-rise, and a garden. With its relief tile surface, the roof of the low structure became the parking deck. In the garden the planners sank one section and laid a bridge across it. Between the rows of box hedges they erected huge stone blocks.

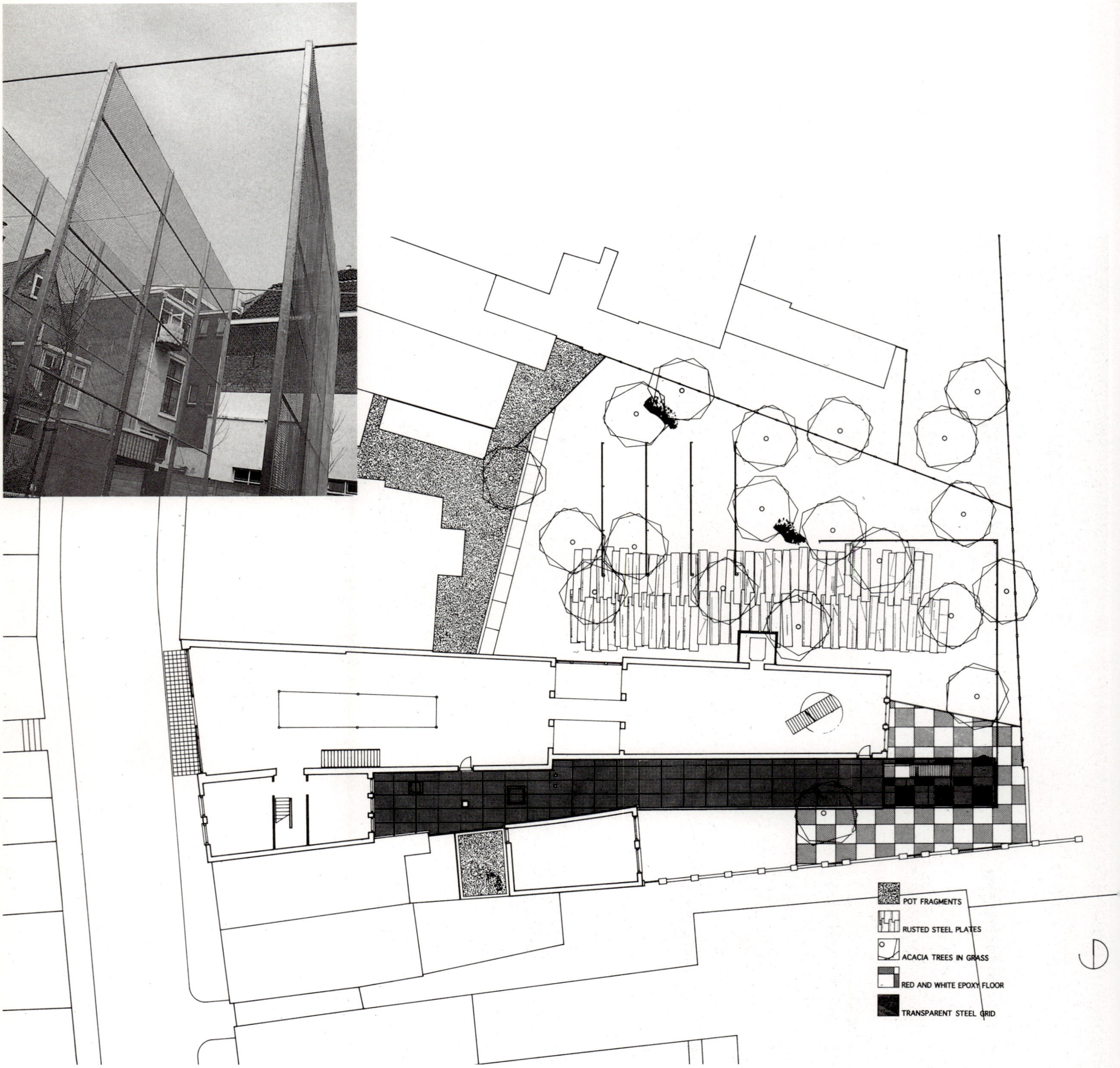

Centrum Beeldende Kunst, Dordrecht
Client: Centrum Beeldende Kunst, Dordrecht
Design: Adriaan Geuze, Han Beumer (West 8), landscape architects
Assistants: Cyrus Clark, Maartje Lammers, Peter Cue
Site: 1200 square metres
Planning: 1993
Construction: 1994–1995
Costs: 200 000 Hfl

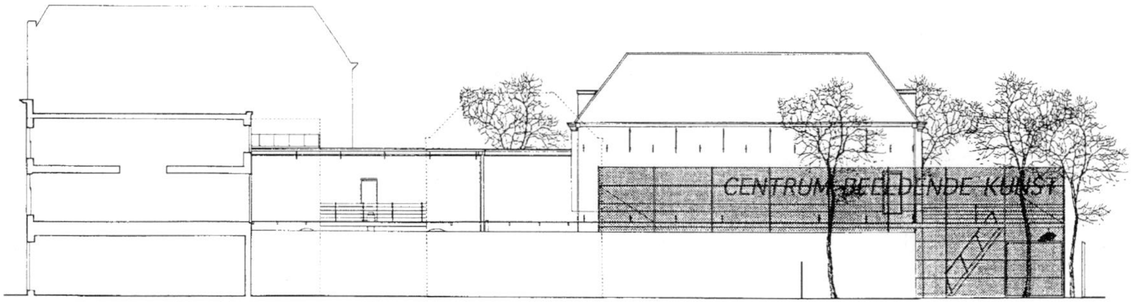

Die Räume des Zentrums für Bildende Kunst in Dordrecht liegen auf unterschiedlichen Niveaus, denn das Zentrum besteht aus mehreren Gebäuden. Der Rundweg, den die Planer von West 8 im Außenbereich anlegten, verbindet diese nun miteinander. Zwischen den Bauten entstand ein enger Patio, in der Höhe wurde eine luftige Dachterrasse angelegt, den Garten zieren Akazien. Eine Stahlträgerkonstruktion ist mit feinmaschigem Drahtgeflecht bespannt – diese transparenten Wände umfassen und ordnen den Raum.

The rooms in the Dordrecht Visual Arts Centre are at different levels because it consists of several buildings. A path added by the West 8 planners now connects them. A narrow patio lies in between, an airy roof terrace is above, acacias decorate the garden. Transparent walls of fine wire mesh on a steel frame enclose and organize the space.

Auf dem Flughafen von Schiphol bei Amsterdam galt es, für den unwirtlichen Innenhof eines provisorischen Bürokomplexes möglichst schnell und kostengünstig eine temporäre Gestaltung zu finden. Die Landschaftsarchitekten setzten zwanzig Birken in den Hof, bepflanzten die Bodenfläche und kombinierten Beläge aus dunklem Kies und aus roten Tonscherben.

At the Schiphol airport in Amsterdam an instant and inexpensive temporary design was needed for the inhospitable inner court of a provisional office building. The landscape architects planted 20 birches in the court and covered the ground with plants and pavements of dark gravel combined with red clay shards.

Courtyard at the Schiphol Airport, Amsterdam
Client: NV Luchthaven Schiphol
Landscape architects: West 8
Design and realization: Adriaan Geuze, Paul van Beek
Site: 12 × 57 metres
Planning: 1993
Construction: 1993
Costs: 25 000 Hfl

verteilt: Restaurant und Auditorium. West 8 entschied sich zunächst für eine Wiese, vollgepflanzt mit federnden, hellen Birken, die einen Kontrast zu den anthrazitfarbenen Platten mit ihrem fossilen Abdruck von Birkenzweigen bilden sollten, mit denen man das Dach der Tiefgarage belegen wollte. Vom Hochbau aus hatte man Sicht auf die wiegenden Kronen und das unbewegliche Dach. Aus dem Flachbau blickte man unter den Kronen hindurch. Doch eine zweigeschossige Garage erwies sich als zu tief und zu teuer. Aufgrund von Sparmaßnahmen sollte nun auf dem Sockel geparkt werden, statt darin. Ein neuer Entwurf folgte, danach ein dritter. Der realisierte Entwurf schließt an den Ökogarten des Nachbargrundstücks an, verstärkt die Höhenunterschiede mit angekarrtem Aushub aus nahegelegenen Baugruben, gräbt einen vertieften Garten in den eigentlichen Garten, legt eine Brücke darüber, die sich unter anderem auf einen der fünf riesigen Felsblöcke stützt, die im Garten verstreut ihren Platz gefunden haben. Auf dem Flachbau prangt ein großzügiger, übrigens unzugänglicher, aber dennoch verheißungsvoller Dachgarten.

Der Garten des Zentrums für Bildende Kunst in Dordrecht (eine aufsteigende Kulturstadt) ist ein Extrembeispiel für energiefressendes Entwerfen bei einem mehr als magerem Budget. Die vorhandenen städtischen Qualitäten wurden gewissenhaft aufgespürt und zunutze gemacht. Auffällig ist, daß auch hier die Höhenunterschiede Teil des Entwurfs sind. Verschiedene Räume wurden über einen Rundweg miteinander verbunden. Ein enger Patio, eine sonnige Dachterrasse, ein Garten mit Akazien, ein Fahrradschuppen angrenzend an einen alten Fußweg, der das Zentrum von der Musikschule trennt, die fröhliche Klänge über den Garten schickt. Jetzt, wo der sogenannte städtische Raum mehr und mehr vom Gestank und Lärm des Straßenverkehrs betäubt wird, ist es vielleicht dieser Garten, der als neuer kultureller Erholungsort dienen kann.

Die Rahmenbedingungen des Gartens in Schiphol haben den Entwurf drastisch beeinflußt. Eine Anlage von provisorischen Bürobaracken, die auf einer Asphaltdecke abgestellt waren, umschloß einen Raum von etwa acht mal 40 Metern. Von dem dort arbeitenden, im Sommer schwitzenden Personal kam die Bitte, »etwas« zu tun: low-budget, provisorisch auf zwei Jahre hin. Zudem war der Hof für Bagger unzugänglich und nur per Kran zu erreichen. Die Lösung: zwanzig Löcher in den Asphalt, ebenso viele Birken hinein, rote Tonscherben und an den äußeren Rand dunklen Kies. Ausgeführt an einem Wochenende.

matched by a similar degree of sensitivity: the garden as an enclosed, secluded place.

The office treats garden design as a more or less separate area of work which is made particularly time-consuming by the fact that designing is approached as a process. For example, the garden in Utrecht which surrounds the head office of a bank came into being in three consecutive stages. The building is a plain, unapproachable, tall block, 85 metres high, from inside which a staff of over a thousand steer global flows of money. Initially, this block was to rest on a base which was to be part of a two-level underground garage and accommodate the communal areas such as a restaurant and lecture hall. West 8 initially decided on an area of grass covered with waving silver-birch trees; these were to provide a contrast to the charcoal-coloured slabs with their fossilized imprints of the branches of birch which were to cover the roof of the underground garage. The high-rise building afforded a view of the swaying treetops and the rigid roof. The low building afforded a view through the crowns of the trees. However, it was decided that a two-level garage would be too deep and too expensive. As a result of cost-cutting measures, parking was to be on top of the base instead of inside. A second design followed and then a third. The design which was chosen and realized reflects the theme of the adjacent ecogarden, emphasizes the differences in height by adding excavated earth from nearby building sites, incorporates a sunken garden in the garden proper, spans a bridge across it, a bridge which has as one of its supports an enormous rocks. The resplendent and generous roof garden on the flat building is, although inaccessible, nevertheless, full of promise.

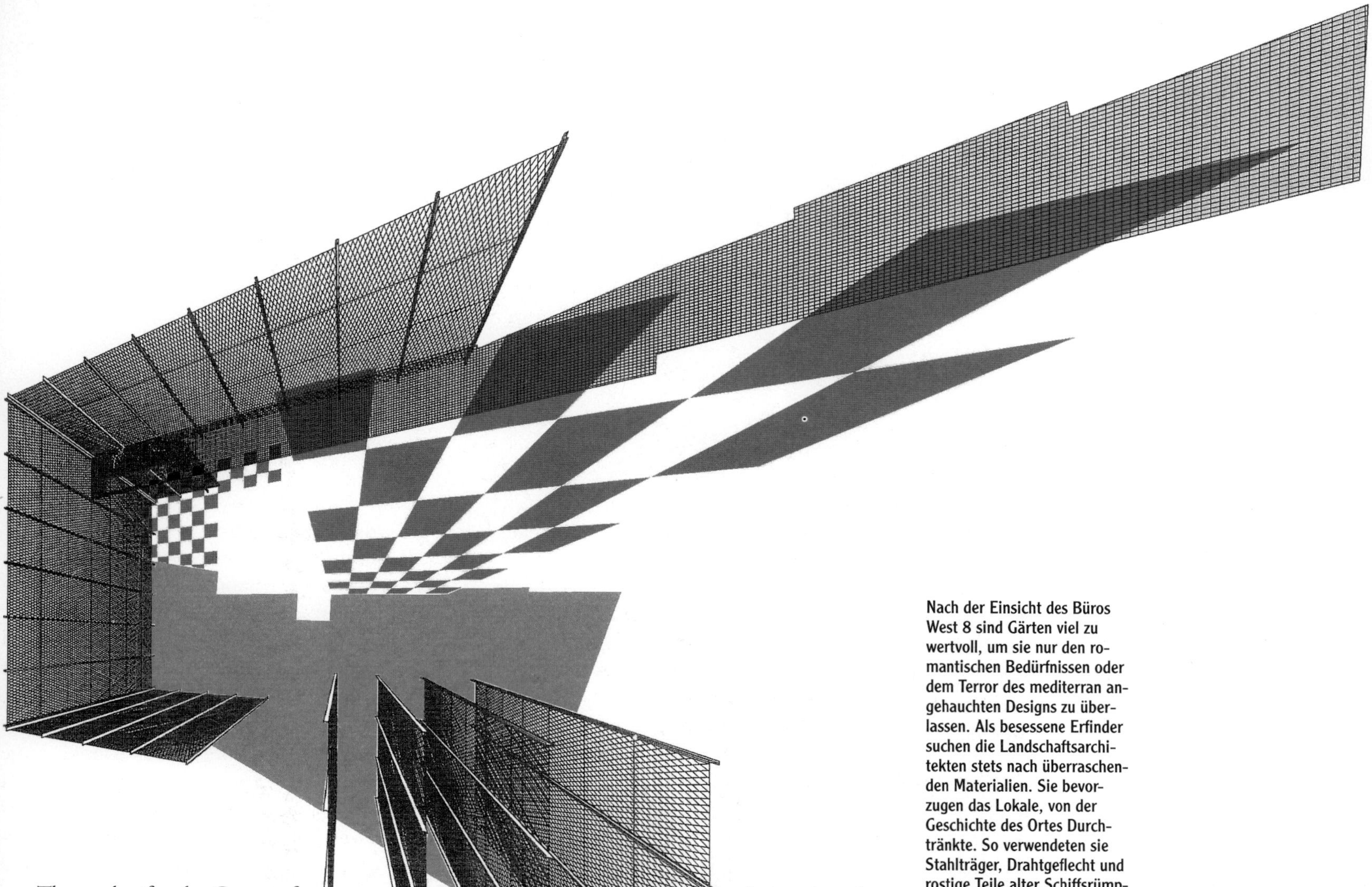

Nach der Einsicht des Büros West 8 sind Gärten viel zu wertvoll, um sie nur den romantischen Bedürfnissen oder dem Terror des mediterran angehauchten Designs zu überlassen. Als besessene Erfinder suchen die Landschaftsarchitekten stets nach überraschenden Materialien. Sie bevorzugen das Lokale, von der Geschichte des Ortes Durchtränkte. So verwendeten sie Stahlträger, Drahtgeflecht und rostige Teile alter Schiffsrümpfe im Freiraum des Kunstzentrums von Dordrecht, einer Stadt mit Schiffsbautradition.

According to the West 8 planners, gardens are much too precious to be relegated to romantic fantasies or the horror of Mediterranean-inspired designs. Obsessed inventors, they are constantly seeking unexpected materials. They prefer local elements, permeated with the history of a place. Hence they use steel supports, wire mesh, and rusty parts of old ships in the free space of the art centre of Dordrecht, a city with a ship-building tradition.

The garden for the Centre of Fine Arts in Dordrecht, which is emerging as a cultural centre, is an extreme example of time-consuming designing on a very low budget. The existing urban qualities were tracked down conscientiously and made use of. What is striking is that differences in height are also part of this design. Different levels were linked with each other by means of a circular path. A narrow patio, a sunny roof terrace, a garden with acacias, a bicycle shed adjacent to an old footpath which separates the Centre from the music school, which, for its part, fills the garden with happy sounds. Now that urban space is being increasingly polluted by the stink and noise of road traffic, it is perhaps this kind of (public) garden which can serve as a new cultural place of recreation.

The conditions which already existed at Schiphol had a major influence of the design of the garden there. A collection of makeshift office buildings which had been put up on an asphalt surface enclosed an area which was approximately eight metres wide and forty metres long. The employees who worked there in conditions which were sweltering in the summer made a request for "something" to be done: low budget, "provisionally", just for a couple of years. In addition, the site was not accessible to bulldozers and cranes would have had to be used.

The solution was this: dig twenty holes in the asphalt, plant a birch tree in each hole, pieces of red clay and a perimeter of dark gravel. A weekend's work.

Der Kromhout-Park in Tilburg, Niederlande

Kromhout Park in Tilburg, Netherlands

Bart Brands

Im Sommer 1991 erhielt unser Büro von der Gemeinde Tilburg den Auftrag für ein Ideenkonzept zur Gestaltung einer neuen öffentlichen Parkanlage im Zentrum der Stadt. Das Gebiet der ehemaligen Kromhout-Kaserne sollte umgenutzt werden. Gefragt war ein moderner Stadtpark, der nicht nur für die angrenzenden Wohngebiete, sondern darüber hinaus für die gesamte Stadt von Bedeutung sein sollte.

Als Vorgabe wurde einzig der Kostenrahmen von der Gemeinde festgelegt. Die sonst übliche Liste aus behördlichen Forderungen und Wünschen seitens der Bewohner entfiel. Diese Freiheit im Parkprogramm bot uns die Chance, einen modernen Stadtpark zu definieren. Die Bewohner von Tilburg werden nun aufgefordert, den Park auf ihre eigene Weise zu entdecken, denn nicht allein der Park bestimmt die Nutzung, auch die Nutzer bestimmen den Park.

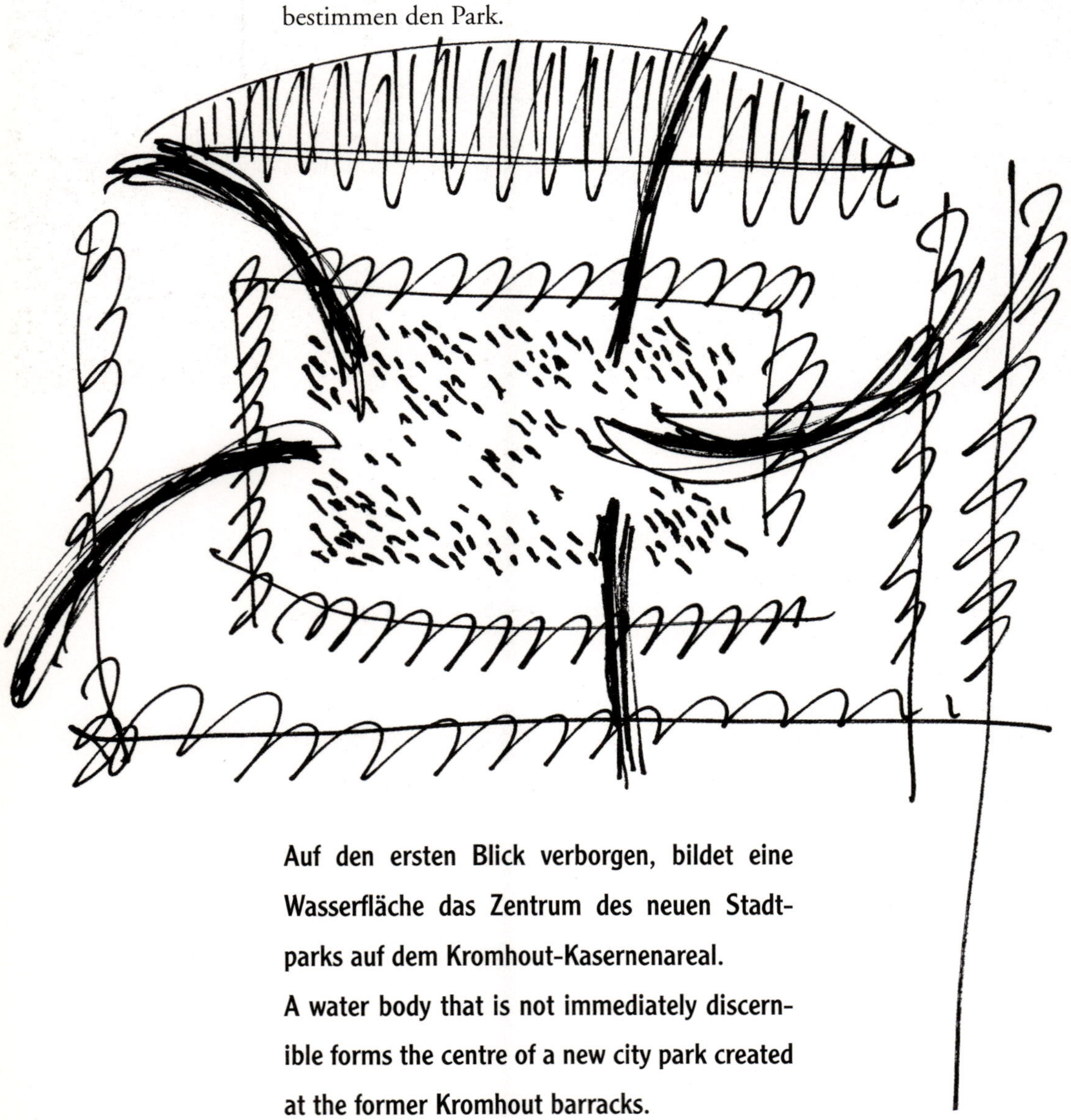

Auf den ersten Blick verborgen, bildet eine Wasserfläche das Zentrum des neuen Stadtparks auf dem Kromhout-Kasernenareal.
A water body that is not immediately discernible forms the centre of a new city park created at the former Kromhout barracks.

In the summer of 1991, our office was commissioned by the municipality of Tilburg, a city in southern Netherlands, to turn the parade grounds of a former barracks near the city centre into a park. What the council had in mind was a modern urban park which would be of meaning not only for the neighbouring residential districts but also for the city as a whole. The only stipulation made concerned the costs, and we were not presented with the usual list of official requirements and wishes on the part of the residents, either. This freedom as far as the park programme was concerned faced us with the opportunity and the necessity to clarify and put into concrete terms our definition of a modern city park.

A significant characteristic of the modern urban park is that it provides opportunities for varied forms of use without specifically designating certain areas or elements to these ends. In the case of Kromhout Park, the residents of Tilburg are thus challenged to discover what the park means to them in their own way. Here the park does not only determine uses; it is also determined by the users.

The site of Kromhout Park is a rectangular piece of property on the southeastern boundary of downtown Tilburg and as already said, was once the parade grounds of a nearby barracks. It is surrounded on three sides by prewar buildings and monumental street trees, and the urban development plan suggests development on the fourth, slightly curved northern side, meaning that our design had to integrate city villas and two other residential buildings accordingly.

A magnificent square of linden and plane trees stands at the centre of the former parade grounds of the Kromhout barracks. This repeti-

tion of a square in a square – with the huge street trees on the outside and the linden and plane trees on the inside – forms the basis of our design.

We increased the scope of the inner square size with a ring of bamboo and rhododendron, thus providing the park with a closed, intimate area both in summer and winter, and established a larger, more open area along the boundaries, oriented towards the residential buildings. This simple measure makes the park easily legible and provides an element of surprise at the same time. We preserved the open character of the area

Mehrere Wege führen auf die Insel im See des Kromhout-Parks. Hier konzentrieren sich Spiel- und Gebrauchseinrichtungen. Jeder Weg besitzt seine eigene Identität, einige bieten Überraschungen für die Mutigen. So klettert man zum Beispiel auf der Wasserlinie hinter einer Betonscheibe eine Schwimmbadleiter hinunter und läuft über Metallroste zur Insel.

Play facilities and park furniture are concentrated along the several paths that lead to the lake and the island in Kromhout Park. Each pathway has an identity of its own and two of them feature surprizes for the brave at heart. In one, for example, visitors can clamber down a swimming-pool-type ladder to the lake and cross over to the island on a zig-zag grid.

Das Plangebiet für den Kromhout-Park ist ein rechteckiges Gelände am Südostrand der Innenstadt – der ehemalige Exerzierplatz der nahegelegenen Kaserne. Das Gebiet ist an drei Seiten mit Vorkriegsbebauung und monumentalen Straßenbäumen umschlossen. Der städtebauliche Plan sah zudem eine Bebauung an der leicht gebogenen Nordseite vor. Die dort projektierten Stadtvillen und zwei weitere Wohngebäude sollten in den Entwurf integriert werden.

Im Zentrum des ehemaligen Exerzierfeldes steht ein prächtiges Karree aus Linden und Platanen. Diese Wiederholung des Rechtecks im Rechteck – die mächtigen Straßenbäume als äußeres und das Baum-Karree als inneres – bilden die Basis des Entwurfs. Das innere Rechteck wird räumlich verstärkt durch einen Ring aus Bambus und Rhododendron. Der Park ver-

Client: City of Tilburg
Design: Bart Brands, Michael van Gessel, Jos Jacobs
Assistants: Francien van Kempen, Rob Lubrecht
Size: 5,7 hectares
Planning: 1991 – 1993
Construction period: 1993 – 1994
Costs: 2,4 million Dutch Guilders

Hoch über dem See kann man die Insel im Kromhout-Park über eine Stahlbrücke erreichen. Ihre filigranen Rahmen wirken wie eine Pergola – ein geschützter Weg.

The island in Kromhout Park can be reached via a steel bridge set high above the water. The filigree, pergola-like structure creates a feeling of intimacy for people crossing the bridge.

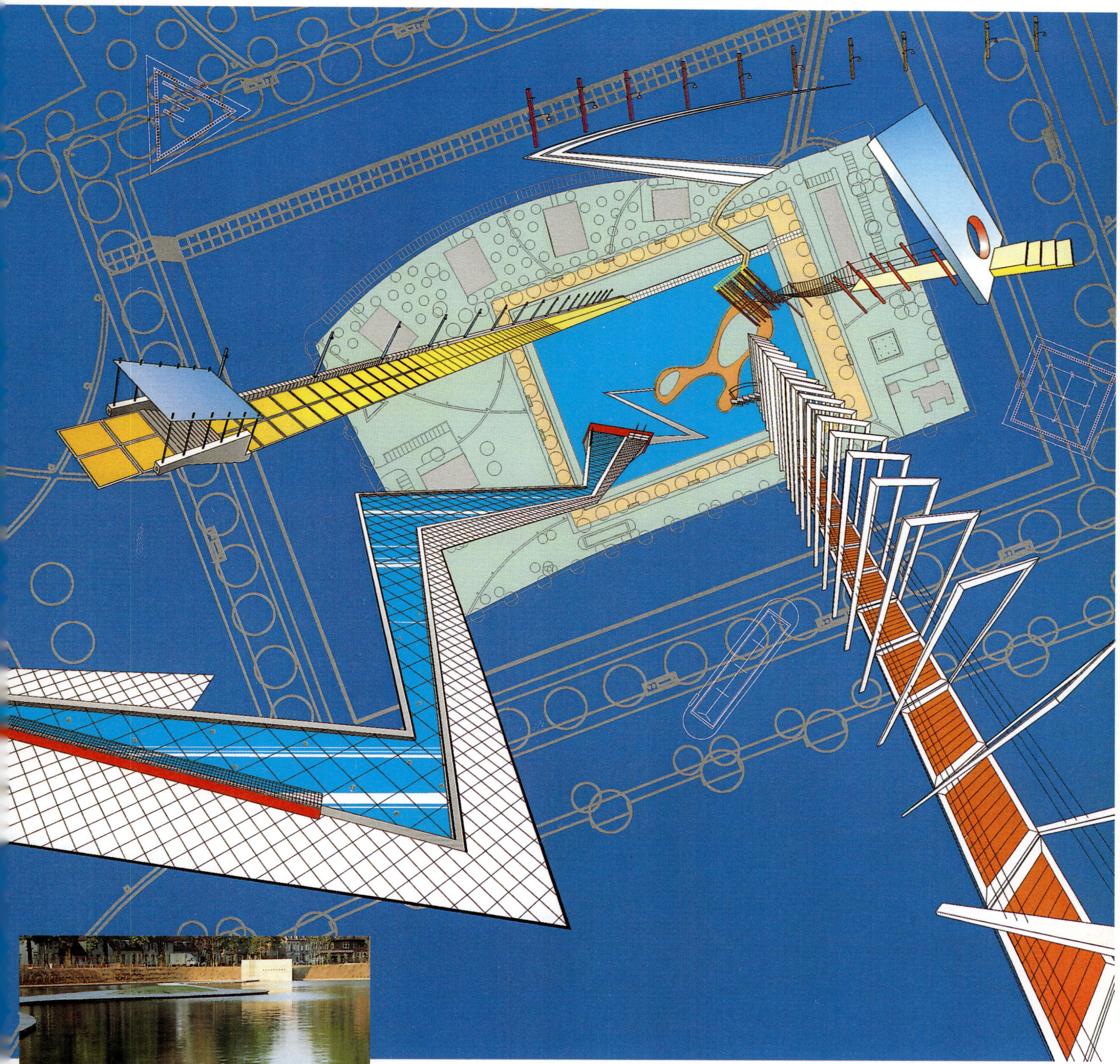

Der Säulenpfad, die Wasserlinie, die Brücke und die Kletterlinie schaffen Verbindungen durch den Kromhout-Park in Tilburg. Sie treffen sich auf der Insel im See. Auf der Kletterlinie gilt es, durch ein enges Loch zu kriechen und eine Hängebrücke zu überwinden (kleines Foto oben). Auf dem Säulenpfad hingegen gelangt man ganz gemütlich durch den Park.

The Column Path, the Water Line, the Bridge and the Climbing Line all converge on the island and lake in Kromhout Park in Tilburg. The Climbing Line, which is intended for children, involves crawling through a small hole and navigating a hanging bridge (small photo above). The Column Path is a more leisurely affair, and features white arrows.

fügt somit im Sommer und im Winter über ein intimes, geschlossenes Zentrum und über einen offenen, den umgebenden Wohngebieten zugewandten Randbereich. Dieser simple Eingriff macht den Park übersichtlich und überraschend zugleich. Das Gebiet rund um das Karree bleibt offen. Eine weite Rasenfläche mit einigen bereits bestehenden Bäumen bietet Raum für Sport und Spiel. In dieser Zone liegen auch die drei kleinen Spielgärten, leicht vertieft angelegt, von einem niedrigen Zaun umgeben und für geschütztes Kleinkinderspiel gedacht. Die Wohnumgebung der Stadtvillen an der Nordseite des Parks ist durch ein Raster aus Kirschbäumen räumlich gefaßt und zum öffentlichen Parkraum hin abgegrenzt.

In der Mitte des Parks erstreckt sich ein großer See. Sein tieferliegendes Wasserbassin ist ein Überraschungselement. Man gelangt nur an vorgegebenen Stellen ans Wasser. Eine Promenade führt entlang der sonnigen Seite des Sees, vier Routen verbinden die höhergelegenen Parkbereiche mit der Insel. Zwei leicht gewölbte Rasenflächen bilden ihre Mitte. Sie sind von einem knapp über der Wasseroberfläche verlaufenden Rand aus Naturstein und Holz umgeben.

Die vier Verbindungsrouten stellen gleichzeitig besondere Gestaltungselemente dar. Die oft in Parks angetroffene weitverstreute Ansammlung von Spiel- und Gebrauchseinrichtungen wird in unserem Entwurf regelrecht zu Linien verdichtet. Jede Linie trägt ihre eigene Identität. Zwei Bahnen sind den etwas mutigeren Parkbesuchern gewidmet: die Wasser- und die Kletterlinie. Die anderen beiden Linien stehen allen Besuchern offen: die Brücke und der leicht abfallende Pfad, die sogenannte Säulenlinie. Sie bilden zusammen eine wichtige Verbindung zwischen Wohngebiet und Stadtzentrum.

Die Wasserlinie führt wie ein Blitzstrahl aus der Südwestecke des Parks zur Insel hinab. Unter den auf Geländehöhe liegenden Stahlrosten führt ein Wasserlauf in Richtung See. Als Überraschung und als Spielelemente sind zusätzlich Fontänen unter den Rosten angebracht. Der auf dem Land verlaufende Abschnitt der Wasserlinie endet in einem Balkon über dem See. Über eine Schwimmbadtreppe gelangt man hinunter, und über knapp über dem Wasser schwebende Gitter weiter zur Insel.

Die Kletterlinie ist als Spielelement insbesondere für ältere Kinder gedacht. Hinter der Uferbepflanzung aus Bambus stellt die blaue Wand den einzigen vom Land aus sichtbaren Teil der Klimmlinie dar. Eine Öffnung in der Mauer bildet den Zugang zur Hängebrücke. In zwei Meter Höhe führt sie über das Wasser zu einem Aussichtsturm auf der Insel.

surrounding the inner square, and it is here that a wide expanse of lawn featuring several established trees provides room for sport and games. It is also here that three small playgrounds, slightly sunken and enclosed by a low fence, are situated, conceived as sheltered areas where small children can play undisturbed.

The residential area formed by the villas to the north is marked by a grid of cherry trees that also delimitates it from the park. Finally, a large lake, a sunken basin which is the main element of surprise, is hidden within the inner square of trees, and can only be accessed at certain defined points. A promenade leads along the sunny side of the lake, with four pathways linking the higher areas of Kromhout Park to the lake and the island set within it. This latter features two slightly raised areas of grass within an enclosure of natural stone and wood that is only slightly higher than the level of the water.

The four paths are not only links but also important design elements. The play facilities and park furniture, which in most parks are usually dispersed, are concentrated in our case along four linear elements, each with its own identity. Two of these elements or links, the Water Line and the Climbing Line, are designed for particularly daring park visitors, while the other two, the Bridge and the Column Line, are intended for everybody. All four connect the residential districts with the city centre.

Water Line. The Water Line runs from the southwest corner of the park to the island like a streak of lightning, with water flowing below steel grids let into the ground. As a surprise and trick element, burladores that shoot fountains up one metre in the air are also located below the grids. The Water Line ends at a balcony-like structure above the lake, with a swimming-pool-type ladder leading down to an angular gridway. This in turn crosses the lake to the island, and has the appearance of hovering above the water.

Climbing Line. The Climbing Line is conceived as a play element for older children. The blue wall is the only visible part that can be seen from the park, and an opening in it provides access to a hanging bridge. This is suspended two metres above the ground and leads to a belvedere tower on the island.

Bridge. A long bridge juts into the lake on the southern side of the park and is connected to the island by means of a narrow flight of steps. Since the trusses on the bridge are only set a metre apart, it was possible to give them a very slender design, and the fact that they are provided with braces at the sides but not at the top creates a feeling of weightlessness and transparency. The light grey of the galvanized steel adds to the general restrained effect, particularly in connection with the grounds as a whole and the lake.

Column Line. In our original design, the slightly sloping path on the northern side of the park was accompanied by rows of columns supporting the busts of current members of the magistracy, which maybe explains why these elements had to be renounced at an early point for cost reasons. The path itself features a pattern of natural stone let into dark concrete, with white arrows pointing the way to the island.

The park was completed in the summer of 1994. We hope it will not only provide plenty of opportunity for future leisure activities but that it also sparks off a lively debate on the meaning of modern-day parks.

An der Südseite des Parks ragt eine langgezogene Brücke in den See. Eine schmale Treppe verbindet sie mit der Insel. Die Träger der Brücke sind im Abstand von einem Meter gesetzt und konnten daher sehr fein gehalten werden. Sie sind an den Seiten, jedoch nicht an der Oberkante miteinander verbunden, was den insgesamt leichten und transparenten Charakter der Brücke verstärkt. Auch das lichte Grau des verzinkten Stahls unterstützt den zurückhaltenden Eindruck dieser Linie in der Gesamtanlage des Parks. In unserem ursprünglichen Entwurf war der leicht abfallende Pfad an der Nordseite des Parks von Säulenreihen von den Büsten gegenwärtiger Mitglieder des Magistrats begleitet. Auf diese Elemente mußte schon frühzeitig aus Kostengründen verzichtet werden. Der Pfad ist über die ganze Länge aus dunklem Beton gefertigt, in den ein Muster aus Naturstein eingedruckt wurde. Weiße Pfeile weisen den Weg zur Insel.

Im Sommer 1994 wurde der Park fertiggestellt. Wir hoffen, daß er Anlaß für rege Diskussionen über die Bedeutung von Stadtparks in der heutigen Zeit geben wird.

Detail aus dem Kromhout-Park, Tilburg: Sitzplatz im oberen Parkniveau.

Detail from Kromhout Park, Tilburg: A masonry bench in the higher area of the park.

Top-Adresse Bahnhofsplatz

Best address in town: Station Square

Martin Knuijt
Christ-Jan van Rooij

Im niederländischen Enschede sind Plätze und Busstation neu gestaltet worden. Sie kurbeln die Entwicklung des gesamten Viertels an.

In Enschede in The Netherlands the squares and bus terminal have been redesigned. They set redevelopment in motion.

Rien ne va plus – in der niederländischen Stadtlandschaft scheinen die Grenzen der Mobilität in Sicht. Der Ausbau des Verkehrsnetzes hält mit dem Anwachsen des Verkehrs kaum mehr Schritt. Nur durch große Anstrengungen kann ein »Verkehrsinfarkt« noch abgewendet werden. Hauptziel: Die Innenstädte müssen zugänglich bleiben, um zu vermeiden, daß einer der lebendigsten Stadtteile zur Ödnis verkommt. Hier helfen die öffentlichen Verkehrsmittel – ihre Linien dienen als Bypässe, um die überquellenden Straßen zu entlasten und den festgefahrenen Autoverkehr von und zu den Zentren wieder zum Fließen zu bringen.

Die niederländische Stadt Enschede liegt an der Grenze zu Deutschland. Mit dem Wegfall der europäischen Binnengrenzen rückt Enschede aus der Randlage in die Mitte einer Wirtschaftsregion. Die 150 000-Einwohner-Stadt hat ihre Textilvergangenheit hinter sich gelassen; nun schickt sie sich an, zum wirtschaftlichen und kulturellen Zentrum aufzusteigen. Eine entscheidende Rolle bei der Transformation der Stadt spielt die Entwicklung des 13 Hektar großen Bahnhofsgebiets.

Ziel ist es, den Verkehrsknoten ans Stadtzentrum anzukoppeln und dabei jenes Gebiet zu erschließen, das jetzt noch ein blinder Fleck im Stadtgrundriß ist. Es könnte sich zu einem lebendigen Geschäftsviertel mit Kulturzentrum verdichten.

Wir halten es für die beste Strategie, den öffentlichen Raum als Motor der städtischen Entwicklung einzusetzen. Noch vor den geplanten Bauten krempeln sie den öffentlichen Raum um – er wird zur Visitenkarte der Stadt. Indem die Stadt hier Ehrgeiz zeigt und ihr Vertrauen in den Ort ausdrückt, kann sie Investoren gewinnen, um Gebäude von hoher architektonischer Qualität zu errichten. Entscheidend für das Gelingen dieser Strategie ist, dem öffentlichen Raum einen Wert als knappes und kostbares Gut zuzuerkennen – und ihn entsprechend hochwertig auszustatten.

Die Eigenheiten der Enscheder Landschaft fließen in unseren Entwurf der Plätze ein – dadurch bekommen die Räume eine zusätzliche Qualität. Es geht beim Wandel der Stadt schließlich um mehr als das bloße Umsetzen eines Programms. Das hier vorhandene natürliche Relief der Landschaft ist in den Niederlanden eine Besonderheit. Der Enscheder Bahnhof, halb Durchgangs-, halb Kopfbahnhof, liegt an einem

Rien ne va plus – the limits of mobility in the Netherlandish urban landscape seem to be in sight. The expansion of the traffic network can scarcely keep up with traffic growth. Only an enormous effort can prevent a traffic 'infarction' at this point. The main goal is to keep inner cities accessible and to prevent some of the most lively parts of town from declining to a wasteland. Public transportation can help. Its routes serve as bypasses, relieving the overcrowded roads and letting the congested traffic in and out of the centres flow again.

The Netherlandish city of Enschede is on the border to Germany. The abolition of inner European frontiers shifted Enschede from its peripheral location to the heart of an economic region. The city with a population of 150,000 has left is textile-manufacturing past behind and is preparing to take off as an economic and cultural centre. A decisive role in the city's transformation is played by the redevelopment of the 13-hectare area around the station. This traffic junction is to be linked to the city centre, thus opening up an area that is now a blind spot in the urban groundplan. It could gel into a business district with a cultural centre.

We thought that the best strategy would be to use public space as a motor for urban development. Even before there are new buildings, we are revamping the public space – it is to become the city's calling card. By showing ambitious initiative and expressing confidence in the site, the city can convince investors to erect buildings of high architectural quality on it. Decisive for the success of this strategy is to recognise public space as a rare and precious commodity – and to furnish it correspondingly in high-quality fashion.

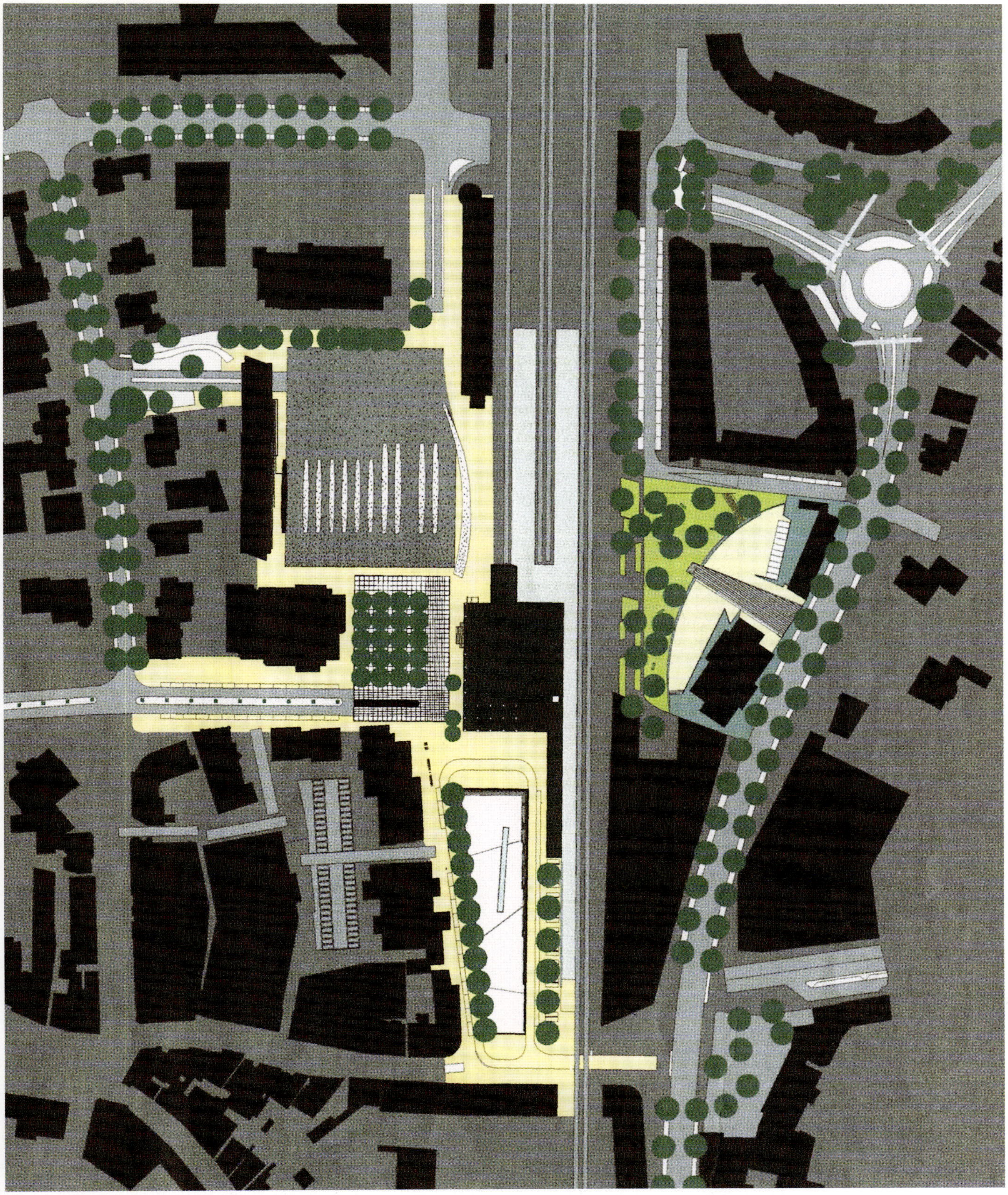

Selten in den Niederlanden: Der Enscheder Bahnhof – halb Durchgangs-, halb Kopfbahnhof – liegt an einem Hang. Die Landschaftsarchitekten des Büros Okra nahmen das Relief zur Grundlage ihres Entwurfes für die Bahnhofsumgebung. Auf dem langgestreckten Bahnhofsvorplatz (im Bild unten) verstärkten sie das Gefälle und setzten ein Wasserbassin auf den Platz – gewissermaßen als »Wasserwaage«. Eine Baumreihe schirmt das Durchgangsgleis ab, eine weitere betont die Blickachse zum Baumplatz. Er ist völlig eben, seine Pflasterung nimmt das Modulraster des Bauwerks auf. Die Asphaltfläche des anschließenden Busbahnhofs hingegen neigt sich wieder dem Hang entsprechend.

Rare in The Netherlands: the Enschede railway station – half through and half terminal station – is on an incline. The landscape architects of the Okra office made the relief the basis of their design for the station area. On the elongated square facing the station they emphasized the slope and placed a pool on the square, virtually a spirit level. A row of trees conceals the track, another underscores the line of vision towards the tree square. The latter is completely level, its pavement picking up the modular grid of the building. The asphalt surface of the adjoining bus terminal, on the other hand, is again inclined to correspond to the slope.

Der Baumplatz bildet die Freiluft-Wartehalle für den Enscheder Busbahnhof. Bäume und Lampenstelen sind im Wechsel in das strenge Quadratraster des Pflasters integriert, Bodenstrahler und Displaysäulen fügen sich ebenfalls in die Geometrie. Von den großzügigen Bänken lassen sich Bussteige und Anzeigetafeln überblicken. Computergesteuert fahren die Busse jeweils einen freien Halteplatz an – sie halten also nicht immer am selben Ort. So können weniger Halteplätze von mehr Buslinien genutzt werden. Ankommende Busse setzen ihre Fahrgäste an einer geschwungenen Rampe ab, die den Busbahnhof von den Gleisen trennt.

A tree square forms the outdoor waiting room of the Enschede bus terminal. Alternating trees and lamp steles are integrated into the severe square grid of the pavement. Spotlights in the ground and display columns also harmonize with the geometry. Departure gates and display screens can be seen from the oversized benches. Buses are directed by computers to whatever gate is free, so they don't always stop at the same place. Thus fewer platforms can be used by more bus lines. Arriving passengers are deposited at a curved ramp that separates the bus terminal from the tracks.

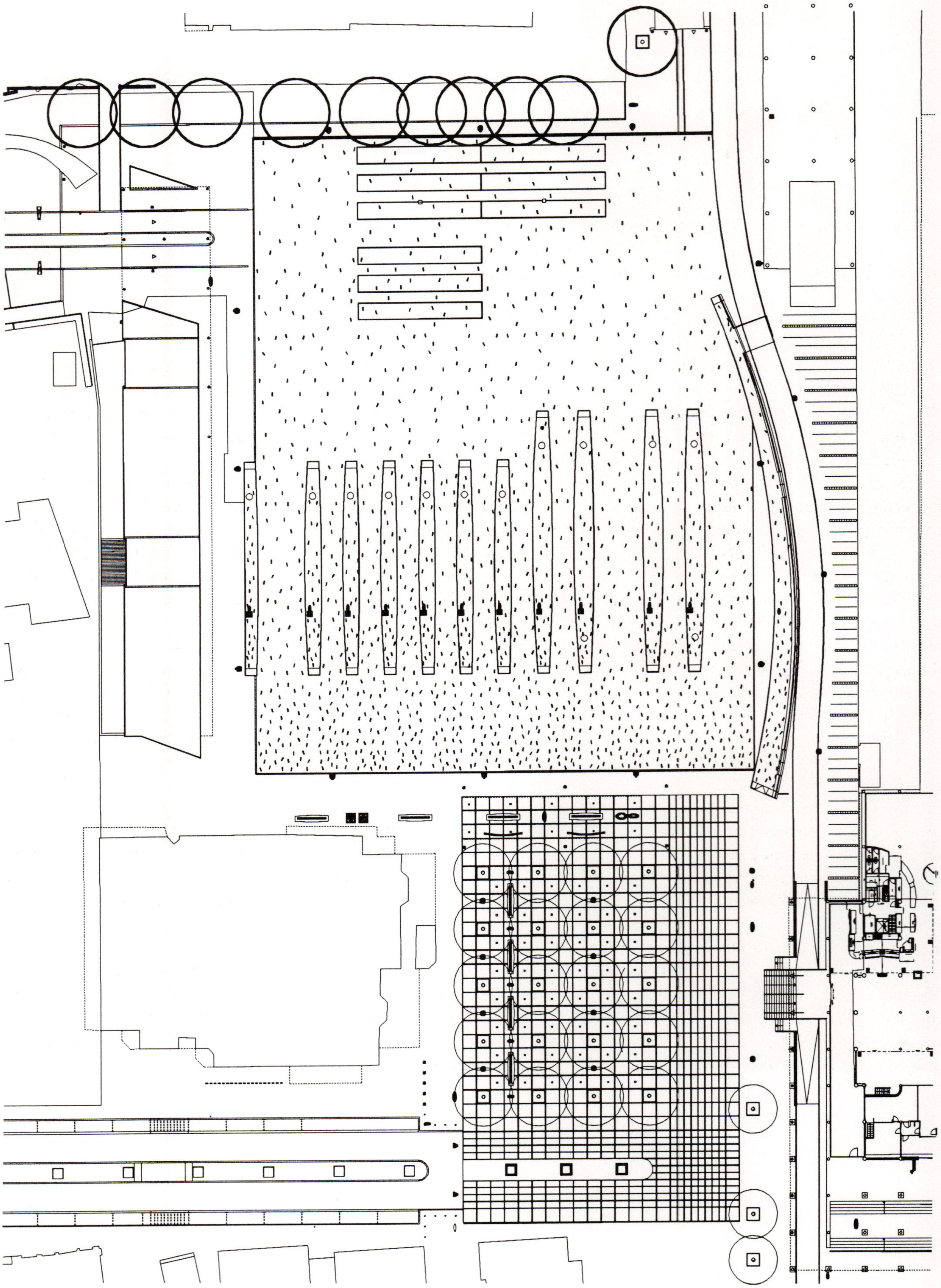

Characteristic features of Enschede topography went into our design of the squares, thus improving the quality of the space. After all, the transformation of a city is about more than the mere realisation of a programme. The natural relief of the local landscape is unusual for The Netherlands. The Enschede station, part terminal and part through station, lies next to an incline. The track going west rises slowly from the level ground up to the dike; the eastward track cuts gradually into the slope. This incline inspired our design for the three squares on the side facing the city centre. On the square in front of the station we emphasized the natural incline by increasing it in the middle of the square. The adjacent elongated pool picks up the height as a 'spirit level'. We practically levelled the square with the trees and covered it with a pavement of modules like those the station is made of. The third square, which is the bus terminal, is as a whole again a slope. The uniqueness of the landscape familiar to the people is thus maintained and makes the city more accessible.

Clear urban spaces can arise when buildings are set up at strategic points. Moreover, our squares must serve as transfer points from one means of public transport to another. The only way for them to become a genuine focus of public life is to be lively spaces where buses, taxis, kiss and ride stations, bicyclists and pedestrians are intermingled as much as possible, and car traffic is limited or moved to the ring roads. The metamorphosis of the station area is thus introduced. The three squares are entirely devoted to the theme of transferring from the railway to other means of transport, and they are related in programme, language of forms, and materials. In ad-

Abhang. Die Zuglinie nach Westen steigt langsam aus dem Gelände auf bis zum Deich; nach Osten schneiden sich die Gleise nach und nach in den Hang hinein. Dieser Hang inspirierte uns zur Gestaltung der drei Plätze auf der Seite des Zentrums. Auf dem Bahnhofsvorplatz betonten wir das natürliche Gefälle, indem wir es in der Platzmitte verstärken. Anschließend nimmt ein langgestrecktes Bassin die Höhe als »Wasserwaage« auf. Den Baumplatz ebneten wir nahezu ein und versahen ihn mit einem Belag, der ebenso wie der Bahnhof aus Modulen aufgebaut ist. Der dritte Platz, der Busbahnhof, ist wiederum in seiner gesamten Fläche geneigt. Das Eigene der Landschaft, das den Menschen vertraut ist, bleibt so erhalten und macht die Stadt leichter zugänglich.

Klare städtische Räume können entstehen, wenn an strategischen Punkten Gebäude errichtet werden. Außerdem müssen die Plätze zum Umsteigen vom einen auf das andere Verkehrsmittel dienen. Nur so werden diese Räume zu echten Brennpunkten der Öffentlichkeit. Menschen treffen sich, wenn verschiedene Transportformen aufeinandertreffen: Busse, Taxis, Fahrräder, Fußgänger. Der Autoverkehr muß eingedämmt und auf die Ringstraßen verlagert werden, Autos sollen nur vorfahren, um Reisende aussteigen zu lassen (»kiss and ride«). Damit wird die Metamorphose der Bahnhofsumgebung eingeleitet. Die drei Plätze stehen ganz im Zeichen des Umsteigens von der Bahn auf andere Verkehrsmittel. Die Plätze sind verwandt in Programm, Formensprache und Material. Daneben haben sie jeweils eigene Charakteristika: der dynamische Busbahnhof, der Baumplatz mit dem Warteraum und der Vorplatz mit dem Wasserbecken.

Der Vorplatz wird für den Reisenden zum lebhaften Tor der Stadt. Hierhin begleitet man Freunde zum Bahnhof, hier steigen gehetzte Geschäftsleute ins Taxi, hier hält das Zugtaxi, und Radfahrer kommen und gehen. Der heute noch chaotische Ort wird durch umfangreiche, aber einfache Eingriffe in einen Platz verwandelt: Eine freie zentrale Fläche schafft den Raum, der von einem neuen Baukörper gegenüber des Bahnhofs begrenzt wird. Der jetzt noch zerstückelte Raum wird zu einer Einheit geschmiedet und leitet über zur Innenstadt.

Der Busbahnhof, der größte der drei Plätze, springt als erstes ins Auge. Er ist im Vergleich zu den anderen Plätzen wesentlich stärker auf seine Funktion ausgerichtet. Oft ist ein Busbahnhof ein großer weitläufiger Platz, oft ohne Bezug zum Maßstab des Stadtzentrums. In unserem Fall haben wir eine zugige Ebene in einen Stadtplatz verwandelt.

The Enschede bus terminal was transformed from an inhospitable asphalt surface into a top-quality urban square. The computer system directing the buses contributes as much to this result as the contemporary materials do. Bus platforms gently curving outwards divide the area into strips. Granite 'glitter' in the asphalt loosens up the rigid structure. The platforms of light concrete with metal borders appear to swim like fish in the dark asphalt. At night a fibreglass light strip creates the impression that the curved arrivals ramp floats above the surface of the square.
The concrete paving of the tree square is also bordered in metal, underscored by the reflections of the lighting at night. Traditional clinker paving frames the asphalt and concrete surfaces of the bus terminal and the tree square, thus relating to the open spaces in the city.

dition, they each have individual characteristics. The station square will be a lively gate to the city for travellers. What is still a chaotic area will soon be changed with comprehensive but simple interventions into a square. A free central surface creates space extending up to a new building opposite the station. The square's cut up parts will be forged into a unified space leading towards the downtown area.

The bus terminal, the largest of the three squares, is the most prominent. Compared to the others it is considerably more oriented to its function. Bus terminals are often large, sprawling spaces, without reference to the scale of the city centre. In our case we have made a windy surface into a city square. The organisation of a bus terminal, as well as its appearance, has changed along with transportation technology. The fixtures of the terminal reflect these dynamics. They are expressed in the curving lines of the gates, the screens displaying departure gates and times, and the furniture, such as the oversized benches where travellers can sit briefly. This bus terminal not only looks high tech, it is. As opposed to traditional bus terminals, this one routes the buses by computer, that is, they are directed to free gates by electronic information systems, allowing fewer gates to be used by more bus lines. As the buses always stop at different gates, the travellers wait elsewhere. They collect in the waiting room,

Von einer unwirtlichen Asphaltfläche hat sich der Enscheder Busbahnhof zu einem hochwertigen Stadtplatz verwandelt. Das Computersystem zur Bussteuerung trägt dazu ebensoviel bei wie die zeitgenössischen Materialien. Leicht geschwungene Bussteige unterteilen den Platz streng in Streifen, in den Asphalt eingelassene Granit-»Sprenkel« lockern die Strenge auf. Wie Fische schwimmen die metallgefaßten Bussteige aus hellem Beton auf dem dunklen Asphalt. Ein Glasfaser-Lichtstreifen vermittelt nachts den Eindruck, die geschwungene Ausstiegsplattform würde gar über der Platzfläche schweben.
Auch das Betonpflaster des Baumplatzes ist metallgefaßt – die Lichtreflexe der abendlichen Beleuchtung betonen dies. Traditionelles Klinkerpflaster rahmt die Asphalt- und Betonflächen des Busbahnhofes und des Baumplatzes und vermittelt so mit den Freiräumen der Stadt.

Die Organisation des Busbahnhofs, aber auch sein Aussehen, ändert sich mit der Transporttechnik. Die Einrichtung des Busbahnhofs strahlt diese Dynamik aus. Sie kommt zum Ausdruck in den geschwungenen Linien der Bussteige, der Anzeigetafeln und der Objekte, zum Beispiel der übergroßen Bänke, auf denen die Reisenden kurz Platz nehmen. Dieser Busbahnhof sieht nicht nur nach High-tech aus, er ist tatsächlich hochtechnisiert. Im Gegensatz zu einem traditionellen Busbahnhof werden hier die Busse computergesteuert, das heißt über elektronische Informationssysteme zu einem freigewordenen Halteplatz geleitet, so daß weniger Haltestellen von mehr Buslinien genutzt werden können. Da die Busse an verschiedenen Bussteigen halten, warten die Reisenden woanders. Sie treffen sich im Warteraum, wo auf Infosäulen die Abfahrten der Busse angekündigt werden. Oder auch auf dem angrenzenden Baumplatz, dem dritten Platz, den wir als »Außenhalle« entwarfen, mit einem Dach aus Baumkronen, die das Licht filtern. Von den geschwungenen Wartebänken aus überblicken die Reisenden den Busbahnhof und können auf Displays die Abfahrtszeiten der Busse ablesen. Die Bänke sind so entworfen, daß viele Passagiere bequem Platz haben.

Auch die Materialien entsprechen unserer Zeit. Die Plätze bestehen aus drei unterschiedlichen steinernen Ebenen. Diese Flächen sind von einem neutralen Klinkerbelag gerahmt, der Material und Farbe der Innenstadt aufnimmt. Auf der anderen Seite des Bahnhofs bildet eine kleine Grünanlage das Gegenstück zu den Plätzen. Dieser Bahnhofsgarten zwischen den neu zu errichtenden Bürogebäuden ist eine »grüne Perle« in unmittelbarer Nähe der Innenstadt. Selbst nachts, wenn wenig Betrieb ist, ist das Verweilen auf den drei Plätzen vor dem Bahnhof sehr angenehm. Besondere Lichteffekte schaffen eine märchenhafte Stimmung, so der Glasfaser-Lichtstreifen in der langen gebogenen Balustrade des Bussteigs für ankommende Fahrgäste, oder auch das Karree aus Lichtsteinen, die abends die Baumkronen auf dem Baumplatz von unten anstrahlen.

Der hohe Einsatz im öffentlichen Raum war nicht umsonst. Schon zeigt sich großes Interesse, hier auch tatsächlich in Architektur zu investieren – trotz der Tatsache, daß die Nachfrage nach Büroraum in der Region um Enschede (der niederländischen Region Twente) im Vergleich zur Randstad relativ gering ist. Die Qualität der neuen Plätze am Enscheder Bahnhof läßt den Ort zum Motor für die Entwicklung des ganzen Gebiets werden. Hier spürt man den neuen Elan der Stadt.

where displays on columns announce the departures. They can also wait on the adjacent tree square, the third square, which we call the 'outdoor waiting room' with a roof of tree foliage filtering the light.

From the curving benches people have a view of the terminal and can see departure information on the displays. The benches are designed such that many passengers can comfortably find seats on them.

The materials also reflect modernity. The squares have three different stone surfaces. They are framed with neutral clinker paving which picks up the materials and colours of downtown. On the other side of the station a small green park forms a counterpart to the squares. This station garden between the future office buildings is a 'green gem' in the immediate vicinity of the inner city.

Even at night when there is little going on, lingering on the three squares is a pleasure. A fairy-tale atmosphere is created by special lighting effects, such as the fibreglass light strip in the long curved balustrade of the platform for arriving passengers, or the square of illuminated stones lighting up the tops of the trees from below at night.

This major investment in public space was not in vain. There is already considerable interest being shown in investing in the architecture on the site, despite the fact that the demand for office space in the Enschede (Twente) region is relatively low compared to the Randstad. It is the quality of the new squares by the Enschede station that makes the site into a motor for the development of the entire district. Here you feel the new energy of the city.

Station area, Enschede, The Netherlands
Client: city of Enschede
Masterplan: Okra landschapsarchitecten; Martin Knuijt, Christ-Jan van Rooij, project architects
Size: 13 hectares
Planning: 1994 – 1995
Costs: NLG 42 million

Realisation of the first stage, bus terminal and station square
Design: Okra landschapsarchitecten; Martin Knuijt, Christ-Jan van Rooij, project architects
In cooperation with: I/AA, Enschede; Sign Design, Binnenbuiten
Size: 1.2 hectares
Planning: 1995; Construction: 1996 – 1997
Costs: NLG 6.5 million

Schouwburgplein Rotterdam – Podium der Stadt

Schouwburgplein, Rotterdam – the city's podium

Klazien Brummel

Rotterdam's Schouwburgplein (theatre square) is by far the most unusual of all city squares in The Netherlands (see Topos 2). Its dimensions are so un-Dutch that it seems more like a broad plain than a square, and yet it is an enclosed space. What makes the Schouwburgplein into an experience is its sensational view of a rapidly growing skyline. On its north side, behind the flat horizontal "De Doelen" concert hall, rise the green and black skyscrapers near the central station. West 8 considers this view one of the square's major characteristics. They therefore wanted to turn the square into a stage from which the Rotterdamers could admire their city.

Starting out with the idea of an empty space, West 8 kept the square as level as possible, raising it by 35 centimetres. It thus makes the impression of a suspended podium, which becomes even more powerful at night when it is brightly lit up around the edges. Besides the choice of materials and the distribution of space according to function, lighting plays an important role in West 8's urban planning designs. Of course light is a typically urban feature – neon lights, laser beams, street lamps, traffic lights, shop windows; a real city never sleeps. What daylight cannot postpone gets lit up at night. Not that urban lighting is always planned in context the way an architectural project is. It occupies no physical space and therefore remains, despite a series of regulations, a rather anarchic phenomenon.

Besides providing urban flair, lighting can underline the theatrical quality of public space. West 8 used it to do the latter: they produced a stage floor. A good square must be able to function as a stage. Although no one can predict exactly how it will be used, seeing as how the city

Der Rotterdamer Schouwburgplein (Theaterplatz) ist von allen niederländischen Stadtplätzen der merkwürdigste (siehe Topos 2). Seine Abmessungen sind so unholländisch, daß er eher einer weiten Ebene als einem Platz ähnelt, und dennoch ist der Raum geschlossen. Was den Schouwburgplein zum Erlebnis macht, ist die sensationelle Aussicht auf eine rasch wachsende Skyline. An der Nordseite des Platzes treten hinter dem flachen Gebäude des Musiktheaters »De Doelen« grüne und schwarze Wolkenkratzer hervor, die in der Nähe des Hauptbahnhofs stehen. Für West 8 gehört diese Aussicht zu den wichtigsten Eigenschaften des Platzes. Der Platz sollte daher eine Bühne werden, von der aus die Rotterdamer ihre Stadt bewundern können.

Ausgehend von der Idee des leeren Raums hat West 8 den Platz so eben wie möglich gehalten,

Ein Platz als Bühne, der sich wie ein Chamäleon verändert: jede Stunde am Tag und am Abend, im Sommer wie im Winter.
The square is a stage, changing chameleon-like from one hour to the next, daytime to evening, summer to winter.

Der Rotterdamer Schouwburgplein liegt im Herzen der Stadt, umgeben von Geschäften, Büros, dem Hauptbahnhof, dem städtischen Theater und der Musikhalle. Das Büro West 8 hat diesen Platz als Bühne konzipiert, von der aus die Rotterdamer ihre Stadt bewundern können.

Rotterdam's Schouwburgplein lies at the heart of the city, surrounded by shops, offices, the station, the municipal theatre and the concert hall. The West 8 office treated this square as a stage from which the Rotterdamers can admire their city.

ihn aber um 35 Zentimeter angehoben, so daß er den Eindruck eines schwebenden Podiums erweckt – ein Eindruck, der sich noch verstärkt, wenn abends der Rand grell erleuchtet wird. In den städtebaulichen Entwürfen von West 8 spielt die Lichtgestaltung neben der Materialwahl und der Flächenverteilung nach Funktionen eine wichtige Rolle. Schließlich ist Licht ein typisch städtisches Merkmal – Neonbeleuchtung, Laserstrahlen, Straßenbeleuchtung, Ampeln, Schaufenster; eine Stadt kommt nie zur Ruhe. Was das Tageslicht nicht aufschieben kann, wird nachts ausgeleuchtet. Nicht, daß dies immer wie etwa ein Architekturprojekt zuvor im Zusammenhang geplant würde. Städtische Beleuchtung nimmt keinen konkreten Raum in Beschlag und ist daher, trotz einer Reihe von Vorschriften, noch immer ein recht anarchistisches Phänomen.

Neben der Möglichkeit, einem Ort durch Beleuchtung städtische Spannung zu verleihen, kann mit Licht die theatralische Qualität des öffentlichen Raums unterstrichen werden. Und das hat West 8 getan: eine Spielfläche inszeniert. Ein guter Platz muß als Theaterbühne funktionieren können. Und obwohl niemand genau vorhersagen kann, wie ein Raum genutzt werden wird – die Stadt macht schließlich damit, was sie will –, lassen sich doch durch Anreize die Aktivitäten bis zu einem gewissen Maße dirigieren. So besteht etwa der Belag des Schouwburgplein zum größten Teil aus perforierten Metallplatten, durch die nachts Streifen von weißem, violettem und grünem Neonlicht heraufleuchten. Jeder, der über den Platz geht, sieht die Streifen direkt vor sich im Rhythmus seiner Schritte vorrücken. Je rascher, desto dynamischer ist der Effekt. Bevor man sich dessen bewußt wird, schaut man nur noch schräg nach unten und beschleunigt die Schritte, in der Absicht, das Licht einzuholen. Und wenn man inmitten von all diesem Metall plötzlich eine große Holzfläche betritt, wird man unwillkürlich aufschauen.

Daneben gibt das Podium des Schouwburgplein seinen Schauspielern nur wenig Requisiten und Bühnenbilder an die Hand. Die Fläche ist über die volle Länge in Streifen unterschiedlicher Funktionen geteilt und die am höchsten aufragenden Objekte sind am östlichen Rand aufgereiht. Drei hohe Türme, die aus Gerüsten errichtet wurden, markieren die östliche Grenze. Sie dienen als Belüftungsschächte für die große Tiefgarage unter dem Platz, erinnern jedoch eher an drei treue Wächter. Jeder Turm gibt in roten digitalen Ziffern einen Teil der Zeit an: 1. 8. 58. In der Nacht leuchten in ihnen grüne vertikale Röhren.

Der Platz als Spielfläche: Licht unterstreicht die theatralische Qualität des Schouwburgplein. Die Beleuchtung reagiert flexibel auf unterschiedliche Aktivitäten: Auf beweglichen Masten montierte Flutlichter beleuchten wie Suchscheinwerfer den Platz. Zu vorprogrammierten Zeiten ändern die Lichtmasten ihre Stellung. Nach Münzeinwurf können auch Passanten die Szenerie manipulieren.

The square as a stage floor: light underlines the theatrical nature of the Schouwburgplein. The lighting adapts to the various activities. Mounted on movable masts, floodlights light up the square like searchlights. The posts change position at preprogrammed times. Passers-by can also alter the stage set with a coin-operated feature.

Zwischen den Lüftungstürmen und einer Reihe auffallend hoher Lichtmasten stehen aneinandergereiht 13 lange Holzbänke. Diese sind nach dem Sonnenstand ausgerichtet und bieten Hunderten von Menschen Platz. Da sie relativ verdeckt plaziert sind, ist dies ein idealer Ort, um voyeuristische Neigungen auszuleben. Von hier kann man den gesamten Platz überblicken. Vor der langen Bank stehen vier extrem hohe Lichtmasten, die sich hydraulisch bewegen und bis auf 35 Meter ausfahren lassen. Die Silhouette dieser Tentakel läßt bei den Rotterdamern Assoziationen zu den vertrauten Kränen aufkommen, die im Hafen, aber auch aus vielen Baugruben und Baustellen der Stadt aufragen. Es entbehrt nicht der Ironie, an den Rand eines nahezu leeren Platzes hohe Kräne zu stellen.

Im Gegensatz zu Theatern, wo die Zuschauer sich sicher im Dunkeln verbergen können, während nur die Bühne im Licht badet, wird das Podium des Schouwburgplein von den Streulichtern der umliegenden erleuchteten Gebäude, Straßencafés und Laternen (die übrigens ursprünglich nicht aufgestellt werden sollten) bedrängt. Wenn der Platz auch nachts seine architektonische Identität behaupten und seiner Umgebung Paroli bieten will, muß er auftrumpfen. Daher wurden auf den beweglichen Masten Flutlichter montiert, die wie helle Suchscheinwerfer den Platz beleuchten. Zu vorprogrammierten Zeiten ändern die Lichtmasten ihre Stellung, oder sie werden von Passanten in Bewegung gesetzt, denn nach Einwurf von einem Gulden kann jeder über eine Bedienungstafel die Szene beleuchten.

Ursprünglich hatte das Büro jedoch an etwas Subtileres gedacht. Die Scheinwerfer an den hohen Masten hätten schwächer ausfallen sollen, um die spärlichen skulpturalen Objekte auf dem Platz auch zur Wirkung kommen zu lassen. An der Südseite liegt beispielsweise eine Reihe kleiner Wasserspiele unter dem perforierten Fußboden verborgen – elegante, wie aus dem Nichts hochsprühende Fontänen. In der Nacht wird dieser Ort durch Streifencodes aus Neonlicht markiert, die das Wasser von unten her anstrahlen. Auch stehen an der Nord- und Südseite fragile, dreieckige Eingänge zur Tiefgarage. Ihre Seitenwände bestehen aus durchbrochenem Glas, ein Detail, das durch die Beleuchtung von innen sichtbar wird.

Der Platz wird von einer kerzengeraden, mit Gittern bedeckten Wasserrinne durchschnitten. In der Nacht wird dieser Kanal durch seine Beleuchtung zu einer auffälligen blauen Trennungslinie. Auf der einen Seite befindet sich das große Kino, auf der anderen Seite liegt die Spielfläche von West 8. In der Nähe des Kinos verändert sich die Atmosphäre des Platzes.

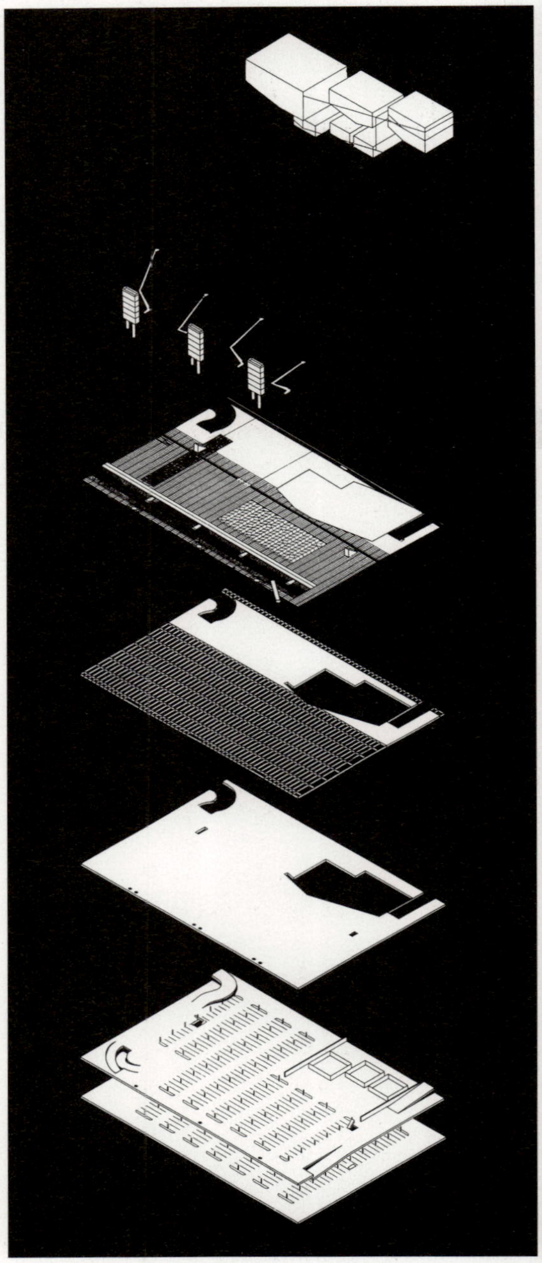

Die Fläche des Schouwburgplein ist über die gesamte Länge in Zonen unterschiedlicher Funktionen aufgeteilt. Die Zonen werden vorgegeben im Bodenbelag, der zum größten Teil aus perforierten Metallplatten besteht, durch die nachts Streifen von weißem, violettem und grünem Neonlicht heraufleuchten.

The entire length of the Schouwburgplain is divided into zones for various functions. They are indicated by the pavement which consists mainly of perforated metal plates with beams of white, purple and green neon light shining up through them at night.

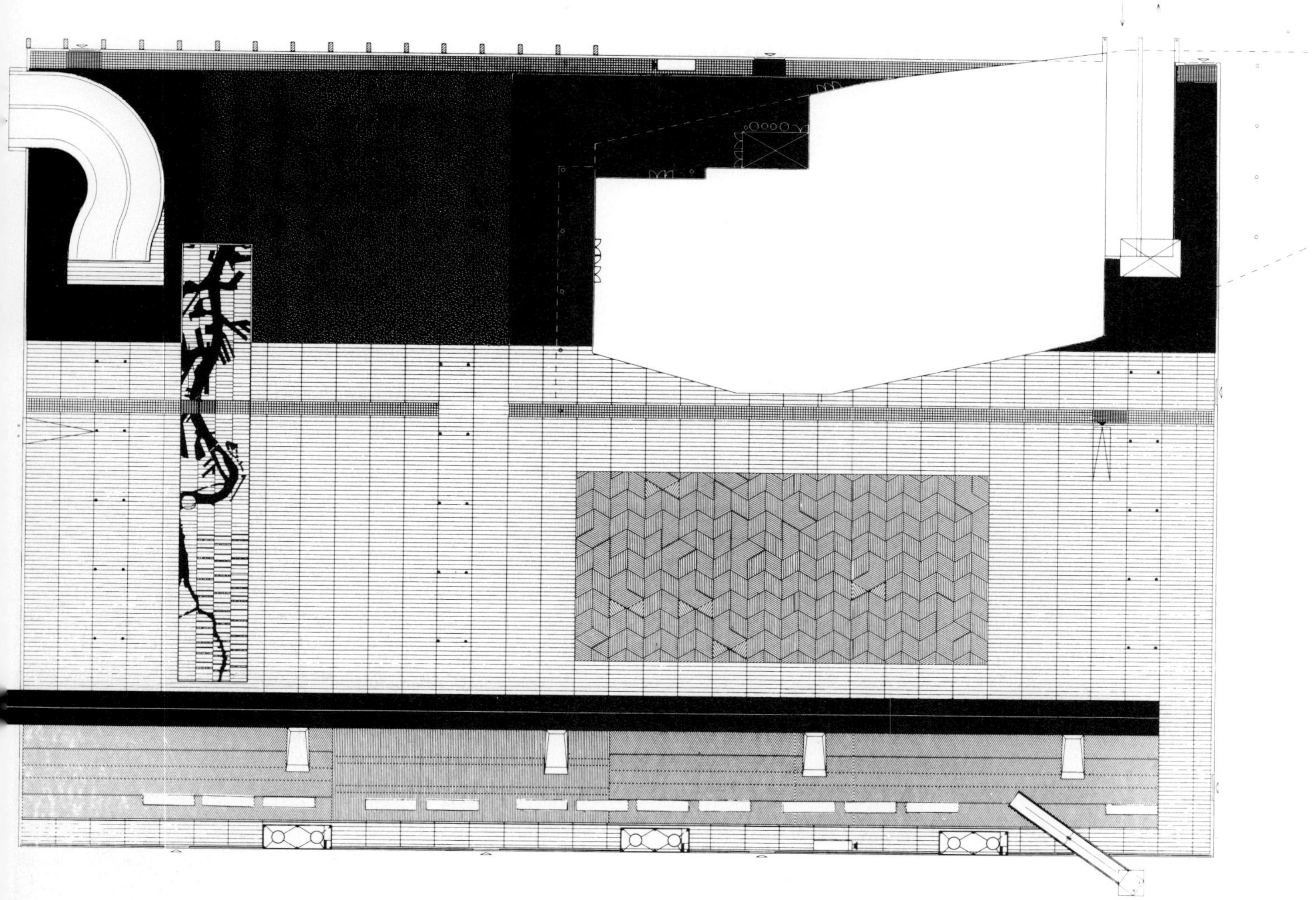

does what it wants with it anyway, to some degree stimuli can incite certain activities. For instance, the pavement of the Schouwburgplein consists mainly of perforated metal plates with beams of white, purple and green neon light shining up through them at night. People going through the square at night see the beams moving ahead right in front of them. The faster they walk the more dynamic the effect. Before they know it, they'll only be looking diagonally down and walking faster to try and catch up with the light. Then when they suddenly step onto a large wooden surface in the midst of all this metal, they will involuntarily look up.

The Schouwburgplain podium supplies only a few more props and sets for its actors. The whole area is divided lengthwise into strips for various functions, and the tallest objects are lined up along the eastern edge. Three tall towers made of scaffolding mark the eastern limit. They serve as ventilation shafts for the large underground car park, though they bring three loyal guards to mind. At night green vertical pipes shine inside them. Each tower provides a unit of the time of day in red digital figures: 1. 8. 58.

Between the ventilation towers and a row of extremely tall lamp posts are 13 long wooden benches lined up end to end. They face the sun and seat hundreds of people. As they are relatively hidden, this is an ideal place to succumb to voyeuristic tendencies. The whole square can be seen from here. The four tall lamp posts can be operated hydraulically to extend by 35 metres. The silhouette of these feelers reminds Rotterdamers of the familiar cranes protruding from the harbour as well as the many construction sites

Szenario der Leere – da der Platz die Perspektive auf die Skyline der Stadt genießt, benötigt er keine weiteren Wände. Der Platz ist folglich als klares Rechteck, dem Dach der darunterliegenden Tiefgarage, definiert. Als Reaktion auf das große Volumen des Kinos ist die Fläche des Platzes völlig eben gestaltet.

A scenario of emptiness – with its view of the city's skyline the square needs no further walls. It is clearly defined as a rectangle, formed by the roof of its underground car park. To counteract the large mass of the cinema, the surface of the square has been designed completely level.

Schouwburgplein, Rotterdam, The Netherlands
Architects: Adriaan Geuze, West 8
Collaborators: Wim Kloosterboer, Dirry de Bruin, Cyrus B. Clark, Erwin Bot, Dick Heydra, Huub Juurlink, Nigel Sampey, Erik Overdiep, Jurgen Beij, Jerry van Eyck
Contractor: Gebr. Van de Heijden BV Construction Company, Duyvis BV Engineering Company
Project: 1990; Construction: 1997
Size: 12,250 square metres; Costs: DM 13,500,000

Man betritt die Einflußsphäre des milchweißen, kolossalen Kinos. Je mehr man sich dem Gebäude nähert, desto mehr verwandelt sich der Platz in eine Art Kombination aus Galerie und Vorhof. Auf der anderen Seite der Trennungslinie gewinnt der Platz seine relative Autonomie zurück.

Die Beleuchtung des Schouwburgplein kann somit nach verschiedenen Funktionen unterteilt werden. Abends werden bedeutsame Objekte und Details durch Beleuchtung, oft von innen heraus, zu auffälligen Markierungspunkten. Und auch die leere Platzfläche braucht, wenn der Abend naht, nicht in Finsternis zu versinken, denn die Flutlichter an den Masten tauchen sie in grelles Licht. Auf diese Weise bewahrt der Platz seine architektonische Autonomie und reklamiert den Raum, der nötig ist, um eine leere Bühne bleiben zu können. Es ist ein anspruchsvoller Platz geworden, über den niemand gleichgültig hinwegschlendern kann. Und es wird sicher eine Weile dauern, bevor er so funktioniert, wie er gedacht ist. Aber schließlich wird die Stadt damit doch machen, was sie will.

West 8 hat den Platz um 35 Zentimeter angehoben, so daß er den Eindruck eines schwebenden Podiums erweckt. Nachts, wenn der Rand grell erleuchtet ist, verstärkt sich diese Illusion. Stündlich ändert das Quartett der Lichtmasten seine Position – ob und wie der Platz funktioniert, liegt in den Händen seiner Nutzer.

West 8 raised the square by 35 centimetres, giving it the impression of a suspended podium. This illusion is reinforced at night when it is brightly lit up around the edges. The quartette of lamp masts changes position every hour. Whether and how the square works is up to its users.

in town. It is not lacking in irony to erect cranes on the edge of an empty square. In contrast to theatres where spectators can hide safely in the dark while the stage is flooded with light, the podium of Schouwburgplein is encircled with lights from the surrounding buildings, outdoor cafés and street lamps (which, by the way, were not originally intended). If the square is to make its architectural presence felt at night and stand up to its surroundings, it has to show off. For this reason floodlights attached to the movable lamp posts shine on the square like powerful searchlights. The posts change position at preprogrammed times and can also be moved by passers-by. Anyone can illuminate the scenery themselves by inserting one Dutch guilder and following the instructions.

Originally, however, the architectural office had thought of something more subtle. The floodlights on the tall posts were to have been weaker, allowing the few sculptural objects on the square to show up as well. On the south side, for example, a series of small fountains concealed in the perforated floor look elegant, as though rising up out of nowhere. At night this place is indicated by neon strip codes illuminating the water from below. On the north and south sides there are fragile triangular entrances to the underground car park. Their side-walls consist of perforated glass, a detail that shows up through the lighting from within.

The square is divided by the perfectly straight line of a gutter covered by a grate. Light makes this channel into a striking blue dividing line at night. On one side is a large cinema, on the other the stage floor by West 8. The atmosphere of the square changes near the cinema as one enters the orbit of the milky white, enormous building. The closer one gets to the cinema the more the square becomes a kind of combined gallery and forecourt. Beyond the dividing line the square regains its relative autonomy.

The lighting of Schouwburgplein can thus be divided according to various functions. With the help of light, often from within, significant objects and details stand out as points of orientation in the evening. Even the empty expanse of the square need not sink into obscurity when evening comes. The floodlights on the posts bathe it in bright light. In this way the square maintains its architectural autonomy and claims the space it needs to remain an empty stage.

Die Planer von West 8 zeigen Sinn für Ironie, wenn sie am Rand des Platzes vier extrem hohe Lichtmasten aufstellen, die sich bis auf 35 Meter ausfahren lassen. Sie erinnern an die hohen Kräne, wie sie die Rotterdamer vom Hafen oder auch von den vielen Baustellen und Baugruben der Stadt kennen.

The planners of West 8 show their sense of irony by placing four extremely tall lamp masts on the edge of the square. These can be operated hydraulically to extend by 35 metres. They recall the tall cranes familiar to Rotterdamers from the harbour as well as the many construction sites in town.

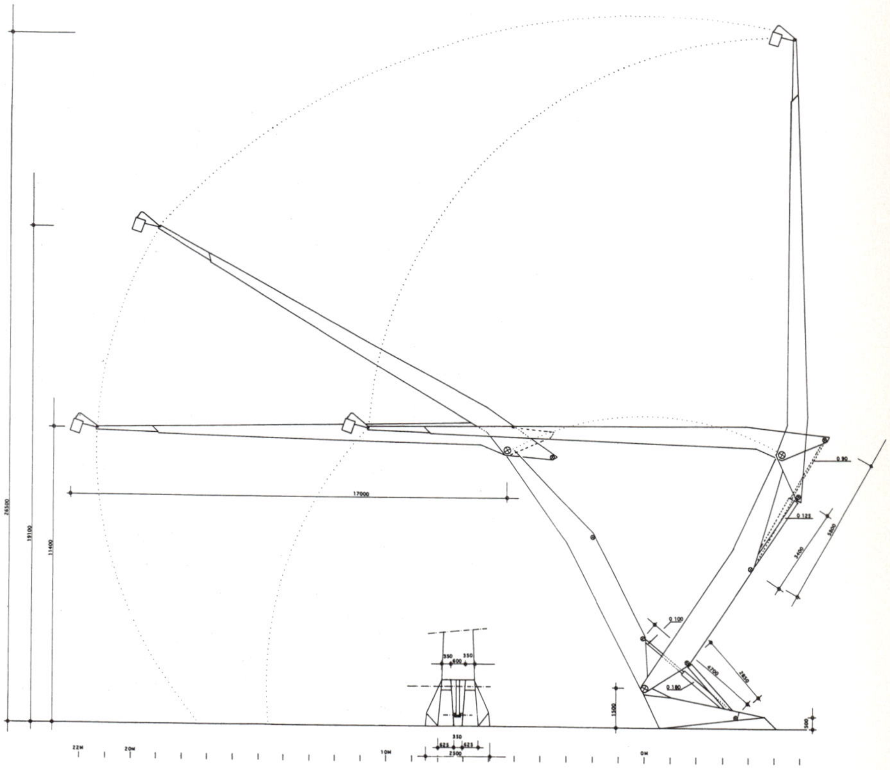

Der Große Markt, Almere

Market Square, Almere

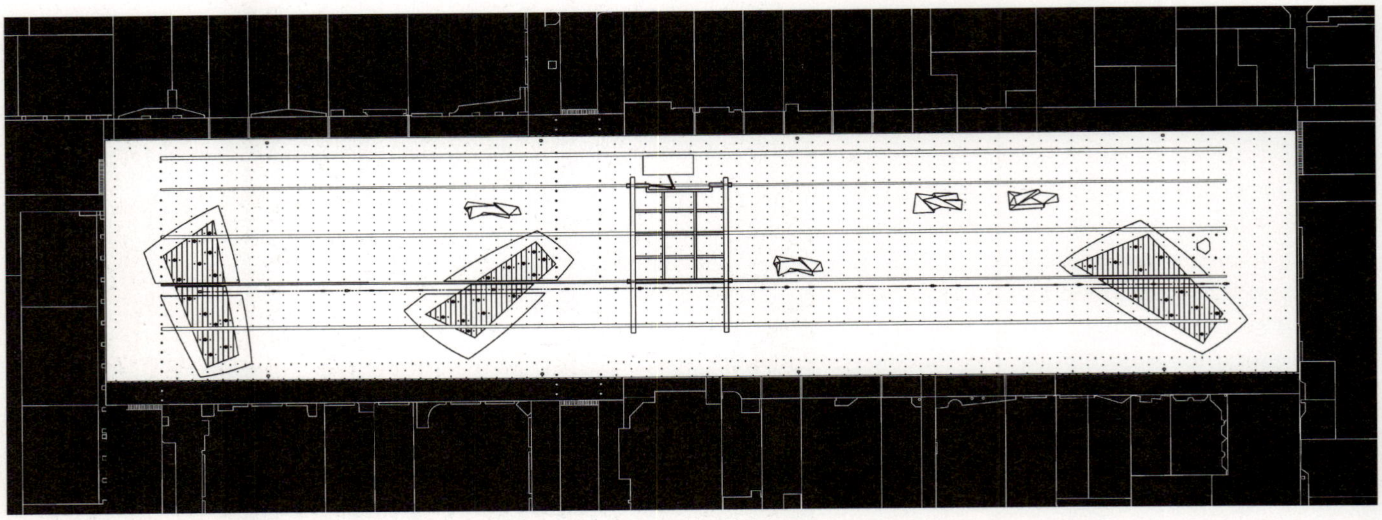

Almut Röwekamp
Petrouschka Thumann

Keine Stadt der Niederlande wächst so schnell wie Almere. Die erst 1974 gegründete »Newtown«, 30 Kilometer nordöstlich von Amsterdam, hat heute 150 000 Einwohner. Die Stadt liegt in Flevoland, ein erst 1968 trockengelegter Polder im IJsselmeer. Zunächst als reine Landbaufläche geschaffen, ist der Polder heute Teil der »Randstad«. Almere will zu den zehn größten Städten der Niederlande gehören, angestrebt werden 250 000 Einwohner. Zunächst wurde in Almere nur fehlender Wohnraum geschaffen, mittlerweile ist es auf dem Weg zu einer vollwertigen Stadt zum Wohnen und Arbeiten. Um diese Entwicklung zu beschleunigen, formuliert der Rat von Almere Aufgaben in verschiedenen Maßstäben, sowohl für die Stadterweiterungsgebiete als auch für das bestehende Zentrum. So entstand die Frage nach einem neuen Impuls für den Großen Markt im Stadtzentrum.

Ausgehen statt Einkaufen: Maßgeschneidert zeigt sich Almeres Großer Markt mit Leuchten, Sitzmöbeln und einem mobilen Podium.

Thanks to customised lighting, seats and a mobile stage, Almere's Market Square is a place where people prefer to linger than to shop.

Möglichkeiten zum Ausgehen, Kneipen, Restaurants, Straßencafés oder kulturelle Veranstaltungen gab es bisher in Almere kaum. Die Identität des Zentrums wurde vor allem durch die Einkaufsmöglichkeiten bestimmt. Lediglich auf dem Großen Markt gab es einige Kneipen. Die überall parkenden Autos verhinderten jedoch ein angenehmes Verweilen. Ziel war es, dem Markt ein neues Gesicht zu geben. Zusammen mit dem

No other Dutch city is growing as swiftly as Almere, which is located about 30 kilometres north-east of Amsterdam on the South Flevoland Polder, a tract of lowland reclaimed from Lake IJsselmeer in 1968 for purely agricultural purposes. Founded in 1974, the new town has 150,000 inhabitants today, and is a component of the Randstad industrial and metropolitan region. It intends to become one of the ten largest cities in The Netherlands and is aiming for 250,000 inhabitants. Originally created as a dormitory town, Almere first concerned itself with housing construction only, but is now on the way to becoming a city in its own right, a place where people not only live but also work. In order to foster this development, the City Council has formulated tasks on various scales, both for urban extension areas and the city's core. It was in this connection that the question of what was to become of Market Square was raised. At the time, the identity of downtown Almere, where Market

Square is situated, was mainly determined by shops and stores. The city as a whole had hardly any pubs, restaurants, street cafés or places where people could go in the evenings, and thus suffered a dearth of cultural events. The only place with a few pubs was Market Square, but the masses of parked cars did not make it particularly attractive. Thus when the Council began to turn its attention to the square, it decided that its appearance needed to be changed.

The concept. Bureau B+B gave the square a simple surface and closed it off to traffic to create a place where urban life can freely unfold. Their design, drawn up in 1996, regards the square space as a setting for a variety of uses. To support this aim, they designed a mobile stage that can be moved on tracks from one end of the rectangular space to the other to enable different uses and introduce changes in appearance. Seating and lighting elements were also designed to enable constant transformation and adapt the space to differing requirements.

The design. Before the reshaping, the square was fragmented into three sections, making it difficult to recognise its generous dimensions at a glance. Now it is a single space from wall to wall, making the surrounding buildings – edifices from the eighties characterised by differing architecture, facade organisation and colours – more readily visible. The square's length is underscored by the parallel lines of the rails, the sluices and the lighting strung on wires. Chestnut trees originally positioned over the area in a regular grid have now been consolidated into three solid groups and pruned to make them more compact. The result offers spatial variety without impinging on the openness of the space and thus affecting its

Deutlich werden nach der Umgestaltung des Großen Marktes die großzügigen Abmessungen des rechteckigen Platzes. Jetzt ist der Platz eine einzige Fläche von Giebel zu Giebel und lädt zum Besuch von Straßencafès und Restaurants ein. Die Bühne, Mittelpunkt des Platzes, kann auf Schienen über die gesamte Platzlänge verschoben werden.

The generous dimensions of Market Square can now be taken in at a single glance. Thanks to the renewal measures, it is now a single space from wall to wall and along with its street cafés, makes an inviting impression. Its main focal point, the stage, can be moved on tracks from one end of the rectangular space to the other.

Die überdachte Bühne, eine Stahlkonstruktion, ist für professionelle, multifunktionelle Nutzungen ausgestattet. Lichtlinien mit hängenden Lampen sorgen für eine zentrale Beleuchtung. Aus sternförmig gelochten Blechen unter den Kastanien strahlen Spots nach oben. Das Licht spiegelt sich in den Verkehrsmarkierungen aus Edelstahl, die in den sandgestrahlten anthrazitfarbenen Terrazzo-Boden eingelassen wurden.

The heavy steel stage, which is covered over at the top, is equipped for professional, multifunctional dramaturgic use. Central lighting is provided by strings of suspended lights. Spotlights installed below the chestnut trees shine up onto the leaves through sheet metal lamps with star-shaped apertures. The lighting effects are reflected by steel traffic setts let into sand-blasted, anthracite-coloured terrazzo.

Bureau B+B wurde eine Strategie entwickelt zur Transformation des Parkplatzes in einen Aufenthaltsort mit allen Formen kultureller Aktivität. Die Planer setzen darauf, dass die Kneipen und Restaurants mehr Straßencafés nach sich ziehen, mehr und mehr Besucher kommen, und so der Platz rund um die Uhr lebt.

Das Konzept. Das Bureau B+B entwarf für den Großen Markt einen autofreien Platz mit einer schlichten Oberfläche, auf dem sich das städtische Leben voll entfalten kann. Der Raum wird als ein flexibler Rahmen aufgefasst, geeignet für vielfachen Gebrauch. Das neu geschaffene Podium macht diese Intention am deutlichsten wahr. Die Bühne ist fahrbar. Sie kann auf Schienen über die gesamte Platzlänge geschoben werden. Unterschiedliche Nutzungen werden möglich, der Platz verändert stets sein Gesicht. Sitzelemente und Beleuchtung auf dem Großen Markt sind ebenfalls auf die ständigen Transformationen abgestimmt und passen den Raum an die jeweiligen Erfordernisse an.

Der Entwurf. Die großzügigen Abmessungen des rechteckigen Platzes waren in der alten Situation nicht erkenntlich, weil der Raum in drei Teil-

suitability for outdoor events. The paving forms a wall-to-wall carpet, in which the sluices, the stage rails and the Corten steel surfaces in which the trees are set are incorporated as integral components. Most of the materials and elements were especially developed and designed with the project in mind. Developing the paving was particularly difficult. On the one hand, it had to bear the weight of heavy vehicles driving into the square in connection with its various uses; on the other hand, the ground on which Almere rests consists of a soft sea floor, and is still settling. Moreover, the architects wanted the paving to make a festive effect and yet still be robust. A choice was made of sand-blasted, anthracite-coloured terrazzo in a particularly long and narrow format. Shining traffic setts made of stainless steel underscore the

Renewal of Market Square, Almere, The Netherlands
Design: 1996
Construction: 1997 – 1999
Client: City of Almere, Centrum product office
Project architects: Bureau B+B; Petrouschka Thumann, Michael R. van Gessel, Frans Boots
Stage and seating element design: Ironyx; Jerry van Eyck
Technical formulation: City of Almere
Costs of the stage: NLG 3.5 million
Costs of the square: NLG 350 per square metre

festive effect. The stage, designed by Bureau B+B in collaboration with a number of artists, has a 16 metre high portal and a 15 x 15 metre footprint. Equipped for professional, multifunctional dramaturgic use, it has a height-adjustable floor, is covered over at the top and can be closed in at the sides, and features a robotic arm ending in a Cinemascope screen that can be turned to face in any direction. Building the heavy steel stage on the polder soil was a technical challenge, and meant anchoring the rails onto piles let deep into the ground to ensure that they do not sink when the stage is moved.

The custom-designed lighting masts are the main protagonists at night. Central lighting is provided by strings of suspended lights, while spotlights arranged along the edges illuminate the

gebiete fragmentiert war. Jetzt ist der Platz eine einzige Fläche von Giebel zu Giebel. Die Ränder, Gebäude aus den achtziger Jahren von sehr unterschiedlicher Architektur mit verschiedenen Giebeleinteilungen und Farben, sind wieder sichtbar. Die parallelen Linien der Schienen, der Abflussrinnen und der an Drähten aufgespannten Beleuchtung unterstreichen die Länge des Platzes. Die ursprünglich in regelmäßigem Raster über den gesamten Platz verteilten Kastanien sind zu drei soliden Gruppen vereint. Sie wurden zurückgeschnitten und zu kompakten Formen modelliert. Die Bäume bieten räumliche Abwechslung, ohne die Offenheit des Platzes und damit die Brauchbarkeit für Veranstaltungen zu beeinflussen. Das Pflaster ist ein einziger, platzbreiter Teppich. Die Abflussrinnen, die Schienen für die Bühne und Flächen aus Cortenstahl, in denen die Baumgruppen stehen, sind Teil dieses Teppichs. Die meisten für den Platz verwendeten Materialien und Elemente wurden speziell für dieses Projekt entworfen. Die Entwicklung des Pflasters war besonders aufwendig. Einerseits sollte der Platz wegen des multifunktionalen Gebrauchs auch für schweren Verkehr zugänglich sein, andererseits ist der ehemalige Meeresboden, auf dem Almere gebaut ist, sehr weich und setzt sich immer noch. Das Pflaster sollte festlich und robust zugleich wirken. Die Wahl fiel auf Steine aus sandgestrahltem anthrazitfarbenen Terrazzo in einem besonders langen und schmalen Format. Glänzende »Pins«, Verkehrsmarkierungen aus Edelstahl, unterstreichen das festliche Aussehen.

Der Entwurf des Podiums wurde in Zusammenarbeit zwischen Bureau B+B und Künstlern erstellt. Es ist ein raumwirksames Portal von 16 Metern Höhe und einer Grundfläche von 15 mal 15 Metern. Die Bühne ist vollständig für eine professionelle, multifunktionelle Theaternutzung ausgestattet. Die Stahlkonstruktion hat einen in der Höhe verstellbaren Boden, ist überdeckt und kann an den Seiten geschlossen werden. Ein Roboterarm, der in jede gewünschte Richtung zu drehen ist, trägt einen Farbbildschirm in Cinemascope-Format. Die Realisierung der schweren Bühne in der Polderstadt Almere war eine technische Herausforderung. Die Schienen, auf denen die Bühne bewegt wird, mussten tief mit Pfählen im Boden verankert werden, damit sie nicht versinken.

Die speziell für den Platz entworfenen Mastleuchten sind die Protagonisten der nächtlichen Atmosphäre. Lichtlinien mit hängenden Lampen sorgen für eine zentrale Beleuchtung, während entlang der Ränder des Platzes angeordnete Spots die Giebel erhellen. Aus sternförmig gelochten Blechen unter den Kastanien strahlen Spots auf die Blätter der Bäume. Das gesamte Licht spiegelt sich in den 3000 im Pflaster eingelassenen Pins. Die Lichtstärke ist je nach Art der Aktivitäten auf dem Platz veränderbar. Während eines Auftrittes kann zum Beispiel die gesamte Platzbeleuchtung so reduziert werden, dass die Inszenierung der Bühne zu ihrem Recht kommt.

Zum Sitzen wurden, ebenfalls in Zusammenarbeit mit den Künstlern, vier versetzbare Sitzskulpturen von 3 mal 9 Metern aus mattem Edelstahl entworfen. Neben diesen Elementen laden Straßencafés zum Verweilen ein. Vor den Restaurants und Kneipen sollen Wintergärten gebaut werden. Die Giebel öffnen sich dann zum Platz hin und das ganze Jahr über ist Straßencafésaison. Die Fundierungen für die Wintergärten sind mit der Neugestaltung des Marktes bereits angelegt.

Der Prozess. Der Erfolg der Gesichtsveränderung des Großen Marktes ist von einer Reihe von Faktoren abhängig. Die Neugestaltung des Platzes ist die erste Maßnahme. Die Gemeinde formulierte Aktionen für einen weiterführenden Prozess. Subventionen sollen den Bau von Wintergärten durch Gastwirte fördern und die Benutzung des Podiums stimulieren. Eine Stiftung wirbt für die Bühne und sorgt für ihre Instandhaltung. Über die Qualität des Platzbildes wacht die Gemeinde mit eigens entwickelten Regeln.

Neben dem Großen Markt wird zur Zeit die gesamte Innenstadt von Almere erneuert. Aufgrund der steigenden Einwohnerzahl werden Bebauung und städtisches Programm verdichtet. Die junge und sehr erfolgreiche Stadt ist für Landschaftsarchitekten und Städtebauer als Auftraggeber einzigartig. So ging der Auftrag mit seiner langfristigen Strategie für den Großen Markt viel weiter als vergleichbare Projekte. Die Stadt stand den Ideen der Architekten sehr offen gegenüber und machte die maßgeschneiderte Entwicklung der Materialien möglich. Das Ergebnis ist ein Platz, der, auch wegen seiner vielfältigen Nutzungsmöglichkeiten, einen wichtigen Beitrag für die neue Identität des Zentrums und der gesamten Stadt liefert. Getreu dem Motto der Stadt: »In Almere ist es möglich«.

walls of surrounding buildings. Further spotlights are installed below the chestnut trees, and shine up onto the leaves through star-shaped apertures let into sheet metal. Three thousand steel setts in the paving reflect the lighting, the intensity of which can be adapted according to the activities going on at the space.

The process. The success of the face-lifting at Market Square is dependent on a number of factors, of which the actual renewal is just a first step; others are to follow according to a continuing process involving measures formulated by the council. Subsidies are to encourage the construction of the winter gardens by the proprietors of the catering establishments, and are also to stimulate use of the stage, for which a foundation has been set up to advertise its availability and take care of its upkeep. The council itself keeps an eye on the square's appearance according to especially developed guidelines.

Due to the growing number of inhabitants and thus the necessity for construction and urban programme consolidation, it is not only Market Square that is being reshaped, but also the whole downtown area. The young and highly successful city is a unique proving ground for landscape architects and the metropolitan town planners, and thus the commission for Market Square went a lot further than comparable projects, particularly in view of its long-term strategy. The city proved to be very receptive to the architects' ideas, and financed the development of some of the materials used. Due to the wide variety of uses that it enables, the refurbished square makes an important contribution to the new identity of the city centre and Almere as a whole, quite in keeping with the city motto, "In Almere, anything is possible".

Halbzeit am Kop van Zuid

Halftime at Kop van Zuid

Lodewijk Baljon

Öffentliche Freiräume sollten die Hafenatmosphäre in den Rotterdamer Docklands bewahren helfen. Einblick in eine Stadt im Werden.

Public open spaces are to help preserve the harbour atmosphere of the Rotterdam docklands: a look at a city district in progress.

Recollections of the harbour. In redeveloping the Kop van Zuid, a derelict former industrial area close to the centre of Rotterdam, the planners were determined to create a city district as a well-formed, cohesive, organised public domain. The basis for this development was found in the history of the place itself. After all, the river is the lifeblood of this city. Recollections of the past can be helpful when exploited for the transformation of the city. Even in physical terms, the investments made in the harbour a hundred years ago determine the quality of the redevelopment today.

A tour of the Kop van Zuid creates expectations. The fact that the site is located on the river, connected to the coast and thus to yet another boundary, enhances this feeling. The Kop van Zuid's authenticity can be found along its quays, where the quality of seemingly 'undesigned' places holds sway. These areas, with their exposed rawness, should be supplemented with sheltered places.

Urban culture on the river. The objective in redeveloping the Kop van Zuid is to stimulate the city district's economic and socio-cultural aspects. This objective cannot be met without the effective development of public space. The quality of the public space determines to a great extent the quality of life in a city. Spatial quality therefore figures as an integrated concept in planning. Quality can come about by taking advantage of local conditions and by creating activity and tranquillity, busyness and calm, and areas with a distinctive atmosphere. The aura of urban culture gives residents and visitors the feeling of participating in the life of the city. They become aware, perhaps even with a sense of privilege, of their position at its centre.

Erinnerungen an den Hafen. Bei der Sanierung des Kop van Zuid waren die Planer fest entschlossen, das veraltete Industriegebiet nahe der Innenstadt Rotterdams zu einem gut entwickelten und geschlossenen Viertel zu gestalten und zu einem Anziehungspunkt für die Bewohner. Ausgangspunkt dieser Erneuerung war die Geschichte des Ortes selbst. Schließlich ist der Fluss der Lebensnerv der Stadt.

Rückblicke in die Vergangenheit können eine große Hilfe sein bei der Umgestaltung einer Stadt. Die vorhandene Bausubstanz wurde vor rund hundert Jahren errichtet und war maßgebend für die Sanierung. Ein Rundgang durch Kop van Zuid übertrifft alle Erwartungen. Die Tatsache, dass der Stadtteil direkt am Fluss liegt und durch diesen mit der Küste als imaginärer Grenze am Horizont verbunden ist, verstärkt diesen Eindruck noch. Das Bedürfnis Kop van Zuids nach Authentizität ist vor allem entlang der Kais spürbar. Hier prägen unsanierte Gebäudekomplexe das Stadtbild. Ihre augenfällige Rohheit sollte durch öffentliche Freiräume, die die Hafenatmosphäre bewahren, ergänzt werden.

Urbane Kultur entlang des Flusses. Bei der Sanierung Kop van Zuids kam es darauf an, die städtische, ökonomische und soziokulturelle Entwicklung dieses Stadtviertels zu stimulieren. Keines dieser Ziele kann jedoch erreicht werden ohne eine wirksame Entwicklung des öffentlichen Raumes – denn die Qualität der öffentlichen Freiräume bestimmt in hohem Maße die Lebensqualität der Stadt und ihrer Stadtviertel. Deshalb wurde bei der Planung besonderer Wert auf die Entwicklung der räumlichen Eigenarten gelegt.

Diese als integrierende Idee zu begreifen, erfordert, die vor Ort herrschenden Bedingungen zu nutzen, aber gleichzeitig auch Aktivität und Ruhe, Geschäftigkeit und Stille und reizvolle Orte zu schaffen. Wahrnehmung städtischer Kultur gibt Bewohnern und Besuchern das Gefühl, unmittelbar am Stadtleben teilzunehmen. Man wird sich bewusst, ein Teil der Stadt zu sein, privilegiert zu sein.

Kop van Zuid liegt inmitten einer heterogenen Landschaft, deren Extreme am Hafen aufeinanderstoßen. Mit der Umgestaltung sollte auch ein neues Verhältnis zwischen Stadt und Landschaft geschaffen werden. Will man die Stadt kennenlernen, so muss man in erster Linie ihre Besonderheiten erleben: die Hafenanlage und den Fluss Maas. Jeden Tag aufs Neue inszenieren sie das Wettergeschehen auf einzigartige Weise – und werden so zum Erlebnis. Der Himmel spielt bei der Wahrnehmung der Landschaft eine ganz entscheidende Rolle. In Kop van Zuid ist er mit seinem veränderlichen Wolkenmeer Teil der Stadtlandschaft. Der Tidefluss lässt sich nicht bändigen. Seine Kraft und sein launisches Wesen sind bis weit in seine Häfen spürbar. Nirgendwo ist etwas wie Gemächlichkeit zu spüren. Vielleicht macht gerade das den Charakter Kop van Zuids aus: störrisch, aber in Übereinstimmung mit der übrigen Stadt.

Kontinuität des städtischen Raums. Die Struktur, das Wesen einer Stadt abzubilden, kann beispielsweise mit Hilfe der öffentlichen Räume geschehen. Um eine Stadt jedoch überhaupt richtig wahrnehmen zu können, muss sie einige charakteristische Elemente aufweisen: Wege und Straßen, Ränder, Mittelpunkte, Stadtviertel und Wahrzeichen – diese Theorie von Kevin Lynch hat nach wie vor Bestand. Um das Neue in das Bestehende integrieren zu können, müssen vor allem die einzelnen Straßen und Wege miteinander verknüpft werden. Ein Netz aus Haupt- und Nebenstraßen entsteht, das die durch das Wasser und die Hafenanlagen geschaffenen Räume ergänzt und das Rückgrat der öffentlichen Freiräume Kop van Zuids bildet. Es entsteht ein Rechteckschema, einem Netzwerk gleich, das gleich-

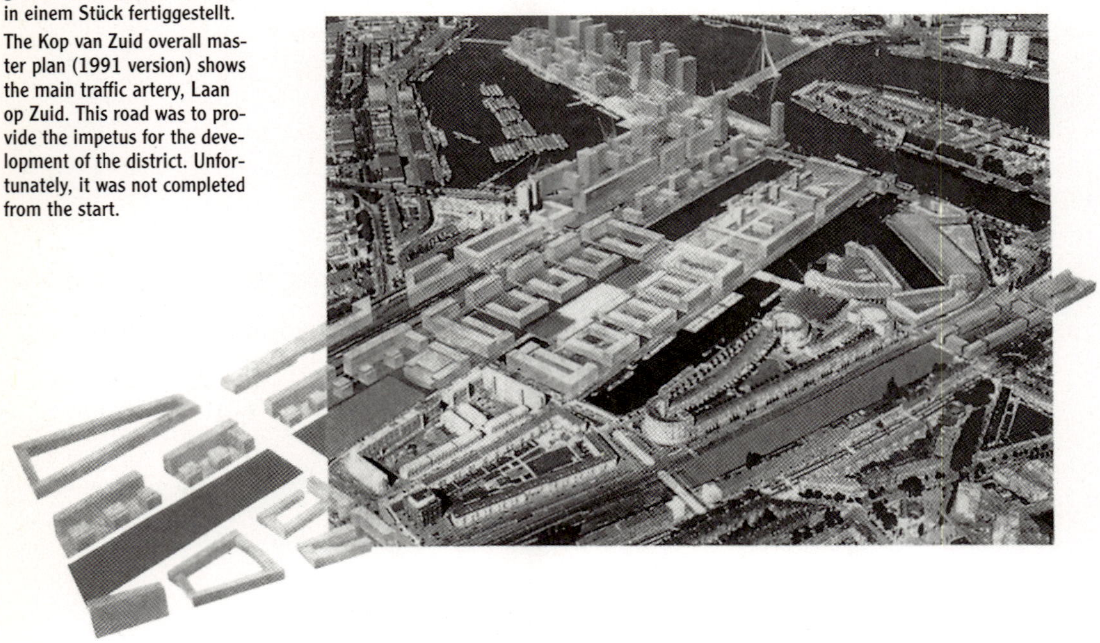

Kop van Zuid-Masterplan Gesamtgebiet (Stand 1991) mit der Hauptverkehrsstraße, der Laan op Zuid. Von ihr sollten wesentliche Impulse für die Entwicklung des Viertels ausgehen. Leider wurde sie nicht in einem Stück fertiggestellt.

The Kop van Zuid overall master plan (1991 version) shows the main traffic artery, Laan op Zuid. This road was to provide the impetus for the development of the district. Unfortunately, it was not completed from the start.

The Kop van Zuid is an urban situation in a landscape setting. Its two contrasting facets meet at the quay, where a new form of interaction between city and landscape is to occur. The harbour and the river are special features in the urban experience on this site. Day after day, they dramatise the changes in the weather. Skies are important in our perception of the landscape. In the Kop van Zuid, they have become a part of the cityscape. The tidal river refuses to be intimidated. Its force and moodiness are felt right up to the harbour. Nowhere is the water really gentle. Maybe this is also the basis of the Kop van Zuid's character: a stubborn character well in keeping with the rest of Rotterdam.

Cohesion around the river. Public space provides an image of a city's structure. The elements described by Kevin Lynch – paths, edges, nodes, districts and landmarks – continue to be relevant. In order to embed new elements into the existing ones, it is important to interweave the roads. The new system of main roads, supplementing the links created by water and quays, forms the backbone of the Kop van Zuid's public space.

A grid-like network now ensures the continuity of the district's urban space, which is one of the most important conditions for a city's functioning. It is a pity, however, that the Laan op Zuid could not be completed from the start as the basis for the Kop van Zuid's development. Undefined green spaces now occupy areas where major links should be developed. As it stands now, the avenue looks grim; it is difficult to instil a sense of cosiness on pavements measuring ten metres across.

The design of the public space is successful. Applying a traditional spatial hierarchy continues

Kop van Zuid, die Rekonstruktion des Südufers der Nieuwe Maas, liegt dem Stadtzentrum zugewandt. Das zentrale Projekt der Stadtentwicklung Rotterdams umfasst eine Vielfalt von Funktionen, Regie führt die Stadt selbst.

Kop van Zuid, the redevelopment of the south bank of the Nieuwe Maas, faces the city centre. The central project of Rotterdam's urban development, it comprises a variety of functions. The city itself is directing the operation.

zeitig Geschlossenheit gewährleistet. Auf diese Weise wird eine der wichtigsten Bedingungen für das Funktionieren einer Stadt, nämlich die Kontinuität städtischen Raumes erfüllt. Es ist jedoch ein Jammer, dass der Laan op Zuid, die Hauptverkehrsstraße des Viertels, nicht von Anfang an fertiggestellt werden konnte – eigentlich sollten von diesem Boulevard wesentliche Impulse für die Entwicklung des Viertels ausgehen. Mehrere Verbindungen konnten deshalb nicht angelegt werden und werden nun schmerzlich vermisst. An ihrer Stelle offenbaren sich im Moment undefinierte grüne Räume. Der Boulevard sieht trostlos aus – es fällt schwer, zehn Meter breiten Bürgersteigen ein Gefühl von Behaglichkeit abzuringen.

Die Gestaltung des öffentlichen Freiraumes ist gelungen – die hierarchische Gliederung bleibt auch nach Jahrzehnten eine altbewährte Entwurfsmethode – sowohl im Grundriss als auch im Querschnitt. Der besonderen Bedeutung des Verkehrs wird in einer nachdrücklich positiven Art Rechnung getragen. Geschlossenheit und Lebhaftigkeit können als Folge dessen in das Stadtviertel einziehen – eine urbane Atmosphäre entsteht. Die Weitläufigkeit der noch unbebauten Flächen in diesem Gebiet lassen das Auto beinahe unauffällig erscheinen. Ob der Laan op Zuid allerdings eines Tages mit Fußgängern belebt werden wird, bleibt abzuwarten. Dennoch bildet er das Gerüst, von dem die anderen Straßen abzweigen: kohäsiv, zweckmäßig und realistisch zugleich. Die Nebenstraßen folgen einer Logik, die ihre Bedeutung und ihre Rolle im Straßennetz stärkt. Einfache, durch verschiedene Belagsarten gekennzeichnete Straßenprofile stärken zudem die Integrität Kop van Zuids, tragen zum Zusammenhalt bei. Auch die Baumpflanzungen orientieren sich am Straßenraster. Das Pflanzensortiment und ihre Anordnung entlang der Straßen und Plätze ist deshalb auch einfach und schlicht. Größere Arten wie Rosskastanie, Ulme, Platane und Linde werden auf beinahe neutrale Art und Weise verwendet: als Elemente, die nur mit geringem Abstand und in strengen Reihen angeordnet sind. Die ohnehin bereits sichtbare Hierarchie der Boulevards, Alleen, Stadt- und Wohnstraßen wird so noch zusätzlich hervorgehoben, horizontale Linien in ihrer Länge betont. Besondere Orte hingegen, wie Verkehrsknotenpunkte, werden zusätzlich optisch akzentuiert. Die Auswahl verschiedener Beleuchtungselemente unterstreicht darüber hinaus die klare Trennung zwischen Nutzung und Freiraum. Das Konzept basiert auf dem Grundgedanken der langen, geraden Linien; organisatorisch und optisch eingesetzt ziehen sie sich wie ein roter Faden durch den Entwurf. Es müssen jedoch noch eine

to be a valuable design method, easy to establish in profile and plan. The important role of traffic is regarded as emphatically positive. The result can be cohesion and liveliness – in short, an urban atmosphere. The spaciousness of the open areas makes cars unobtrusive. Whether these areas will also be enhanced by the liveliness of pedestrians remains to be seen.

The Laan op Zuid forms the trunk from which the other roads branch off, in cohesive, practical and realistic fashion. The roads have their own logic, as the plan demonstrates. Street profiles developed with specific materials, simple forms and ground surfaces provide a pronounced unifying effect. Tree plantings depend on the road. Their arrangement and assortment are kept simple in order to differentiate the boulevards, avenues, city streets and residential streets clearly. The larger varieties in the main assortment, horse chestnut, elm, plane and linden, are arranged in closely spaced, orderly, austere rows. Thus the hierarchy of the roads becomes apparent in terms of space. The length of horizontal lines is emphasised. Special places, such as nodes, are made to stand out. The lighting elements further underscore the hierarchy of use and space.

The key to the plan is the use of long lines, both organisationally and visually. Realising a connection with the rest of Zuid still requires tying up a lot of loose ends.

Planning process. The plan was presented in visual form right from the start. Urban planning, architecture and ground surface design were always integrated, thus demonstrating how the open space components interlock and making clear that one cannot flourish without the other. The attractive cityscape thus proposed was needed to convince the parties involved of the location's interesting possibilities. The opportunities for organising the public space were a persuasive factor for potential developers. With substantial investments in the public space, the government is demonstrating that it takes the quality of the area seriously. This is a definite development strategy, financially covered on the basis of well considered and worked out details. The minimal budgets typically allotted to public space in The Netherlands were dismissed at an early stage. Profiles, schematic detail drawings and materials for the entire network of roads and quays forming the basis for the public space are solid and high-quality.

The design is based on long lines and large surfaces expressly to enable long-term developments. However, small-scale interpretations of the large areas are slow in getting started. The large dimensions are turning out to be inhibiting. No enriching elements have evolved from daily use so far. Perhaps more attention should be paid to temporary activities. Festivities and events can attract the people of Rotterdam to the area, making it a component of their urban experience.

As far as we can judge at present, the attempt to produce an integrated design has been successful.

Details on the river. Attempts to organise public space tend to be like tribal wars. The battle over public space results in barricades of countless pillars, blocks and strips. Public space is often a sum of individual interests. With each interest group grabbing a little piece of the pie, cohesion becomes impossible. The ground surface has to be a durable yet inconspicuous floor for the city. An effective floor creates space and connects buildings.

Vielzahl loser Enden miteinander verknüpft werden, um dieses Gebiet mit dem übrigen Stadtviertel zu verbinden.

Planungsprozess. Von Beginn an wurde der Entwurf anhand von Plänen und Modellen anschaulich präsentiert. Dabei wurden neben stadtplanerischen und architektonischen Aspekten auch Detaillösungen, wie Materialauswahl und Oberflächengestaltung, berücksichtigt. Dieser integrierte Ansatz veranschaulicht, wie die einzelnen Elemente des öffentlichen Raumes ineinandergreifen. Er macht deutlich, dass das eine nicht ohne das andere wachsen und gedeihen kann. So entstand eine verführerische Stadtlandschaft – nur mit ihrer Hilfe konnten diejenigen überzeugt werden, die an der Planung beteiligt und an der Entwicklung des Potentials Kop van Zuids interessiert waren. Dabei spielten die Chancen, die die Entwicklung des öffentlichen Freiraums in sich barg, eine wichtige Rolle, um potentielle Entwickler für Investitionen gewinnen zu können. Darüber hinaus investierte die Regierung eine beträchtliche Summe in das Stadtviertel und macht auf diese Weise deutlich, wie sehr sie an der Entwicklung und Förderung Kop van Zuids interessiert ist. Die Voraussetzungen für die Entwicklung des Planungsgebietes sind demnach mehr als günstig: Neben der abgesicherten Finanzierung verfügt Kop van Zuid über eine klare Entwicklungsstrategie, die auf wohl überlegten und ausgearbeiteten Details beruht. Auf eine Finanzierung mit geringen Budgets, die für die Entwicklung des öffentlichen Raumes in den Niederlanden sonst typisch ist, wurde bereits in einer sehr frühen Planungsphase verzichtet. Querschnitte, schematische Detailzeichnungen und die Auswahl der Materialien für alle Straßen, Wege und Anlegestellen wurden mit einer soliden Sorgfalt ausgearbeitet. Sie bildet die Grundlage für die Entwicklung des öffentlichen Raumes in Kop van Zuid.

Lange Linien und große Oberflächen kennzeichnen das Planungskonzept. So soll eine Entwicklung auf lange Sicht hin ermöglicht werden. Die Vielzahl möglicher Interpretationen bedeutet allerdings auch, dass mehr Zeit benötigt wird, um den Prozess in Gang zu setzen. Die großen Flächen scheinen auf den ersten Blick eher von Nachteil, lassen sie doch eine Vielzahl möglicher Nutzungen zu. Bis zum jetzigen Zeitpunkt konnten keine Anregungen aus der alltäglichen Benutzung gewonnen werden. Möglicherweise sollte künftig mehr Aufmerksamkeit auf temporäre Aktivitäten gerichtet werden. Festivals und Events könnten die Bewohner Rotterdams animieren, hierher zu kommen und das Viertel zu einem festen Bestandteil der Stadt zu machen. Soweit wir das zum jetzigen Zeitpunkt beurteilen können, ist der Versuch, ein integriertes Konzept für Kop van Zuid zu entwickeln, erfolgreich verlaufen.

Einzelheiten über den Fluss. Manche Versuche, Konzepte für den öffentlichen Freiraum zu entwickeln, muten wie Stammeskämpfe an. Der Kampf um öffentlichen Raum führt dazu, dass Barrikaden aus unzähligen Pfeilern, Blöcken und Begrenzungen errichtet werden anstatt Freiraum zu gestalten. Oftmals ist öffentlicher Freiraum eine Summe individueller Interessen. Der Zusammenhalt, das Zusammenwachsen eines Viertels wird mit jeder Interessengruppe, die ein kleines Stück des Kuchens erhaschen möchte, unwahrscheinlicher. Freiräume müssen strapazierfähig aber möglichst unauffällig sein. Nur so sind sie für die Stadt von Nutzen, schaffen Raum und verbinden die einzelnen Gebäude miteinander.

Alle an der Freiraumplanung Beteiligten haben bei dieser Planungsaufgabe Professionalität bewiesen; nicht nur hinsichtlich ihres handwerklichen Geschicks und ihrer Liebe zu ihrem Beruf, sondern auch in ihren Entwürfen und in der Ausführung ihrer Pläne. Eine nicht zu unterschätzende Rolle spielt hier sicherlich auch die abgedeckte Finanzierung, die zur Profes-

It is gratifying to see the professionalism, both in workmanship and professional pride, demonstrated by those organising the open space within the Kop van Zuid in the design and implementation of their plans. (A contributing factor is that the necessary budgets were guaranteed.) Such professionalism shows particularly in the details. It is through details that we deal with our environment. A successful detail is an expression of a greater concept, its most concentrated expression. Now that the riv-

Durch seine exponierte Lage ist Kop van Zuid Wetter und Gezeiten ausgesetzt. Die großen Freiflächen lassen eine Vielzahl von Nutzungen zu. Temporäre Aktivitäten sollen die Bewohner Rotterdams animieren, das Viertel zu einem festen Bestandteil der Stadt zu machen.

Because of its unprotected site, Kop van Zuid is exposed to the weather and the tides. Its large open areas allow a variety of uses. Temporary activities are to encourage Rotterdam's population to see the district as a genuine component of the city.

er's surroundings are to be adapted to daily use by the city's inhabitants, the relationship between the river's scale and the human scale needs to be determined. Details must be in proportion to the scale of the river and the docklands. They should either have robust dimensions to measure up to their environment or such small ones that they do not figure. This places designers in the position of having to decide whether something has to be massive and rugged-looking or so slender and almost vulnerable that it invites no competition.

sionalität beiträgt. Diese Perfektion drückt sich insbesondere in den Details aus. Sie sind es, mit deren Hilfe wir mit unserer Umwelt interagieren. Ein erfolgreiches Detail ist Ausdruck für einen bedeutenden Entwurf: Es drückt die Planungsidee in extrem komprimierter Form aus.

Die Umgebung des Flusses soll so gestaltet werden, dass sie der täglichen Nutzung der Bewohner standhalten kann; deshalb muss das Verhältnis zwischen dem Maßstab des Flusses und des menschlichen Maßstabes neu bestimmt werden. Die Details müssen im Verhältnis zur Dimension des Flusses und der Docklands stehen. Sie sollten eine entsprechende Größe haben, um an ihre Umgebung angepasst zu sein oder so klein sein, dass sie nicht mit ihr in Konkurrenz treten. Hier gilt es zu entscheiden, ob ein Detail mas-

Qualitätvolle Materialien sollen der täglichen Nutzung standhalten, schlicht, haltbar und zeitlos sein. Verwendet wurden Klinkerziegel, Basalt und Granit. Trotzdem sind bereits jetzt Abnutzungsspuren zu erkennen.

High-quality materials are to stand up to daily use and be simple, durable and timeless. Clinker, basalt and granite were used. Nevertheless, traces of wear are already apparent.

In designing the ground surface and selecting materials, the objective was to create an uncluttered, solid background tending toward neutrality. In exceptional cases, there is room for something lighter to put this austere background into perspective. Materials were selected for their durability and timelessness. The usual practice in The Netherlands is to elevate the absolute minimum to the level of a standard. In the Kop van Zuid, however, it seems that with a single stroke of the pen the standard was set at exclusiveness. High-quality materials enable a simplicity that could otherwise degenerate into bareness. The durability of the clinker brick is not only technically but also aesthetically attractive. Most of the other materials chosen will also age gracefully.

The quality of a ground surface design often lies in the way familiar problems have been solved in a slightly different way. The Kop van Zuid features extra broad kerbs (robust, uncompromising and therefore a timeless, inconspicuous border for the pavement) and red pedestrian crossings (a necessary visual support giving the Wilhelminaplein a festive colour). There are round spots on the asphalt, their visual contrast attracting attention to their interesting graphic forms, thus improving traffic supervision. The basalt wearing course on the pavement tiles is colourfast and wear-resistant. This paving material is not easily soiled and its deeper tint co-ordinates better than the pavement with the rugged-looking brick facades. Finally, there are timeless granite cobblestones on the quays.

Comments on some spots. The end of the Erasmus Bridge on the Kop van Zuid marks the convergence of major parts of the plan: the entrance to Zuid, Wilhelmina Pier, Hof van Zuid, Laan op

Zuid, and the city boulevard along the Rijnhaven. The spot is called Wilhelminaplein, and its multiple components and proximity to the river make it difficult to establish its character. Uniform paving cannot solve the problem. Moreover, Wilhelminaplein has to compete with magnificent views of the adjacent water. The spot has been designated a square but it is primarily a traffic hub. An exceptional paving material has been used on the pier and around Wilhelminaplein: elongated yellow tiles reminiscent of wooden jetties and the 'boardwalk look' so popular with today's designers. But the difficulties associated with their elongated shape (20 x 60 cm) and light yellow colour are poorly dealt with. The square behind the Entrepot is an empty space awaiting events that do not occur. It is an ill-favoured spot as a meeting place: neither on a crossroads nor on the beaten track. The question of a quay's scale in relation to human scale was answered successfully along the Binnenhaven. A double quay with a retaining wall sporting an elegant balustrade forms a comfortable link between the houses and the harbour. Unfortunately, the boxes with their sockets are waiting in vain for inland navigation vessels to moor.

Maintenance, an issue emphatically included during the planning process, has deteriorated. The design details were thoroughly considered during the preparation phases; materials and processing methods were selected precisely with maintenance in mind. Nevertheless, neglect is already apparent. Perhaps not everyone is as enthusiastic as the planners. Nevertheless, it is important especially during the current construction phase, when people think the public space looks fragmented and disorganised, that the completed

siv und rauh aussehen soll oder so klein und beinahe verletzlich gestaltet ist, dass es nicht mit den umliegenden konkurriert. Bei der Freiflächengestaltung und der Auswahl der Materialien stand das Ziel im Vordergrund, einen schlichten Hintergrund zu schaffen, der fast neutral erscheint. In einigen Ausnahmefällen jedoch wird der Hintergrund durch einige wenige Besonderheiten in den Mittelpunkt gerückt. Die Auswahl der Materialien erfolgte hinsichtlich ihrer Haltbarkeit und Zeitlosigkeit. In den Niederlanden ist es gängige Praxis, auch das absolute Minimum zumindest auf ein Standardniveau anzuheben. Doch es scheint, als ob in Kop van Zuid mit einem einzigen Füllerstrich der Standard auf ein exklusives Niveau angehoben worden ist. Qualitativ hochwertige Materialien ermöglichen eine Schlichtheit des Entwurfs, die sonst wohl eher in Nüchternheit oder Leere resultieren würden. Seine lange Lebensdauer macht den Klinkerziegel nicht nur technisch, sondern auch ästhetisch attraktiv. Das Material erscheint fast zeitlos. Die meisten Materialien werden aber auf eine ansprechende Art und Weise altern und verwittern.

Oftmals liegt die Qualität der Freiflächengestaltung darin, altbewährte Methoden anzuwenden und diese ein wenig zu novellieren: großzügige Bordsteinkanten (robust, kompromisslos und deshalb eine zeitlose, unauffällige Abgrenzung zum Bürgersteig); rote Zebrastreifen (eine notwendige optische Unterstützung, die dem Wilhelminaplein einen beinahe festlichen Glanz verleiht); runde Sprenkel auf dem Asphalt (ihr optischer Kontrast und ihre interessante graphische Form verlangt Aufmerksamkeit); die basaltähnliche Oberfläche der Gehwegplatten (dieser Belag ist farbecht und verschleißfest und verschmutzt nur langsam; der abgedunkelte Farbton betont die rauh wirkenden Ziegelfassaden) und zeitlose Granitkopfsteinpflaster an den Anlegestellen.

Anmerkungen zu einigen anderen Orten. Erasmusbrug ist ein wichtiger Ort in Kop van Zuid. Hier treffen wichtige Bestandteile des Entwurfs aufeinander: der Eingang zum Stadtviertel, der Wilhelminapier; der Hof van Zuid; der Laan op Zuid und der Stadtboulevard entlang des Rijnhaven. Die Vielzahl der Elemente und ihre Nähe zum Fluss macht die Bestimmung des Charakters dieses Ortes sehr schwierig und kann deshalb nicht mit der Verwendung ein und desselben Belages gelöst werden. Die Probleme von Wilhelminaplein rühren von der Tatsache her, dass er mit den großartigen Aussichten, die sich hier über das angrenzende Wasser bieten, konkurrieren muss. Wo die Brücke auf das Land trifft und wo Anlegestelle, U-Bahn,

Höhepunkt Kop van Zuids inmitten der Stadt: Die Erasmus-Brücke (Entwurf: Ben van Berkel), wichtige Verbindung von der Kernstadt zum Süd ufer.

The culmination of Kop van Zuid is in the middle of town: Erasmus Bridge (design: Ben van Berkel) forms the major link between the heart of the city and the south bank.

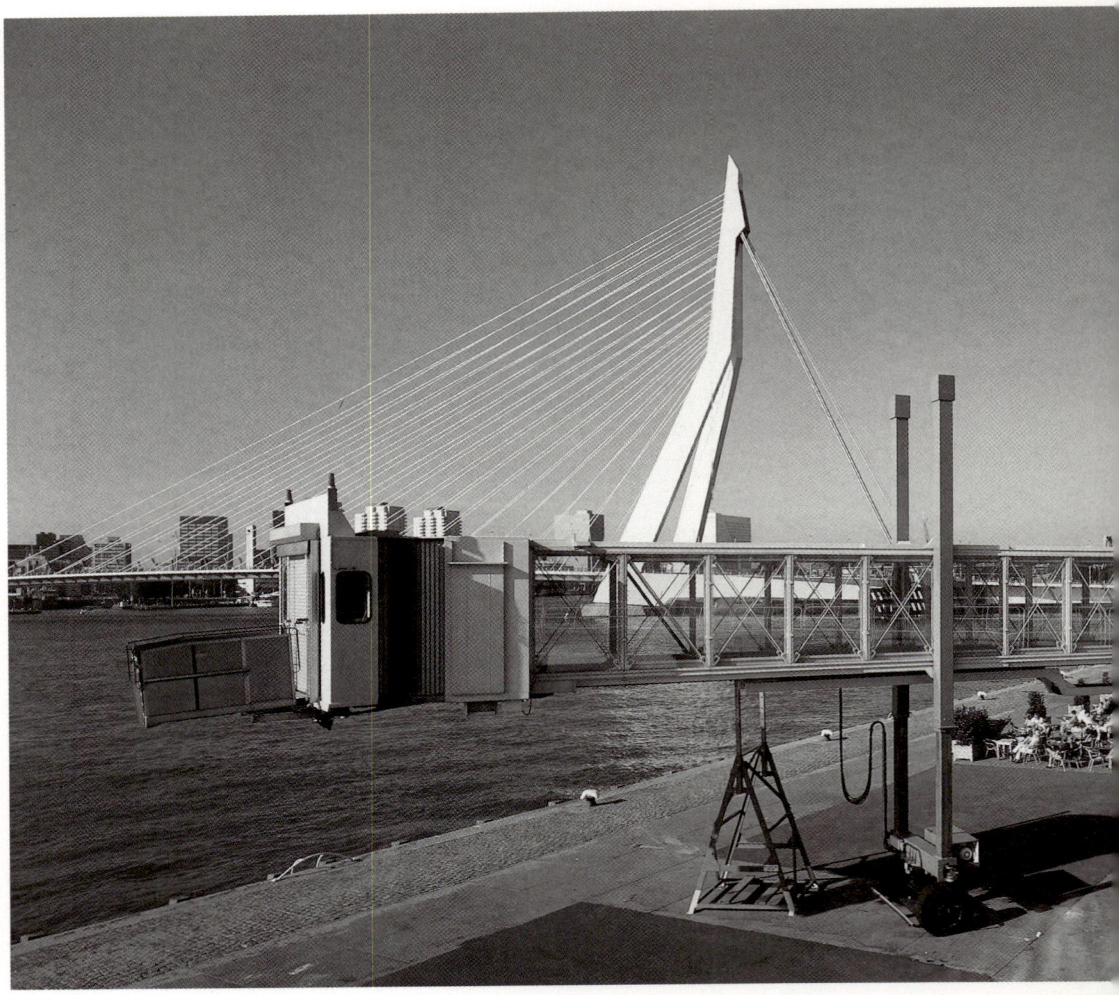

parts look the way they should and thus promote careful usage. Is Rotterdam's sloppiness typical of a working city? Does it mean that after something has been built people lose interest, their ambition giving way to weeds and litter? With the development of the Kop van Zuid, the River Maas has come to feel more like a part of the city. People can see an impressive panorama along its banks. They see the city at a distance and are right in the middle of it at the same time. Crossing the bridge is a glorious experience with the sensation of space it creates within the city. As for more recreational uses, there is still the question of how inviting public spaces at such exposed

spots can be in our climate. Through consistent and meticulous design of the public space, the planners of the Kop van Zuid have succeeded in transforming the docklands into an addition to the city centre. This has been accomplished by preserving the city's collective recollections while adding an openness that the future can absorb.

Allee und Kai zusammentreffen, entstand ein Platz, der heute jedoch mehr ein Verkehrsknotenpunkt ist. Im Bereich der Schiffsanlegestelle und des Wilhelminaplein wurde ein außergewöhnliches Belagsmaterial verwendet: länglich-runde gelbe Platten, die an hölzerne Landungsbrücken erinnern und heute bei den Planern sehr beliebt sind. Allerdings bereitet die längliche Form der Platten (20 mal 60 Zentimeter) und ihre hellgelbe Farbe Probleme. Der Platz hinter dem Entrepot ist leer; es ist ein unschöner Ort und nicht als Treffpunkt geeignet, genauso wenig wie eine Kreuzung oder ein Trampelpfad.

Die Frage nach der Maßstäblichkeit einer Anlegestelle wurde entlang des Binnenhafen recht gut beantwortet. Ein für zwei Schiffe angelegter Kai mit einer Stützmauer, umgeben von einer eleganten Balustrade, verbindet Häuser und Hafen miteinander. Leider wartet man hier vergeblich auf Schiffe.

Ein Thema, das noch während des Planungsprozesses ausdrücklich berücksichtigt wurde, wird zunehmend vernachlässigt: Bewahrung und Erhaltung. Alle Einzelheiten wurden hinsichtlich dieses Leitgedankens sorgfältig während der Vorbereitungsphase geplant; Materialien und Ausführungsmethoden gewissenhaft und präzise. Trotzdem sind bereits jetzt Nachlässigkeit und Abnutzung erkennbar. Es mag sein, dass nicht jeder so enthusiastisch ist wie die Planer selbst. Dennoch es ist wichtig, dass die bereits fertiggestellten Bereiche ihr Aussehen beibehalten und so einer behutsamen Nutzung zugeführt werden. Dies gilt insbesondere für die Ausführungsphase, wenn der Freiraum die Menschen durch seine Fragmentierung und Disorganisation beeindruckt. Ist Rotterdams Nachlässigkeit typisch für eine Arbeiterstadt? Bedeutet dies, dass nach der Fertigstellung das Interesse verlorengeht und so Unkraut und Straßenabfällen der Weg geebnet wird?

Mit der Entwicklung Kop van Zuids wird der Fluss Maas mehr und mehr Bestandteil der Stadt. Entlang seiner Ufer können die Bewohner ein beeindruckendes Panorama entdecken: Sie können die Stadt in einiger Entfernung sehen und befinden sich gleichzeitig selbst in ihrer Mitte. Es ist ein wunderbarer Augenblick, die Brücke zu überqueren – sie ist der Höhepunkt eines solchen Ortes inmitten der Stadt. Es stellt sich die Frage, wie verführerisch Freiraum, der der Erholung dient, sein kann, wenn er an einem solch exponierten, vom Klima beeinflussten Ort liegt. Nur durch konsequente und genaue Planung des Freiraumes ist es den Planern gelungen, die Docklands als eine Ergänzung des Stadtzentrums umzugestalten – obwohl sie Erinnerungen beibehalten und dem Ort eine Offenheit verliehen haben, die von der Zukunft aufgegriffen werden kann.

Zutphen: Atmosphäre schaffen durch Kontraste

Zutphen: Creating an atmosphere through contrasts

Christ-Jan van Rooij
Martin Knuijt

Alte holländische Städte stehen in enger Verbindung zum Wasser. Dies gilt besonders für die ehemaligen Hansestädte wie Zutphen. Charakteristisch für sie ist der Kontrast zwischen der vom Wall umschlossenen Stadt und dem weiten flachen Umland. Diese Charakteristik spiegelt sich im öffentlichen Raum wider. Verschlungene Straßen und althergebrachte lokale Materialien mischen sich mit dem, was über das Wasser herangeschafft werden konnte. Zahlreiche Gebäude und öffentliche Räume, Weinhaus, Gemüsemarkt, Saatgutmarkt, Holzmarkt und Grafenhof zeugen noch von den mittelalterlichen Aktivitäten. Wie auch in vielen anderen Stadtzentren geriet allmählich die Qualität des öffentlichen Raums immer mehr ins Hintertreffen und der Verschleiß wurde sichtbar.

Der Masterplan für das Zentrum Zutphens besinnt sich auf die Tradition. Qualitätvolle Materialien sollen den öffentlichen Raum aufwerten. The master plan for Zutphen reflects a consciousness of tradition. High quality materials are supposed to raise the value of urban open space.

Qualitativ hochwertige Räume zu schaffen ist ein zeitraubender und langwieriger Prozess. Konsequenz bei der Verwendung von Materialien ist daher von essentieller Bedeutung für die Stadt als Ganzes. Manchmal ist das Material allein nicht genug. Material an sich erzählt keine Geschichte, nur im Zusammenhang und in seinem Kontext erzählt es über die Stadt, den Ort und das Programm. Der Masterplan für die Innenstadt von

Old Dutch towns are closely connected with water. This goes especially for the former Hanseatic towns like Zutphen. One of its main characteristics is the contrast between the town enclosed by a rampart and its far-reaching flat surroundings. This trait is also reflected in urban open space. Winding streets and old traditional local materials are combined with those which could be brought over on the waterway. Numerous buildings and public places, the wine house, the grocery market, the seed market, the wood market and the count's courtyard are tokens of medieval activities. As with many other town centres the quality of urban open space gradually deteriorated.

To create high quality spaces is a time-consuming and lengthy process. Being consistent concerning the use of materials is, therefore, of essential significance for the town as a whole. Sometimes the material taken by itself is not enough. Material alone does not tell history, but only conveys to us things about a town, a place or a programme in relation to its context. The master plan of the inner town of Zutphen was made to guarantee the unity between design and atmosphere. The new material will remain an integral part of the town for a long time. Material is not the design equipment but the language of a plan. It is an expression of a design conception by the tangible parts of the design. In its essence the material touches upon the innermost being of a conception. Because of the commonly neglectful designing practices concerning urban spaces it is necessary to deal with the material and with details in greater depth. The art of the detail is not the aim of the design, but the translation of a conception into a limited space which finally opens up to the whole. Starting from the conception materials are used which can be derived from that conception. Sand, wood, metal ore, stone, gravel, trees and loam are converted into concrete, terrazzo, cut polyester concrete, glass, glued wood, sealing material, high-grade steel, blocks of natural rock, epoxy resin, rubber and bricks. The materials are in a technical sense transformed and manipulated to the limiting point of their feasible applications. In Zutphen steel is used in contrast to the traditional pavements. It shoots up from the ground, so to speak, and bends itself to an object to sit on. Other materials are chosen because they catch the light, and can refract it into contrasts or into nuances of a certain colour spectrum. An often used contrast is light and dark. In Zutphen you can easily observe how materials react to changed conditions. Materials absorb the weather conditions. Whenever it rains stones become darker, and start to shine, in the sun they turn white. The colour spectrum of the lit up shopping windows is reflected by the paved surface. The material adopts the colour of its surroundings, and becomes an integral part of it.

In the evenings the lights enhance the medieval atmosphere of the buildings. Gentle light shines on the roof ledges and the brick facades. It is this indirect lighting that spreads a velvet fairy-tale-like gleam over the town without revealing the light sources within one's view of the street. Contrasts in material and light produce an exciting view. Especially in northern Europe, where the skies are often overcast and where it rains often, they are especially effective. The strongest contrasts, like black and white, rough and fine textures, dull and shiny materials create a sense of

Zutphen wurde erstellt, um die Einheit von Entwurf und Atmosphäre zu gewährleisten. Das neue Material wird über lange Zeit hinweg Bestandteil der Stadt bleiben. Material ist nicht die Ausstattung, sondern die Sprache eines Entwurfs. Es ist der Ausdruck des Entwurfskonzepts in fassbaren Bestandteilen. Material berührt in seiner Essenz das tiefste Wesen des Konzepts. Wegen der oft nachlässigen Gestaltung der Stadträume ist es notwendig, sich intensiv mit Material und Details zu befassen.

Die Kunst des Details ist nicht Entwurfsziel, sondern die Übersetzung des Konzepts in einen Raum, der schließlich aufgeht im Ganzen. Ausgehend vom Konzept werden Materialien verwendet, die man herleiten kann. Sand, Holz, Erz, Stein, Schotter, Bäume und Lehm werden zu Beton, Terrazzo, geschliffenem Polyesterbeton, Glas, Leimholz, Schiffshaut, Edelstahl, Natursteinblöcken, Epoxidharz, Gummi und Backstein. Die Materialien werden in technischem Sinn bis an die Grenze ihrer Anwendungsmöglichkeiten transformiert und manipuliert. In Zutphen wird der Stahl als Kontrast zu den traditionellen Bodenbelägen verwendet. Er schießt aus dem Grund und biegt sich zu einem Sitzobjekt. Andere Materialien werden gewählt, weil sie Licht einfangen und zu Kontrasten oder aber zu Nuancen eines bestimmten Farbspektrums brechen können. Ein häufig genutzer

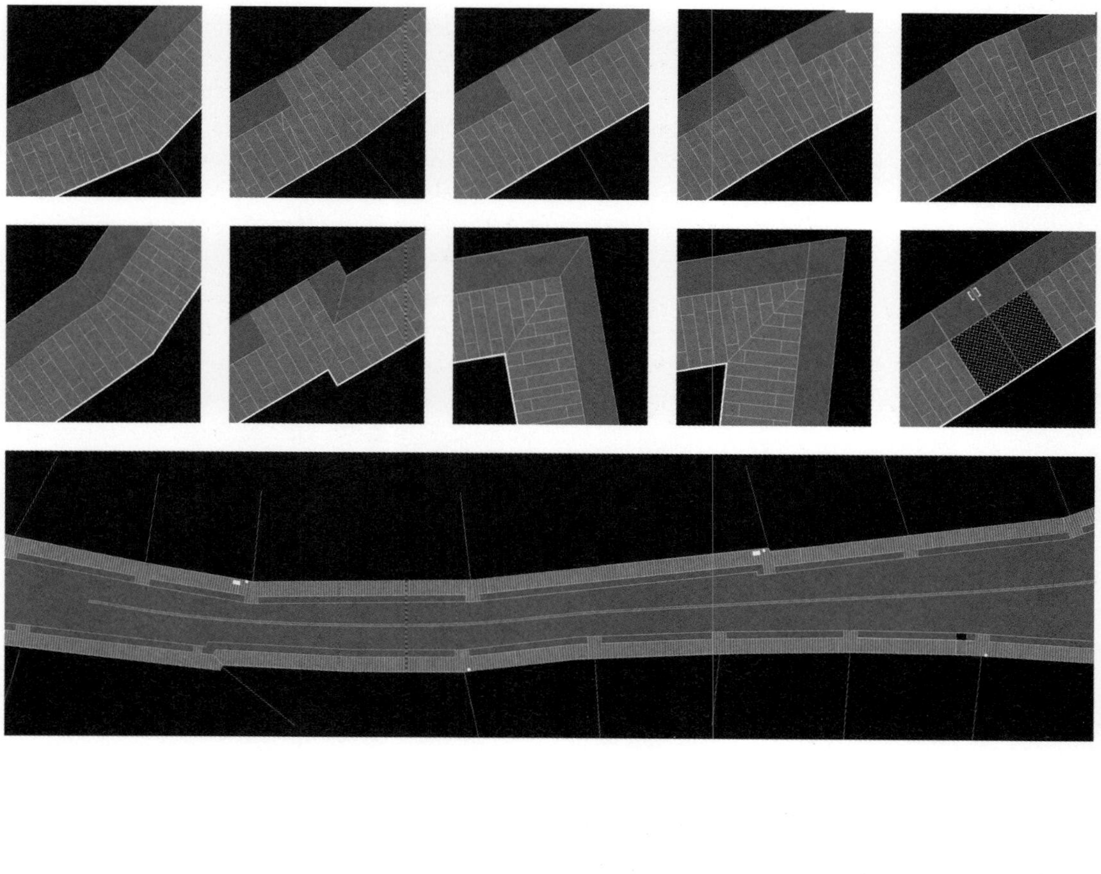

Der Masterplan sieht qualitätvolle Materialien für die Innenstadt von Zutphen vor: Roter holländischer Klinkerstein und Steinbänder aus belgischem Blaustein ergänzen sich spannungsvoll in der Langen Hofstraat.

The master plan has designed high-quality materials for the town centre of Zutphen: Red Dutch bricks and strips of Belgian blue stone complement each other in a scintillating manner in the Langen Hofstraat.

Kontrast ist hell-dunkel. In Zutphen lässt sich gut verfolgen, wie Material auf veränderte Bedingungen reagiert. Materialien absorbieren die Witterung. Wenn es regnet, wird der Stein dunkler und beginnt zu glänzen, bei Sonne ist er weiß. Das Farbspektrum der erleuchteten Schaufenster spiegelt sich im Straßenbelag wider. Das Material absorbiert die Farbe seiner Umgebung und wird zu deren Bestandteil.

Abends unterstreicht die Beleuchtung die Atmosphäre der mittelalterlichen Gebäude. Sanftes Licht strahlt auf Dachgesimse und Backsteinfassaden. Es ist diese indirekte Beleuchtung, die einen samtenen märchenhaften Schimmer über die Stadt breitet, ohne dass die Lichtquellen im Straßenbild zu sehen wären. Kontraste in Material und Licht erzeugen ein spannendes Bild. Gerade im Norden Europas, wo der Himmel oft bedeckt ist, und es viel regnet, sind sie besonders wirkungsvoll. Die stärksten Kontraste, wie schwarz-weiß, grobe und feine Texturen, matte und glänzende Materialien, schaffen Räumlichkeit. Das Glitzern des Regens, der Widerschein von Licht und der Schattenfall, Textur und Fühlbarkeit, raue und glatte Materialien werden erfahrbar in den Straßen.

spaciousness. The shimmering of the rain, the bright reflections of light, the outlines of the shadows, texture and perceptibility, rough and smooth materials are especially susceptible to experience in the streets. Urban space within the Zutphen town centre is gradually changing. What is so beautiful about the Dutch town is that it forms a unity between scale and material, but can at the same time be very rich in the variations of form. The shopping centre of Zutphen is provided with streets paved with bricks and a modern variant of sidewalks. The market places are laid out with surfaces of natural stone throughout the area, and designed with asymmetrically arranged sidewalks. The 's Gravenhof square around which the administration centre has always been concentrated is turned into a paved

Sanftes indirektes Licht betont die mittelalterlichen Gebäude. Einen Kontrast dazu bieten die eigens für Zutphen entworfenen Sitzelemente Ziezo aus gefalzten und polierten Edelstahlplatten.

Gentle, indirect light enhances the medieval buildings. A contrast is formed to them by the seating elements made of folded and polished high-grade steel designed especially for Zutphen.

area of natural rock with footpaths for the important buildings which in turn determine their position. The Lange Hofstraat forms the most important connection between the administration centre and the market places. It constitutes, so to speak, a brace between two main focuses of interest. The character of the squares paved with monumental natural rock is continued along the Lange Hofstraat by matching the stone paving in the market places. Broad, blue strips of stone pavement accentuate the bends of the street.

The transformation of the town centre of Zutphen is very gradually taking form. The finished areas provide an inspiring incentive for the projects to come. Meanwhile, the blueprints for the market places and town squares are already in their advanced stages.

Der öffentliche Raum in der Zutphener Innenstadt verändert sich langsam aber stetig. Das Schöne an der alten holländischen Stadt ist, dass sie in Maßstab und Material eine Einheit bildet, in der Form aber sehr abwechslungsreich sein kann. Das Einkaufszentrum erhält Straßen mit Backsteinpflaster und einer modernen Variante der Gehwege, die Marktplätze bekommen ein Natursteinpflaster über die volle Breite sowie asymmetrisch angeordnete Bürgersteige. Der Platz 's Gravenhof, um den sich seit jeher das Verwaltungszentrum konzentriert, wird zu einem Natursteinplatz mit Gehwegen für die wichtigen Gebäude. Zwischen dem Verwaltungszentrum und den Marktplätzen stellt die Lange Hofstraat die wichtigste Verbindung dar. Sie ist die Klammer zwischen zwei Schwerpunkten. Der Charakter der mit Naturstein gepflasterten Plätze setzt sich in der Lange Hofstraat fort in einer zum monumentalen Pflaster passenden Pflasterung der Märkte. Breite blaue Steinbänder begleiten die Krümmung der Straße. Ganz allmählich nimmt der Umbau der Zutphener Innenstadt Gestalt an. Die fertiggestellten Bereiche geben den Anstoß für die folgenden Projekte. Inzwischen sind die Entwürfe für die Marktplätze und Stadtplätze weit fortgeschritten.

Renewal of the open urban space in Zutphen, The Netherlands
Client: City of Zutphen
Landscape architects: Okra, Utrecht (project architects: Christ-Jan van Rooij, Martin Knuijt, Boudewijn Almekinders)
Planning team: Koen Schrauwen, landscape architect; Mirjam Jansen, technical engineer; Amal Kafu, architectural designer
Size: 32 hectares in the historical centre of Zutphen
Planning: 1997 – 1999 (master plan), 1997 – 2003 detailed plans
Construction: 1998 – 2004
Costs: NGL 10.55 million for the first four stages

Tilburg: Magnolien im Schieferbeet

Tiburg: Magnolias in a bed of slate

Adriaan Geuze

Der Garten einer Versicherungsfirma lädt Mitarbeiter wie Anwohner an seine Wasser-Tische und auf seine Rasen- und Schieferplateaus.

The garden of an insurance company lures employees and nearby dwellers to its tables of water and its lawn and slate plateaus.

Der Hauptsitz der Interpolis-Versicherung liegt in der Achse des Tilburger Bahnhofs. Das Gebäude ragt im Norden eines dreieckigen Grundstücks auf und lässt Raum für einen etwa zwei Hektar großen Garten. Wir gestalteten ihn als einen ruhigen, introvertierten Ort, von der Umgebung abgeschlossen durch Hecken und einen dunkelgrünen Stahlzaun mit stilisierten Stechpalmen-Blättern. Tagsüber steht der Garten den Mitarbeiterinnen und Mitarbeitern der Firma ebenso offen wie den Tilburger Bürgern. Das Verwaltungsgebäude des Architekten Abe Bonnema forderte eine Gartengestaltung, die ihm etwas entgegensetzen würde. Wir pflanzten deshalb Douglasien in lockeren Gruppen. Ihre langen, schmalen Schatten bieten dem Hochhaus Paroli. Die Rasenflächen erscheinen als tektonische Platten, gerahmt von dunkelgrauen Stützmauern aus Be-

The headquarters of the Interpolis insurance company is located on the axis of the Tilburg railway station. The building rises in the north of a triangular plot, and leaves enough space for a garden of about two hectares in size. We designed it as a quiet, introverted place sealed off from its surroundings by hedges and a dark green steel

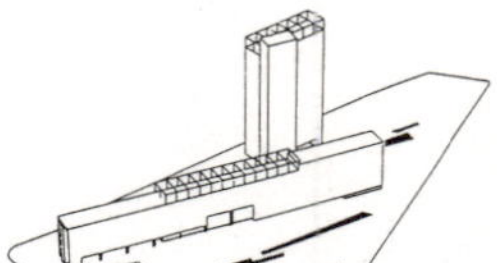

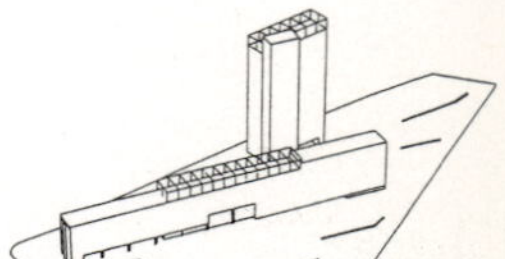

fence with stylised holly leaf ornaments. During the day the garden is open to the employees of the company as well as to the people of Tilburg. The administration building of the architect Abe Bonnema called for a garden design which stood in contrast to it. Therefore we planted Douglas firs in loose clusters. Their long, narrow shadows easily stand up to the building. The lawn areas look like tectonic plates framed by dark grey supporting walls of concrete. The long extended tables of water, the shortest of which measures 20 metres and the longest 85 metres, are especially eye-catching. Together with their water lilies they offer a habitat for frogs. The stage-like, non-parallel arrangement of the basins continuously opens up new impressive sight lines to the visitor. Soft footpaths covered with red-brown mulch lead through the garden. On their way visitors find places to rest here and there on the wide rims of the tables of water or upon the wood-topped supporting walls. The employees can even work outdoors here on their laptops which have a wireless link to the intranet of the company.

At the foot of the building we designed a plateau made of plates of slate. Laid out according to different angles they form tectonic plates similar to the lawn areas. In spring the light-coloured blossoms of the Magnolia trees present a marked contrast to the massive, dark, rough

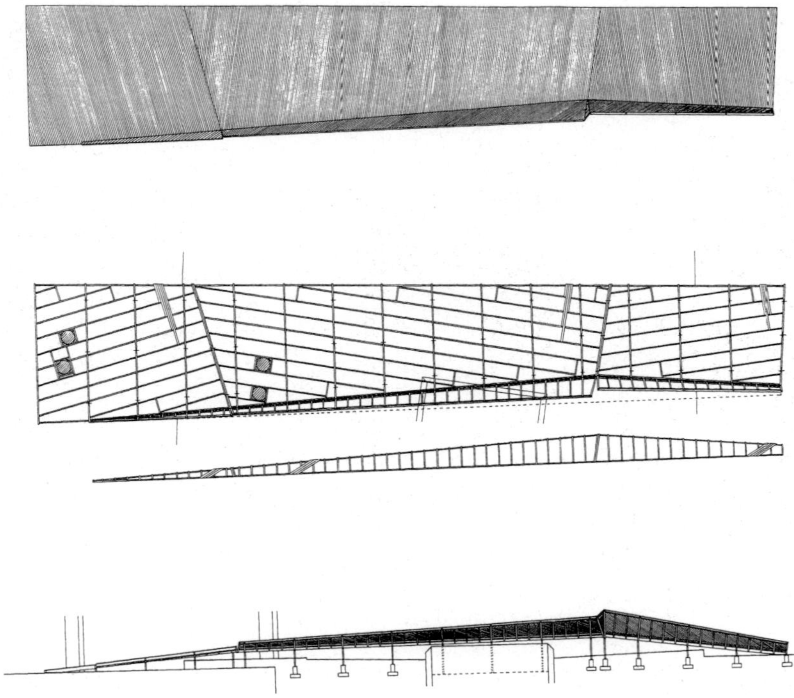

Vom Dach des Bürohochhauses lässt sich die Tektonik des Gartens mit Elementen aus Rasen, Wasser, Mulch und Schiefer gut erkennen. Douglasien mit ihren langen, schwarzen Schatten setzen dem Hochhaus klare Vegetationsvolumina entgegen. Als repräsentativer Eingang überbrückt ein mehrfach geknickter Steg (Pläne links) die Schieferfläche am Fuße des Gebäudes.

From the roof of the office high-rise the structure of the garden with its lawn, water, turf and slate elements can be easily identified. Douglas firs with their long, black shadows set distinct volumes of vegetation over and against the high-rise building.
Forming the representative entrance a footbridge with several bends (plans, left) spans the slate area at the base of the building.

ton. Besonders auffällig sind die langgestreckten »Wasser-Tische«, deren kleinster 20 Meter und deren größter 85 Meter in der Länge misst. Mit ihren Wasserlilien bieten sie einen Lebensraum für Frösche. Die kulissenartige, nicht-parallele Anordnung der Becken eröffnet den Besuchern immer wieder neue, starke Blickachsen. Weiche, mit rotbraunem Mulch bedeckte Fußwege führen durch den Garten – auf ihrem Weg finden die Besucher hier und da Plätze zum Ausruhen auf den breiten Rändern der Wasser-Ti-

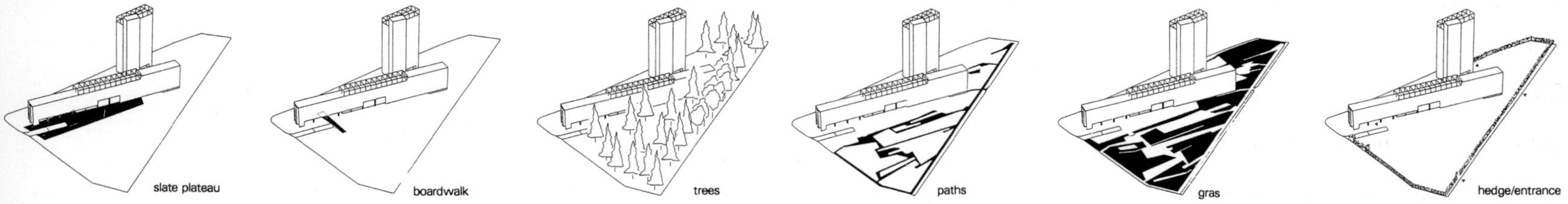

sche oder auf den holzgedeckten Stützmauern. Der Garten soll der Erholung und der Muße dienen, aber man kann in ihm auch arbeiten: Die Versicherungsangestellten können sich mit ihrem kabellos ans Intranet der Firma gekoppelten Laptop einen Arbeitsplatz im Grünen suchen.

Am Fuße des Gebäudes gestalteten wir ein Plateau aus großen Schieferplatten. In verschiedenen Winkeln verlegt, formen sie ähnlich wie die Rasenflächen tektonische Platten. Im Frühjahr bilden die duftigen, hellen Blüten der Magnolienbäume einen auffälligen Kontrast zu dem massiven, rauhen, scharfkantigen und dunklen Schiefer. Vom Gebäude leitet eine Holzbrücke über das Schieferplateau zur Eingangsebene des Gartens. Zusätzlich zu den zwei Toren im Metallzaun bildet dieser Platz den dritten, repräsentativen Eingang zum Garten.

and sharp-edged slate. There is a wooden bridge that leads from the building over the slate plateau to the place of entry into the garden. This place forms a third more presentable entrance in addition to the other two in the metal fence.

Interpolis Garden, Tilburg, The Netherlands
Client: Interpolis Verzekeringsmaatschappij
Design: West 8 landscape architects and urban planners, Rotterdam
Size: 2 hectares
Planning: 1997
Construction: 1998

Im Frühjahr heben sich die zarten Magnolienblüten vom scharfkantigen Schiefer ab. Die kantigen Betonmauern setzen sich deutlich von den weichen Mulchbeeten ab.

In spring the delicate Magnolia blossoms present a marked contrast with the sharp-edged slate. The edged concrete walls purposely contrasts with the soft mulch flower beds.

Authors

Gerrie Andela, born in 1953, studied art history at Groningen University in The Netherlands and carried out research work at the Institute for Art History and Architecture in Groningen. She is also the author of various articles on landscape architecture in The Netherlands.

Lodewijk Baljon, born in The Hague in 1956, has his own landscape architecture office in Amsterdam. His PhD thesis on La Villette formed the basis of his book Designing Parks, published in 1992. He lectures at the Academy in Amsterdam.

Bart Brands, born in 1962 studied at the Horticultural College and the Department of Urban Development at the Academy of Architecture both in Rotterdam and Amsterdam. While he was studying, he worked for the municipalities of Diemen and The Hague and went on to join the B+B office in Amsterdam in 1989. Since 1997 he has run his own practice, Karres en Brands, together with Sylvia Karres.

Klazien Brummel, is an art historian specialised in landscape architecture. She works as an editor and writer for different media, including journals, books, websites and television.

Adriaan Geuze, born in 1960, studied landscape architecture at the Agricultural University of Wageningen and gained his diploma in 1987. He founded West 8 landscape architects in Rotterdam in 1987.

Jan de Graaf, born in 1952, studied architecture and urban planning at the Technical University of Delft. He teaches architecture history and urban development theory at the Rotterdam Academy of Architecture and writes regularly on town planning and landscape architecture topics. For 2002 he supervises the design project "To the Sea" by the National Planning Office, The Hague.

Martin Knuijt, born in 1966, studied landscape architecture at the Agricultural University of Wageningen in 1991. He worked in various interdisciplinary teams before joining the Okra office with three other landscape architects in 1994. His projects to date include the design for the masterplan for open spaces in the inner city of Rotterdam and the inner city plan for Amsterdam, and use and mobility studies. He has also published widely on urban planning.

Bart Lootsma, born in Amsterdam in 1957, received a diploma in architectural history and theory at Eindhoven Technical University in 1984. He then went on to work as an assistant at the master classes held by Laurids Ortner at Linz Art Academy before becoming head of the Design Department at the Academy of Fine Arts in Arnhem, Holland.

Winy Maas, born in 1959, studied landscape architecture in Boskoop and at the Technical University in Delft. He worked with Bureau B+B in Amsterdam, Kuiper Compagnons in Rotterdam, for UNESCO in Nairobi, OMA in Rotterdam. He is a co-founder of MVRDV, lecturer at several universities and has contributed articles to a number of journals.

Frits Palmboom, born in 1951, studied architecture at Delft Technical University and joined the Rotterdam Department of Urban Development in 1981, where he worked on the Prinsenland project, among others. He opened his own office in 1990 and has been working on construction projects in collaboration with Jaap van den Bout since 1994. He teaches at various universities and is the author of "Doel en Vermaak in het Konstruktivisme" (1979) and "Rotterdam, verstedelijkt landschap" (1987).

Almut Röwekamp, born in Aachen in 1979, studied landscape architecture at the Agricultural University in Wageningen, The Netherlands, with studies abroad at the Technical University in Delft and the Agricultural University in Frederiksberg, Denmark. From 1997 to 1999 she worked at the landscape architecture firm of Veenebos en Bosch in Arnheim. Since 2000 she has been working for the B+B office for urban planning and landscape architecture in Amsterdam.

Michiel den Ruijter, born in 1945, studied landscape architecture at the Agricultural University in Wageningen. Since 1973 he has taught landscape architecture part-time at the Larenstein International Agricultural University in Boskoop and

Velp, The Netherlands. From 1985 to 1993 he was the director of landscape architecture and design of the international horticultural exhibition, Floriade, held in The Hague-Zoetermeer in 1992. He founded his own office, DEN.etc landscape architecture and urban design, in Dieren in 1993. He has published numerous writings in specialist journals and books.

Tjerk Ruimschotel, born in 1949, studied architecture at Delft University of Technology, during which time he started to teach and publish in the areas of urban design and land art. From 1985 to 1987, he did research on colonial architecture in Indonesia. Before working for the municipality of The Hague as chief urban designer, he was engaged in several large-scale housing projects. After a brief interlude with B+B, he now owns his own firm.

Robert Schäfer, born in 1954, studied landscape planning in Berlin and journalism in Stuttgart. He became editor-in-chief of Garten + Landschaft in 1985 and of Topos - European Landscape Magazine, which he founded, in 1992.

Petrouschka Thumann, born in 1970 in Amsterdam, studied architecture at the Technical University in Delft, specialising in architecture and landscape. In 1994 she worked for the Van Berkel en Bos architecture office in Amsterdam. Since 1996 she has held guest lectureships at the TU Delft and the State University for Architecture in Rotterdam. In 1995 she began working for the B+B office for urban planning and landscape architecture in Amsterdam. She has been a member of the team of directors of B+B since 2001.

Marieke Timmermans, born in 1956, studied landscape architecture at the Academy of Architecture, Amsterdam. From 1988 to 1995 she ran her own office in Scheveningen. From 1989 to 1992 she participated in the City Core project in The Hague. Since 1995 she has been working in the B+B office for urban development and landscape architecture in Amsterdam. She now owns her own office in Amsterdam.

Harmen van de Wal, born in 1966, studied architecture at the Technical University, Delft. From 1992 to 1994 he worked for the Netherlands Institute for Architecture (NAI) in Rotterdam. He has done freelance work and is a lecturer at the Academy of architecture, Rotterdam. Since 1997 he has been working at the B+B office for Urban development and landscape architecture in Amsterdam. He now owns his own office in Rotterdam.

Christ-Jan van Rooij, born in 1963, is a landscape architect and partner in Okra landscape architects office. He studied landscape architecture at the Agricultural University of Wageningen. From 1990 on he worked for the city of Apeldoorn and for the Stichts Cultureel Erfgoed foundation in Utrecht. He founded the Okra office with three other landscape architects in 1994. His activities concentrate on design management and the realisation of large-scale urban planning projects.

Martine van Vliet was born in 1970. She studied landscape architecture in Melle, Belgium, and Boskoop and the Academy of Architecture in Rotterdam. In 1993 she began working at the Tedder/Timmermans landscape architecture office in The Hague. 1995 she worked at the Niek Roozen landscape office in Weesp. Since 1996 she has been with the B+B office for Urban Development and landscape architecture in Amsterdam.

Cor Wagenaar, born in 1960, studied history at Groningen University in The Netherlands and currently carried out research work at the Institute for Art History and Architecture in Groningen. He takes considerable interest in the open space planning of Rotterdam, as proved by the subject of his dissertation and his recently published book "Die neue Stadt, Rotterdam im 21. Jahrhundert, Utopie und Realität," 1993.

Photo Credits

Fotodienst Universiteit Groningen: 8-11, 15-17
Gemeentearchief Rotterdam: 13, 18
J. Vrijhof: 19
KuiperCompagnons: 29-35
Jeroen Musch: 36-41
"Rotterdam verstedelijkt landschap": 42, 43
Jannes Linders: 43
Frits Palmboom: 45, 46, 47
Gruppe Opbouw: 48
"Alexanderpolder, new urban frontiers": 50, 51
Jeroen Musch: 68-72
West 8: 73-81
Tom Noz: 82-87
Frank Colder / Picture 7: 88-94
West 8: 95
Jeroen Musch: 97, 100, 101, 103, 104
Nico Bick: 105
Stadtentwicklung Rotterdam: 108
Aeroview/Dick Sellenraad: 109
Kop van Zuid: 112-116
Frank Colder: 119, 120, 121 left
Okra landschapsarchitecten: 121 right
Jeroen Musch: 122-124

Translations

English/German
Beate Rupprecht: 42, 53, 60, 95
Cora Lorke: 107
Lisa Diedrich: 122
Dutch/German
Beate Rupprecht: 36, 68, 73, 88, 118
German/English
Almuth Seebohm: 6, 68, 88
Judith Harrison: 20, 82, 102
Peter Zusi: 36
Felicity Gloth: 73
Bruce Roberts: 118

Impressum

in cooperation with Birkhäuser – Publishers for Architecture, P.O.Box 133, CH-4010 Basel, Switzerland

A CIP catalogue record for this book is available from the Library of Congress, Washington D.C., USA.

Deutsche Bibliothek Cataloging-in-Publication Data – CIP-Einheitsaufnahme

Im Blickpunkt: Niederlande : beispielhafte Ideen und Konzepte für Stadt und Landschaft = The Netherlands in focus. - München : Callwey, 2002
ISBN 3-7667-1512-7

Printed on chlorine-free pulp. TCF

Printed in Germany

ISBN Callwey
3-7667-1512-7
ISBN Birkhäuser
3-7643-6671-0